Alois Mailander
A Rosicrucian Remembered

Samuel Robinson

PANSOPHIC PRESS
Oberstdorf, Germany

First published in Great Britain 2021

First edition

Published by Pansophic Press
info@pansophers.com

ISBN: 978-0-6453946-0-3

www.pansophers.com

For our community

My greatest debt of gratitude goes to

Dr. Christine Eike & Dr. Erik Dilloo-Heidger

Contents

Introduction

One of the greatest untold histories of Rosicrucianism and the Theosophical Society at the turn of the 19th century surrounds the activities of a certain Rosicrucian guide, or "Master," who provided spiritual instruction to several prominent esoteric figures. Among his students, Gustav Meyrink, Franz Hartmann, Friederich Eckstein, Karl Weinfurter, and Carl Kellner are the most renowned.

Referred to as "Brother John" by his students, and unlike outspoken occult figures such as Aleister Crowley and Rudolf Steiner, the humble Alois Mailänder never sought fame or public acknowledgement of any kind. This is made apparent by the veiling of his identity in all published mentions relaying Mailänder's presence to the public by his students.

Who was this mysterious Rosicrucian guide who incited such inspiration and devotion to cause at least 54 members of the Theosophical Society to pledge themselves as his disciples?[1]

This volume provides source material that unveils his character, his teachings, and his following.

---

[1] Meyrink reports this number in his "Transfiguration of the Blood" manuscript, first only kept in his estate Meyrinkiana. It was never intended for public viewing but was published after his death in Gustav Meyrink and Eduard Frank, *Fledermäuse: Erzählungen, Fragmente, Aufsätze* (Frankfurt: Ullstein, 1992).

1

The literature on Mailänder is sparse, so when my friend Richard Cloud drew a comparison between him and a known description of Rudolf Steiner's unidentified teacher, it sent waves through the occult world. Several decried the comparison while others raised positive questions, especially because many had never heard of Alois Mailänder, a poor weaver and Rosicrucian seer from Kempten.

In this southernmost part of Germany, in 1877 Mailänder experienced a spiritual awakening and, thereafter, reputedly delivered Rosicrucian visionary type sermons following the enthusiastic spirit of Jacob Boehme's Christian Theosophy.[2] With the gift of his Inner Word, Mailänder established a spiritual circle named the "Bund der Verheißung" (Covenant of Promise), whose members initially comprised the men and women who worked at the Kempten factory.

Accordingly, during his immergence into deep revelatory states of consciousness, Mailänder began uttering divine pronouncements. Was the "spirit of John" speaking through him or was he the embodied reincarnation of John himself? Both possibilities have been put forward, which I aim to settle by presenting the gathered evidence.

The spiritual heritage of Mailänder's community, aside from literary sources like Jacob Boehme and associated Rosicrucian writings, originated directly from the spiritual community of Die Allgäuer Erweckungsbewegung or the "Allgäu Revival Movement," where Kempten is located. The movement arose at the end of the 18th century through the efforts of two Catholic priests, Martin Boos und Johann Michael Feneberg. The Allgäu Revival Movement was originally Catholic, but its strong leanings

[2] Roger Heil, "Okkultistische Sekte im Dreieichenhain der Jahrhundertwende," *Landschaft Dreieich*, 1990, 120–25.

towards Protestant pietism saw over four hundred believers convert to Protestantism, Catholic priests among them. This book demonstrates their spiritual doctrine was taken up by Mailander's circle as their spiritual heirs.

Closer to the Bund, two figures emerge as spiritual sources behind Mailänder. The first is Frau Gabele, Mailänder's mother-in-law, who was a known seeress in Kempten, and who was called upon to heal ailments and exorcise spirits. The second is Prestel, a Rosicrucian dimly lit in the pages of history.

After the decline of the Rosicrucian fraternities in Germany at the turn of the 19th century, it became quite unusual to find a living example of a Rosicrucian wielding the operative art of alchemy. Yet Mailänder's initiator, Prestel, reportedly practiced alchemy and passed on a sweet smelling sample of the Philosopher's Stone, which Franz Hartmann carried upon his person for the rest of his life in a small vial. The presence of Prestel whispers hints of an older heritage transmitted from the fading era of the Rosicrucians immediately before him.

Together, the combined forces of the Allgäu Revival Movement, Frau Gabele, and the Rosicrucian force of Prestel provide the spiritual lineage to Alois Mailänder's Rosicrucian Bund der Verheißung.

We shall also see that the writings Mailänder devotedly studied, such as the Philadelphian writings of Jane Lead which he expanded upon, places him squarely in continuance of the great Christian Theosophers.

Alongside Mailänder, the Bund der Verheißung had a second leader in Nikolas Gabele, Mailänder's brother-in-law. The books he loaned to members of the Theosophical Society tell us much about the doctrine of this circle and how Mailänder developed his esoteric Rosicrucian system.

Within the Bund der Verheißung, Gabele was called "Salomonus," and each member was provided a spiritual name by Mailänder, which served to activate their inner spiritual drive, nature and destiny.[3]

Given the surge of organized Theosophical groups in the wake of Madame Helena Petrovna Blavatsky and her 1877 work "Isis Unveiled," is no wonder a spiritual guide such as Alois Mailänder did not remain isolated for long in Kempten. This is partly because Franz Hartmann was also from Kempten and the Theosophist Wilhelm Hübbe-Schleiden was in talks with Nikolaus Gabele in 1884. It didn't take long for the news to leave Kempten, possibly stirred by Hartmann's move to publish two fascinating pieces about Mailänder, both of which are included in this volume.

The first was titled "Practical Occultism in Germany," published in September 1885 in *The Theosophist*. Then Hartmann manufactured a kind of interview with Mailänder in May 1886 for the same publication. Therein, Mailänder remained anonymous and was addressed only as the "German Adept." In reference, Madame Blavatsky stated, "there is only one Adept in Germany, and he lives in Kempten. But he is not of our school."[4] The discovery of a real and living Rosicrucian master must have been hot on the lips of the Theosophists who, apparently, could hardly contain such exciting secrets amongst themselves.

Consider that Madam Blavatsky had primed her occult audience to seek out hidden teachers with her grand tales of encounters with "the masters" who acted as spiritual guides in her lifetime. Her Master Morya, Saint Germain, Egyptian Tuitit

[3] Ibid.

[4] "Auch Helena Blavatsky hatte gesagt, dass es heute in Deutschland nur einen Einge-weihten gebe und der lebe in Kempten. Er gehöre aber nicht zu ihrer Schule." In Rolf Speckner, "Friedrich Eckstein Als Okkultist," *Der Europäer* 18, no. 09/10 (2014): 10.

Bey, and Tibetan Koot Hoomi were apparently magnificent supernatural beings who occasionally met her "in the body" and lived impossibly long lives. They could travel without train tickets or passports and communicate across continents in the astral. However, these masters were still hardly accessible to many others. Enter Alois Mailänder, an adept in the flesh, and within reach.

It was the Theosophist Mary Gebhard who snapped up Mailänder in 1886 and brought him out of Kempten. She led the very first Theosophical Lodge ever established in Germany, the Theosophische Societät Germania. Her wealth, with other Theosophists, could support Mailänder's family, even buying them a homestead with land. From this moment, the German Theosophical movement entered a new phase of activity, which wasn't predominantly guided by eastern mysticism, but by a Rosicrucian objective. Theosophists from as far as England now came to visit Mailänder to receive his guidance.

Until now, the full impact of Alois Mailänder and his spiritual alchemy has never been told, which is why this book is dedicated to restoring these significant events to their rightful place in occult history.

At the same time, this book does not engage in speculation as to what kind of impact Alois Mailänder might have had on figures such as Rudolf Steiner and the occult fraternities connected to the Ordo Templi Orientis, the activities of which proliferated after Mailänder's death in 1905. Certainly, because Mailänder was a major force behind the Viennese occult circle of Friederich Eckstein and Carl Kellner, the knock-on effect will demand fresh examination, even revision, of the known history of Rudolf Steiner and his form of Rosicrucianism, along with exploring Mailänder's impact on several occult movements. I have reserved such conclusions, connections, and my own speculations for this book's sister volume, *The Rosicrucian Fraternities in the Wake of J.B Kerning and Alois Mailänder.*

This volume is foremost intended to deliver translated source materials on Mailänder himself to provide a basis for further scholarly exploration. In part one of this book, titled "What Do We Know About Alois Mailänder?" and spanning over 80 pages, I have provided my observations and drawn certain conclusions regarding the life of this mystic and in particular, the nature of his practical method.

I presented many of these findings to the public for the first time at the Rosicrucian Salon of the Arts event in London. Hosted by the Society of Rosicrucians in Anglia, this talk was held at the Atlantis Bookshop on October 16, 2021. A video recording of this lecture and its meditation is available on YouTube.

In truth, the events surrounding Mailänder were difficult to uncover. Mailänder's disciples, such as Franz Hartmann and Gustav Meyrink and their Theosophist associates, never openly wrote about Mailänder by name. Whenever they referenced him in their writing, the Theosophists simply used the letter "M." or "J." to denote "Mailänder" or "Johannes," or referred to "der Führer." Within private notebooks, never intended to be publicly disseminated, they all wrote "J." or sometimes the name "Johannes" in full.

Openly published items occasionally appear, yet they typically veil Mailänder's identity, such as the example in Hartmann's *Magic White & Black*, where he describes only the words of an "unlearned person." [5]

Only in the private notebooks of Wilhelm Hübbe-Schleiden do we find the name "Mailänder" ever placed in direct connection

---

[5] Franz Hartmann, *Magic, White and Black: Or, The Science of Finite and Infinite Life*, 3rd ed. (London, 1888), 311.

with his spiritual name "Johannes." This enabled Emil Bock and Roger Heil to identify the real man behind this Theosophical master.[6] Each wrote a single chapter on Mailänder, which have remained the only reliable published sources until now. A third mention of Mailänder of any consequence appears in Willy Schroedter's 1952 *Rosicrucian Notebook*, where he writes of Mailänder's circle:

> Around 1890 there was a mystic school, well-known amongst informed circles, situated in Darmstadt, which was led by an, in other respects uneducated and almost illiterate, weaver called Mailänder. Those who belonged to it included, among others, Karl Weinfurter, Gustav Meyrink, Dr. Franz Hartmann, Helena Petrovna Blavatsky, the Indian Babij and Chief of the Austrian General Staff, Schemua. So Mailänder must have been a rather unusual man.[7]

---

[6] Hübbe Schleiden's diaries name Johannes and Mailänder in letters to Paula. That Hübbe Schleiden actually calls him Mailänder in his Indian diary and these other diaries and letters from 1896, is how Bock got to know who this mysterious J. was and could obtain his real name. Bock discovered Mailänder in Hübbe Schleidens diaries and Bock had access to the 150 letters addressed from Mailänder to Hübbe Schleiden. He quotes them in his "Life and Times of Rudolf Steiner." Bock. 2008. Third edition. Page 206. The Hübbe-Schleiden estate was divided into two halves by Clemens Driessen. The larger part went to the University of Göttingen. The other part went to Paula Hübbe-Schleiden. This was given to Emil Bock after Paula's death. In September 2021 they were rediscovered in the Emil Bock collection at the Anthroposophical Archive in Dornach. Anthroposophical archivist Martina Maria Sam translates a few of them in ARCHIVMAGAZIN. Beiträge aus dem Rudolf Steiner Archiv, Nr. 11 / 2021, Alois Mailänder und die frühe theosophische Bewegung. See Emil Bock, The Life and Times of Rudolf Steiner, vol. 1 (Edinburgh: Floris Books, 2008), 206; Martina Maria Sam, "Beiträge aus dem Rudolf Steiner Archiv: Alois Mailänder und die frühe theosophische Bewegung," ARCHIVMAGAZIN, no. 11 (2021).

[7] His book contains just one page and a half describing the school. See Willy Schrödter, *A Rosicrucian Notebook: The Secret Sciences Used by Members of the Order* (York Beach, Me: Weiser, 1992), 131.

Schroedter barely dedicates more than a single page in his book to this Rosicrucian circle. Fortunately, Roger Heil dedicated five entire pages to Mailänder's group, and the Anthroposophist Emil Bock dedicated a total of nine pages to Mailänder in his coverage.[8] Yet, the present book goes well beyond the published sources. Utilizing unpublished archive manuscripts, primarily from Wilhelm Hübbe-Schleiden and with knowledge of Mailänder's working system, it was possible to scour through Theosophical magazine publications and piece together every fragment to reveal a faithful account of Alois Mailänder's activity, drawing out the facts from those who resolutely kept true to their oath of secrecy.

In my own journey, unveiling Mailänder had a cascading effect. Knowing that his students wrote of him in a veiled manner meant that, once certain facts were known, many pieces of obscure literature became relevant — particularly items that have largely gone unnoticed, or which appeared unremarkable to scholars of occult history. Suddenly, previously insignificant mentions of a "J" or "M" or "baptism of the blood," and the events those items described, became important missing pieces of a puzzle, fitting into just the right place to render the entire picture of Mailänder's story into clarity.

Franz Hartmann's largely forgotten book, *Unter den Adepten und Rosenkreuzern,* hereafter called *Under the Adepts,* is one of those wonderful pieces. Published in 1910, Hartmann provides direct quotes from a therein unidentified Rosicrucian master, although it must also be said Hartmann left many veiled mentions of Mailänder scattered throughout Theosophical magazines. Unfortunately, *Under the Adepts* has often been

---

[8] Heil, "Okkultistische Sekte im Dreieichenhain der Jahrhundertwende"; Bock, The Life and Times of Rudolf Steiner, 1:203–11.

confused for one of Hartmann's other two books, *With the Adepts* and *Amongst the Adepts*, causing this volume to go unnoticed by the English-speaking world. Hartmann published sections of the same content in the Theosophical *Lotusbluten* magazine in 1900.[9]

This volume also provides the first translation of that material into English.

However, Hartmann's overall presentation of Mailänder's Rosicrucian teachings is often coloured by his own eastern influenced Theosophical interpretations. For Hartmann, the Rosicrucianism of Mailänder is yoga. Therefore, this book contains only the most relevant sections from *Under the Adepts*.

The most important treasure this volume has to offer has never been seen before in any English language publication. Its original title is the *Seelenlehre*, or the *Soul Teaching*, as it was called by Alois Mailänder. This was forgotten in the notebook collections of Mailänder's student Wilhelm Hübbe-Schleiden (1846-1916). Upon closer inspection, one part of Hartmann's *Under the Adepts* is a shorter version of the same.

The *Soul Teaching* came into my possession thanks to the generosity of Dr. Erik Dilloo Heidger. We became aware of each other after recognizing we were working on the same endeavour: to uncover the story of Alois Mailänder and his Rosicrucian path of spiritual alchemy. At the time Erik was preparing the *Soul Teaching* and *44 Letters to Gustav Meyrink* for publication in German, I was preparing a book series on the bodily mysticism of J.B Kerning and its adoption by Mailänder. We were excited to share notes.

---

[9] "Under the Adepts," by Hartmann (2013), was originally published as Franz Hartmann, "Unter den Adepten: vertrauliche Mittheilungen aus den Kreisen der indischen Adepten und christlichen Mystiker," *Lotusblüten* 16 (1900): 648–81.

However, our team was actually a trio. One of the scholars of Rosicrucian history featured on our Pansophers.com site named Dr. Christine Eike had been working on translating German materials with me to clarify the history of Kerning and Mailänder. She became a vital member of the team, sorting out the treasure trove of materials Erik had discovered. Christine spent months with Erik painstakingly scouring through the diary notebooks of Wilhelm Hübbe-Schleiden. One of her prized talents gracing our project was that she could accurately read Hübbe-Schleiden's devilishly awful and most scribbly handwriting. Christine proved to be sharp as a fox when it came to recognizing the importance of many statements in the material and her willingness to challenge our ideas helped me hone our arguments.

Given the year and worldwide situation, all three of us made the most of the COVID-19 lockdowns in 2020 by diving deeply into preparations for this book. The clanging of keyboards passed the time quickly.

Mailänder's *Soul Teaching* can now finally be revealed to our audience. The publication of the German edition by Dr. Erik Dilloo Heidger coincides with the launch of this volume. I personally translated the *Soul Teaching* into English and Christine edited the translation for exactitude. The content itself is a series of 437 spiritual statements Mailänder addressed to his students. Diary notes show that his disciples were expected to make hand copies for others in the Bund der Verheißung, yet only when explicitly permitted to do so.

In purpose, the concepts outlined in the *Soul Teaching* are intended to provide an understanding of our inner mechanisms, or inward properties, enabling us to have a proper inner dialogue and understanding of ourselves during our quest for rebirth. Its subject is the interaction between God, the spirit, the soul, and the human body. How do they interact? How can we learn to hear the soul within? Inward tools of self-understanding are presented through the mind, the heart, the will and, most importantly, through the blood. All these inward devices are brought together in the *Soul Teaching* to not only awaken an inner dialogue, but to allow the gradual opening of these properties to receive the Inner Word.

Dr. Erik Dilloo-Heidger's recent publication of Mailänder's forty-four letters written to Gustav Meyrink, when read in combination with this volume, reveal much about the spiritual character of the man behind the *Soul Teaching*.[10] Those letters show Mailänder's compassionate nature and his constant faith that our sufferings in life, whatever they may be, are not without purpose. Mailänder believed our sufferings would serve to purify us in preparation for spiritual rebirth. Throughout the letters, Mailänder remains consistent about this message, which he hoped to instil within his disciples.

Readers will find I have excluded speculation as much as possible, paying respect to the resources. While this telling of Alois Mailänder's life will serve scholars, as a long-time practitioner of the J.B Kerning and Mailänder methodologies for over a decade, I hope this volume will foremost serve to inspire a new generation of Rosicrucian students to take up Mailänder's practical spiritual alchemy.

Certainly, Gustav Meyrink predicted that, "The time is coming when the doctrine of this alchemy will be erected once more for many."[11] Looking at our large community, the time for its revival is happening now.

Therefore, this publication is also a call to action. The teachings presented herein are not intended or destined to merely sit on

---

[10] Alois Mailänder, Erik Dilloo-Heidger, and Chris Allen, *44 Letters to Gustav Meyrink (English Translation)* (Norderstedt: Books on Demand, 2020).

[11] Meyrink. *The White Dominican*. (Dedalus, Translated Mike Mitchel. 1994). Page 112.

the shelves in closed books, gathering dust as historical items of passing interest. Instead, they vibrantly call us to a practical awareness of our physical body. In my own experience, I have concluded that the practical undertaking of Mailänder's teachings complements all other esoteric practices, even taking them further, by providing a solid foundation to make metaphysical experiences and wisdom pregnant within our bodies. From the poetic, psychic and subtle, to whatever ritualistic revelations we may experience, all of which Mailänder might classify as drawing out the Baptism of Water, he takes us further by essentially saying *now draw it all into the body through the blood.*

Although this book is not intended to be a manual of practical instruction, for those who wish to spiritually meditate on the meaning of Alois Mailänder's teachings, this volume is your doorway to not only obtain an outline of his Rosicrucian doctrine but also to seize it in your being.

In the chapter titled "The Spiritual Alchemy of the Bund der Verheißung," I have shared my own conclusions on Mailänder's practical method which might support practitioners today.

You are now given the key. Opening the door is up to you.

Samuel Robinson

Oberstdorf, December 2021

Notes on Source Materials

All referenced items found in the notebooks and diary of Wilhelm Hübbe-Schleiden were found by Christine Eike and Erik Dilloo Heidger, who scoured through the old hand-written notebooks remaining in Hübbe-Schleiden's estate. There are three notebooks and three diaries in total.

These come from the Special Collections and Conservation Manuscripts and Rare Books Niedersächsische Staats und Universitätsbibliothek - SUB Göttingen.

The notebooks date from 1884 to 1887.

The NOTEBOOKS are:
- 1884/85 numbered Cod_Ms_Huebbe-Schleiden_1012_4
- 1885/86 numbered Cod_Ms_Huebbe-Schleiden_1012_5
- 1886/87 numbered Cod_Ms_Huebbe-Schleiden_1012_6

The DIARIES are:
- Cod_Ms_W_Huebbe_Schleiden_1013_15 Tagebuch 1896
- Cod_Ms_W_Huebbe_Schleiden_1013_16 Tagebuch 1896
- Cod_Ms_W_Huebbe_Schleiden_1013_18 Tagebuch 1896

The SOUL & FORM TEACHINGS are:
- Cod_Ms_W_Huebbe_Schleiden_1018_Seelenlehre
- Cod_Ms_W_Huebbe_Schleiden_1018_Formen_Lehre

The notebooks comprise casual notes, addresses, names, things to be done. The diaries are more systematic, including events recorded for certain days.

Hübbe-Schleiden's diaries and notebooks show that Mailänder's students copied the Formenlehre and Seelenlehr to work through. One version, for instance, was copied in 1892.

Hübbe-Schleiden also wrote a diary when he was in India in 1894. Of course, it wasn't meant for the public and was published by Norbert Klatt in 2009. In it, Hübbe-Schleiden referred to Mailänder as Johannes only once. Otherwise, he wrote his full name. In another diary from 1896, when he stayed with Mailänder for quite some time, he mostly wrote about him as Johannes.

The examination of Hübbe-Schleiden's diary from 1896 showed that in August and September of 1896, Hübbe-Schleiden spent several weeks in Dreieichenhain. At that time, he "read in the records of Crescentia" and subsequently copied *The Doctrine of the Soul* for his adopted daughter, Paula, who was accepted as Mailänder's personal pupil in the summer of 1896. Norbert Klatt notes in his 1993 book *Theosophy and Anthroposophy* that the copy we found most likely belonged to Paula Hübbe-Schleiden. Thus, the *Soul Teaching* copy we have is from 1896.

The original text, as handed down by Hübbe-Schleiden, is continuous and unstructured. The classification and numbering system was introduced by Erik Dilloo Heidger. The cover pages from part three of this book are from Hübbe-Schleiden estate documents 1018_Seelenlehre and 1018_Formen_Lehre.

Content included in square brackets [...] was offered by Hübbe-Schleiden as possible reading variants.

A series of five subheadings were added to the series of statements found in the *Soul Teaching* to distinguish separate subjects. These five titles were added by Hübbe-Schleiden himself. They are:

- From the Spiritual World
- The Truth

- Proverbs of Truth
- The Enigma of Truth
- A Dialogue of Feeling

They are included to represent an authentic translation of the manuscript. Although it is unlikely Mailänder intended their inclusion, they represent an appreciation of his ongoing years of instruction.

Hübbe-Schleiden's copy of the *Soul Teaching* is not originally from the hand of Mailänder's circle but is rather a copy. In his diary from 1896, Hübbe-Schleiden wrote the following entry on October 1st:

> In the morning I copied the Form Teachings for Paula, and all the additions since 1892 as an addendum to the Form Teachings and the Knowledge Lecture (Part I. Soul Teachings, Part II. Doctrine of Gods) for myself.[12]

In other words, the two scripts existed before 1896, at least since 1892, and supplements were added by 1896. In any case, the *Soul Teaching* could thus have been expanded at any time in between.

We do not know exactly who made the copies, but the so-called "Gabriele" coordinated it in some way.

From the above quote, we can conclude:

First: In addition to the *Soul Teaching* and the *Form Teachings*, there was also a *Doctrine of Gods* (Götterlehre), which made up the second part of the epistemology or Knowledge Lecture (with the *Soul Teaching* being the first part). We have not yet found this second part in any estate, but it may turn up in the future.[13]

---

[12] Cod_Ms_W_Huebbe_Schleiden_1013_18.

[13] The original page quite clearly shows that there is a "Formenlehre" and an "Erkenntnislehre". It states the "Erkenntnislehre has two parts: the Seelenlehre and

Second: Not only the words of Alois Mailänder were written down, but also those of Nikolaus Gabele. However, it can be assumed, based on what we know about this group, that Mailänder's words carried more weight and were more numerous.

To the cover of Hübbe-Schleiden's copy of Mailänder's *Form Teachings* was attached a torn-off sheet of loose paper. You can still discern two small text fragments on it:

> "I want to be strong" (1896) ". [I] thank you, that you are my helper!"

The text from the *Form Teachings* is found in the SUB Göttingen Huebbe_Schleiden_1013_18 Tagebuch 1896.

Now, regarding Franz Hartmann's account of Mailänder:

In some of his published accounts of Mailänder, it is clear Hartmann took liberties in describing the teaching of this Rosicrucian group. One must distil the material to absorb the essence and be wary of any possible injections of Blavatsky's Theosophical influences into Hartmann's content.

Hartmann's book, *Under the Adepts*, consisted of two sections. The first section presented his introduction to the group. The second section, "Memorable Recollections," contains recorded dictations made by Mailänder and Nicholas Gabele and should be considered Hartmann's version of Mailänder's *Soul Teaching*.

Hartmann describes "Memorable Recollections" as a personal diary account of what transpired during his time in that circle; it compares well with Meyrink's version of events and is therefore considered reliable.[14] "Memorable Recollections" is presented in

---

the Götterlehre. The title page of the Soul Teachings shows that it is part 1 of the "Erkenntnislehre".

[14] Hartmann, "Unter den Adepten," 1900.

its entirety in chapter four. Although not stated by Hartmann, this preserved another version of the original *Soul Teaching* itself.

The last item of that chapter, "A German Adept," is the first clear representation of Mailänder's Rosicrucian voice to the public. Hartmann presented his words through an interview in *The Theosophist* in May 1886. In the interview, Hartmann introduced several of his own Theosophical ideas and stated that he did not record Mailänder but reproduced the answers from his own memory.

In part five, I provide Meyrink's *Transfiguration of the Blood (Verwandlung des Blutes)*, sometimes titled *Metamorphosis of the Blood*. The text is very interesting because it mentions Jakob Lorber, Johannes, Friederich Eckstein, Kerning, and Yoga all within a single text, demonstrating a complete awareness of the esoteric practices kept hidden behind the Theosophical Society's closed doors at the time.

Meyrink's final typoscript of 1930 is included for comparison with his *Verwandlung des Blutes*.

Part One

What Do We Know About Alois Mailänder?

A Rosicrucian Forbearer

Outside the small church of Gschnaidt in Altusried, in March 1845, a local farmer looked out upon the snow and witnessed a miracle. Strange symbols had been impressed deep into the snow and not a footprint was in sight to account for their origin. Local legend tells us these figures were oracles that observers could interpret. We'll start our story here because this occurred in close proximity to Mailänder.

The location of the 1845 miracle took place just outside of Kempten and is now a site of pilgrimage in commemoration. Another church nearby called Heiligkreuz (Church of the Holy Cross) is famous for its Blutwunder, or "blood miracle," recorded in 1691, and another site of pilgrimage is the monastery in Schwabelsberg. All three sites can be reached by following a walking path from Kempten. The distance from Kempten to Gschnaidt and back is just fifteen kilometres.

We will return to the locations of these miracles in a moment in search of that unnamed farmer who witnessed the strange symbols in the snow. First, we must explore the heritage and activities of Mailänder's Rosicrucian initiator, a man only named as "Prestel" by all accounts.

Of the three leaders of Bund der Verheißung, one brother P. was the easiest to identify, for Willy Schroedter writes, "We are interested in someone else who belonged to this group, one P., a Rosicrucian. He was named Prestel and had the ability to convert base metals into noble ones."[15]

Schroedter continues:

> Now, Prestel was one of those who came to Germany. He was a nomadic and mysterious old man. He was a master joiner by profession, but could produce magical phantasmagoria, etc. In his possession there was a bottle containing a grey salt. According to him, it was the unfinished elixir of life. He always kept it near the warm kitchen stove. One day a real blue serpent appeared in the bottle and Prestel said, "I am going to die." He did die, too. The elixir was never perfected. After his death, it was passed on to a certain Gabele in Darmstadt who became his brother-in-law and, today, this unfinished product is in one of the cities of Southern Germany.[16]

Hartmann's *Magic: White & Black* contains a very important footnote regarding Prestel:

---

[15] Schrödter, *A Rosicrucian Notebook,* 132.

[16] German alchemist and occultist G.W Surya was the source for Willy Schroedter's statements. But the original text contains a strange detail concerning Prestel's origins. G.W Surya actually wrotes, "Auch hatte P. (ein Rosenkreuzer in Italien) die Macht, unedle Metalle zu veredeln. Einige Proben davon befinden sich in meinem Besitz." Thus, Prestel, a carpenter by trade, but its unlikely he was Italian considering the name Prestel is from the Kempten region. In G.W. Surya, *Der Triumph der Alchemie (Die Transmutation der Metalle)* (Leipzig: Altmann, 1908).

There lived about ten years ago a person whose name was Prestel, within a short distance of the town where we are now writing, who was a reputed Rosicrucian and Alchemist. We personally knew this man and are well acquainted with two of his still living disciples. This man was generally known as an eccentric and mysterious person. He possessed great powers of projecting the images formed in his own mind upon the minds of others, so that they believed to see things which, however, had no objective existence. For instance he was once waylaid by an enemy, and as the latter bounced upon him, he caused him to see a terrible sight of a scaffold and an executioner, so that the person was terrified and ran away; and it was not Prestel who told this story, but the man himself who attacked him. The former kept silent about it. -- Now, this man was not a full-fledged Alchemist, and could not make gold and the Elixir of Life, because, as he said, he could not find a woman sufficiently pure, and at the same time willing, to assist him in his labours. For, as it is known to all Alchemists, it requires the co-operation of the male and the female element to accomplish the highest process. This person could therefore not make pure gold. But he could change the nature of metals so that they would obtain certain chemical qualities, differing from substances of the same kind. He could, so to say, ennoble metals, so that, for instance, Iron or Brass would not rust if exposed to air and water, and we are now in possession of a Rosicrucian Cross made of brass, which, although it is over twenty years old, and has been exposed to salt-water air, and to climates where every other inferior metal rusts, is still as bright as it has been when first received, and it never needed any cleaning or polishing. -- This person also had the power to cause combustible substances to become incombustible, and he could perform many of the alchemical processes described in the books of T. Tritheim, abbot of Spandau. He insisted that he could have made himself to live a thousand years if he had found a suitable person to assist him in his alchemical work.[17]

Thus, in the above, Franz Hartmann states that Nikolaus Gabele and Alois Mailänder were both Prestel's disciples, which is supported by Karl Weinfurter in a similar description of the relationship between Mailänder and Prestel: "This leader had been initiated by a brother of the Order of the Rosicrucians, who came to him of his own free will and informed him of certain things which the former needed."[18][19]

Regarding Prestel's alchemical ability, Franz Hartmann states, "P. also had the power to transmute base metals into noble ones and I possess some examples of this."[20] Schroedter adds to this, "Hartmann received from Prestel the gift of a cross that he had made from transmuted metal." Hartmann also confirms that, "I have carried it about with me for many years on my travels, even in India."[21]

Schroedter continues with another gift from Prestel, "At this point, Dr. Franz Hartmann undid a small screw at the end of the cross. 'Here in this hole,' he said, 'there is a drop of the elixir

---

[17] Originally a footnote in Hartmann, *Magic, White and Black*, 216; Franz Hartmann, *Der weisse und schwarze Magie oder das Gesetz des Geistes in der Natur* (Leipzig: Friedrich, 1894), 235.

[18] Karel Weinfurter, *Der brennende Busch: der entschleierte Weg der Mystik* (Bietigheim, Württemberg: K. Rohm Verlag, 1980), 200.

[19] Hartmann said Prestel, "could perform many of the alchemical processes described in the books of T. Tritheim, abbot of Spandau," and quotes Tritheim in his Pronous in the Temple of Truth: "The fire resides within the heart and sends its rays through the whole body of man, causing it to live; but it no light is born from the fire without the presence of the spirit of holiness." In Franz Hartmann, *In the Pronaos of the Temple of Wisdom: Containing the History of the True and the False Rosicrucians : With an Introduction Into the Mysteries of the Hermetic Philosophy* (Theosophical Pub. Society, 1890), 121.

[20] Franz Hartmann, *Lotusblüten* 16 (1900): 154, footnote 1.

[21] This also suggests Hartmann knew Prestel before he met Blavatsky and returned to Kempten in 1885.

of life. Just smell it!' I did so and a sweet, fine vanilla like odour wafted toward me. I have never been able to forget this smell. This happened and was seen and smelled in Algund near Merano in the year of Our Lord 1910!"

Returning to the Kempten church miracles, two of those sites factor into our Mailänder investigation.

The miracle in Kempten at Heiligkreuz, or Church of the Holy Cross, revealed itself in 1691 when according to legend, on the eve of the Holy Apostle Jacob, one Elisabeth Wegerin was busy turning hay in the square where the church stands today. Suddenly, she saw blood splatter half a shoe high in five places on the surface of a small oval tablecloth, lasting half an hour. These five fountains of blood have been associated with the five wounds of Christ on the cross. Several eyewitnesses confirmed the testimony by taking an oath and two rakes kept in the church are said to have shown the blood stains for some time after the event.

Mailänder's group now becomes tied to the scene by Willy Schroedter, who records that:

> "This man Mailänder," said Meyrink, stressing that the latter had never told a lie, "saw one winter's day... near the Church of the Holy Cross, the snow stained as red as blood in a certain place, and declared that an adept of the Middle Ages (Paracelsus, 1493—1541) had buried some of the red tincture and that the red coloration in the snow had been caused by emanations from this tincture." The "blood" was impressed at five places around the Church and many others saw it besides Mailänder.[22-23]

---

[22] Schrödter, *A Rosicrucian Notebook*, 132.

[23] Meyrink also describes the Paracelsian origins in his description of John the Imposter in Gustav Meyrink, "Hochstapler der Mystik," *Allgemeine Zeitung*, 1927.

Therefore, it appears that Mailänder and Prestel had some sort of prequel story to account for what they considered to be the actual, and more alchemical, origins of these five fountains of blood.

Mailänder's and Prestel's ties to the second miracle of signs in the snow is somewhat elusive. Yet, given the above circumstances, I would share a special hypothesis regarding a painting hanging inside the foyer of the chapel of Gschnaidt in Altusried. Commemorating the snow miracle of 1845, it reads:

> Here in Geschneite, one afternoon in March 1845 from one to three o'clock, in a four to five inches deep snow, a farmer and a merchant observed an incalculable imprinted number of different writings and signs of all kinds, without any connection or context. Neither human footsteps nor other traces of a living creature could be discovered. The interpretation of this phenomenon will not be difficult for the observer of our time.

Painting inside the chapel of Gschnaidt in Altusried

Who were the two unnamed figures, farmer and merchant, who saw the signs in the snow?[24]

In Kempten archive documents, one Prestel is named as Franz H. Prestel in full, and recorded as a "Schreiner," which is a carpenter. This indeed matches Hartmann's description of his profession. Yet this does not fit with the two professions named in the Geschneite painting in Altusried. The Kempten document elaborates that this Prestel came from Kindberg, which is near Kempten, to Altusried in the year of 1845, so at least the timeline fits. It was my eagle-eyed friend Christine Eike who discovered that this Franz H. Prestel applied for the rights to work as a carpenter in the very same location of Altusried at that time![25]

Additionally, Christine discovered an enticing 1885 entry in the notebooks of Wilhelm Hübbe-Schleiden, which introduces one new detail:

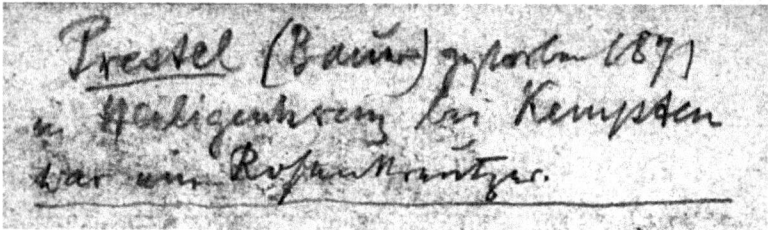

Prestel (Bauer) gestorben 1871 in Heilig[en]kreuz bei Kempten war ein Rosenkreuzer.[26]

---

[24] The painting reads, "Bauren nebst einem Gewerbsmanne" so it's not clear if the witness was two people or one farmer with a second person who was a tradesman/craftsman. The German means "in addition" or "as well" so it could be a single man.

[25] The file reads: "Altusried - Application of Franz H. Prestel from Kindberg for the operation of the purchased carpenter's rights in Altusried." Original, "Altusried - Gesuch des Franz H. Prestel von Kindberg zum Betrieb der erkauften Schreinergerechtsame zu Altusried." "Findmitteldatenbank Der Staatlichen Archive Bayerns, Bezirksamt Kempten (No. 1-2788),"

[26] Heiligkreuz is spelt as Heiligenkreuz. Wilhelm Hübbe-Schleiden, "Wilhelm Hübbe-

Translation: Prestel (Farmer) died in 1871 in Heilig[en]kreuz at Kempten was a Rosicrucian.

Although Theosophists record Prestel as a carpenter, the information doesn't necessarily conflict. Many farmers practiced a trade as well. Therefore, knowing that Mailänder's circle had a fascination with the blood miracle of the neighbouring Church of the Holy Cross, there is a high chance the farmer who witnessed the snow miracle of March 1845 was indeed our farmer and Rosicrucian, Prestel, who arrived to Altusried that year.

March 1845 happens to fall upon Mailänder's second birthday and adopting a somewhat superstitious view of such signs, we might speculate this month obtained some significance for Rosicrucians considering the Great Comet of 1843. This comet appeared in the very month of Mailänder's birth, first observed on March 5th and remained visible for a total of 45 days in the sky. Its trailing light blazed over the heavens so brightly and it developed such an extremely long tail that during its passage, people believed it heralded the end of the world. We don't know what occurred in March of 1844, but I might speculate it appears to have become an auspicious month for those in Kempten when viewed alongside the oracular snow miracle.

We do not know if such signs spurred Prestel to seek out a worthy candidate to impart his knowledge to.[27] Although Franz Hartmann confirms that Mailänder was instructed by Prestel from the time of his youth and Weinfurter states Prestel was his Rosicrucian initiator and came to Mailänder "of his own free will and informed him" of some special knowledge that Mailänder

---

Schleiden's Notebooks" (SUB Göttingen, 1884/85 numbered Cod. MS Hübbe Schleiden 1012: 4, 1884 1885), 20.

[27] Oral tradition explains Prestel sought out Mailänder as a boy. But this cannot be proven in literature.

needed. As the last living genuine Rosicrucian, it is quite probable that Prestel wished to impart his knowledge to a successor.

The Covenant of Promise

"His figure was youthful and strong, his face expressed knowledge and happiness, his eyes seemed to penetrate into the innermost depths of my soul."[28] This is how Franz Hartmann describes Alois Mailänder when introducing him to Theosophists as the "German Adept" in 1886. It was quite fortunate for Franz Hartmann, as an avid seeker of wisdom, that he came from the same town as Mailänder and Prestel.

Recalling Willy Schroedter's account that Hartmann personally received from Prestel the gift of a cross made from alchemically transmuted metal, and our discovery that Prestel died in 1871, this would imply that Franz Hartmann came into contact with Prestel before this date and that he was the first out of the Theosophical Society's ranks to have discovered the Bund der Verheißung community.[29] Hartmann confirmed that he had carried this alchemically transmuted metal cross "with me for many years, even in India," supporting that he already knew Prestel before departing to Adyar with Madame Blavatsky.

Call it good fortune or destiny that the paths of the Bund der Verheißung and the Theosophical Society, which ran parallel for a time, would soon intertwine. Wilhelm Hübbe-Schleiden states in his notebook that he first met Nikolaus Gabele at the house of the Countess Spreti during the Christmas of 1884.[30] She

---

[28] *The Theosophist* 7, no. 80 (May 1886): 534–37.

[29] Franz Hartmann (1838-1912) would have been 33 years of age when Prestel died.

[30] Her name was Caroline von Spreti, geb. Hartmann (1842-1915). See Hübbe-Schleiden, "Wilhelm Hübbe-Schleiden's Notebooks," 1884 1885.

was Franz Hartmann's sister. Hartmann would only return from his excursion to India in May 1885, although he states that he knew the Gabele family for twenty years prior due to the famed seership of Frau Gabele, which coincides well with his story of receiving the alchemical cross earlier from Prestel.[31] Given the timeline, Alois Mailänder must have engaged in Theosophical affairs from 1885 onward.

The important position Mailänder would soon hold as a type of Rosicrucian master, veiled behind the Theosophical Society in Germany, Austria, and Prague, is quite remarkable considering his humble origins as the illegitimate son of Anna Mailänder, a factory worker from Schleis in South Tyrol.[32] In 1853, he moved to Kempten and solidified his ties to the Gabele family. First he married the sister of Crescentia Gabele (born Messmer), who was the wife of Nikolaus Gabele, also called "Salomon" in the circle.[33] After his first wife died, he married Karoline Gabele in 1874, sister to Nikolaus Gabele. They had one son, Anton, who was born in 1876 but died at one year of age.[34] Mailänder and Gabele, as the other leader of the Bund der Verheißung, must have known each other for quite some time because Prestel had taught them together in their youth. Nikolaus Gabele's mother was the famous local seer.

Mailänder was of Catholic background and Nikolaus Gabele was Old Catholic, but we find little in their teachings related to

---

[31] Twenty years prior brings Hartmann's contact to the 1860's which is before Prestel died.

[32] Alois Mailänder was born near Ravensburg in Swabia Germany.

[33] Meyrink says that John the evangelist is the head of the order and vicar of Solomon. See Gustav Meyrink, *The White Dominican* (England; USA: Dedalus; Ariadne, 1994).

[34] Mailänder personal record from Dreieichenhain city council provided by Gernot Schmidt.

Catholic matters. The localities of both Ravensburg and Kempten were pietist enclaves where a personal connection to God and spiritual revelations were held in higher regard than attending church.[35] Given the environment, it is easy to understand how the religious culture of the Covenant of Promise drew heavily upon alchemical Christian Theosophy and Rosicrucianism.[36]

Gustav Meyrink noted the Theosopher spirit, comparing Mailänder to Boehme:

> He resembled in many of his experiences the seer Jacob Boehme, who today is known to every educated person as a wonderful person; he surpassed him as a clairvoyant in many respects, but sky-high he surpassed him through the mentioned realization that leaving the world is wrong, however sublime this escape from the world may seem.[37]

Generally, Mailänder's students considered him a Christian mystic and Rosicrucian.[38]

Emil Bock tells how a thirty-three-year-old Alois Mailänder became a Rosicrucian seer in 1877 and about the early days of the Covenant of Promise:

> He (Nikolaus Gabele) was not the head. The real centre of this circle, which consisted of older and younger workers from the weaving mill and their wives, was a certain Alois Mailänder.

---

[35] Mailänder, Dilloo-Heidger, and Allen, *44 Letters to Gustav Meyrink (English Translation)*, 24.

[36] "Christian Theosophy" and "Theosopher" refers to Christian pietist mysticism and not Blavatsky's Theosophy.

[37] Gustav Meyrink, "Die Verwandlung des Blutes. Meyrinkiana," in *Nachlass von Gustav Meyrink (1868-1932) – BSB Meyrinkiana*, Bayerische Staatsbibliothek, vol. VI:14, Repertorium des Nachlasses von Gustav Meyrink (1868-1932), Sonst Nummer: BSB-Hss Meyrinkiana. BSB-ID: 12773438 (München, 1970), fol. 15.

[38] Hartmann calls him a Christian mystic. See Hartmann, "Unter den Adepten," 1900.

Seven years earlier, in 1877, this group of friends had a strange experience. Nikolaus Gabele, who was a year younger than Mailänder, suddenly begun to speak about Christian matters, and while he spoke, a great enlightenment had broken in upon the soul of the then 33-year-old Alois Mailänder. From that moment on he was a Christian seer.

Completely without the help from modern education, in the most simple living conditions, he worked first in his own small circle. He was called the 'Brother John' because it was believed that John spoke through him. The other members of this group were also given names. So Nikolaus Gabele had the name Solomon, and since they didn't really know the language, they said 'Solomonus'. All had biblical names, e.g. Noah, Adam. They spent the few free hours which they had together. Alois Mailänder, who was 40 years old at the time (when Hübbe-Schleiden met him early 1885) worked a 15 or 14 hour day in the weaving mill, where artificial light was used all day, and received two German marks a day for it. It was similar for the others. But in the evenings they gathered together and it was then that Mailänder-John put himself in a particular enlightened condition and, out of certain clairvoyance, answered the questions which were put to him.[39]

Emil Bock mentions two items of particular interest in understanding Alois Mailänder that we will explore. The first is the use of Biblical names within his circle and the second is Mailänder's gift of seership.

The coverage of Bock's *The Life and Times of Rudolf Steiner*, it should be said, contains additional details because Bock had access to one hundred and fifty letters written by Mailänder. The

---

[39] Emil Bock, *Rudolf Steiner: Studien zu seinem Lebensgang und Lebenswerk : Vortrage vor Mitgliedern der Anthroposophischen Gesellschaft* (Stuttgart: Verlag Freies Geistesleben, 1961), 181.

entire collection of these letters has only recently resurfaced and because it is not yet accessible to the public it is partly difficult to distinguish what is Bock's own opinion, where he made mistakes and what is factual in his coverage.

It is true that Biblical names were given to members of the group, although not of such primordial figures as Adam and Noah. Thanks to Mailänder's letters to Gustav Meyrink and Wilhelm Hübbe-Schleiden's diaries, we know a handful of the spiritual names Mailänder gifted his students.

Of the students, Meyrink was called Ruben-Juda, as seen in Erik Dilloo Heidger's recently published *44 Letters to Gustav Meyrink*. Meyrink's first wife was called Maria. Wilhelm Hübbe-Schleiden's spiritual name was Daniel. Gabele's wife Crescentia was named Gabriele. Mailänder's wife was named Ruth. Gabor Gabele was called Elias. Franz Hartmann was Emanuel. Günther Wagner, a later dedicated disciple of Rudolf Steiner, was called Tobias within the Bund.[40]

1896 Diary entry - Günther Wagner is named "Tobias" by Johannes

Such given names, according to Mailänder, acted as a symbolic spiritual sickle to cut out the ripe fruit, grant power to stir up the soul life, and act as a verbal key to open the book of our inner being.[41]

---

[40] Wilhelm Hübbe-Schleiden, "Tagebuch von Wilhelm Hübbe Schleiden (Diaries)" (SUB Göttingen Cod. MS W Hübbe Schleiden 1013: 16 1896, 1896).

[41] The Soul Teaching statements are listed in Part III of this book. See statements 134, 152, and 357.

Believers of Die Allgäuer Erweckungsbewegung or "the Allgäu Revival Movement," which arose at the end of the 18th century in the same region of Kempten, also called each other Biblical names. For example, Boos was called Joseph, Feneberg was called Nathanael, and his two attendees were given the saint names of Markus and Silas.[42] This causes us to pause and consider to what extent Mailänder drew upon this older pietistic heritage.

The Allgäu Revival Movement was initiated by Martin Boos (1762-1825) and Johann Michael Feneberg (1751-1812). Both were Catholic priests with strong leanings towards Protestant pietism after absorbing the teachings of Johann Arndt together with Zinzendorf and his Moravian Brethren and other enthusiastic Theosopher books. Martin Boos' followers were called the Erweckten Brüder, or the "Awakened Brethren," and sought "Christ in us and for us," placing special emphasis in following the heart over reason. They were known to have circulated pietistic literature amongst themselves, as later found in Mailänder's Bund.[43] The believers also called their movement a Bund and behaved like siblings, exchanging kisses and hugs.[44]

Furthermore, the Awakened Brethren emphasized receiving a true "baptism in the spirit" and awakening through a "baptism

---

[42] Rahel Christine Hahn, "'Ach, er ist ein armer Sünder und hätte verzweifeln müssen': zu Theologie und Frömmigkeit des katholischen Priesters Martin Boos (1762-1825)" (Master Thesis, Vienna, University of Vienna; Evangelisch-Theologische Fakultät, 2015), 17;39. Furthermore, Boos had a chaplain at his side since January 1810, one Josef Rechberger, a native of Linz, who recruited for Boos right at the beginning of his work and was given the significant epithet "Timotheus." Ibid., 78.

[43] One of the books Boos read was "Passionspredigten" by Hermann Daniel Hermes 1784. Boos wrote, "Hermes Sermons on the Passion make such a deep impression on my sinner's heart that I cannot describe it to you." Hermann Daniel Hermes who was caught up with Johann Christoph von Wöllner and his plans to establish the Golden Rosenkreuzers as a religious and governmental authority. See Ibid., 134.

[44] Geschwisterkuss und Umarmung. Ibid., 26.

of fire," which they called Feuertaufe and Geistestaufe, as would Mailänder.[45]

Martin Boos' writings cover much ground concerning rebirth, baptism in the spirit and fire, and the birth of Christ in the souls of believers. In a letter dated May 31, 1797, Boos provided an impressive description of those who had undergone their spiritual rebirth in the Wiggensbach village, which is located on the outskirts of Kempten. Therein, Boos mentions visions of flames, occurrences of miracles, and "spiritual birth pains," requesting authorities to have "patience and faith."[46] These themes, particularly the notion of experiencing spiritual birth pains, are subjects dear to Mailänder's spiritual path.

When viewing the significant stature women held within the earlier Awakened Brethren, it is quite possible that women similarly held far weightier spiritual positions in Mailänder's Bund der Verheißung than surviving manuscripts today evidence. It is clear that Nicholas Gabele's wife Crescentia (spiritual name Gabriele) and Mailänder's wife Karoline both played central roles within the Bund. Meyrink's letters reveal how Gabriele took care of many duties in the organizing of Mailänder's circle. Not only did she pen Mailänder's letters and apparently edit the manuscripts of the Soul and Form Teachings, but she furthermore held serious conversations concerning spiritual subjects with Mailänder's visiting disciples.

Modest laywomen played a central role in the Allgäu Revival Movement.

Two figures especially emerge, Magdalena Fischer and Therese Erndt. Related to Boos' title of Joseph, the first was called Maria

---

[45] Hahn, "Ach, er ist ein armer Sünder"; Alois Mailänder, *Seelenlehre - Formenlehre*, ed. Christine Eike and Erik Dilloo-Heidger, 1st edition (BoD – Books on Demand, 2021). Mailänder's Soul Teaching statement 152 reads "Durch die Feuertaufe."

[46] Hahn, "Ach, er ist ein armer Sünder."

after awakening others to their spiritual rebirth in Christ. Both women were addressed as Gebär-Mütter, or "Birth Mothers," meaning they were representative vehicles of Maria on earth, even living "wombs" whereby their function was to "give the Saviour to the people as Mary once did" to communicate him to the world, "not like it was as in the past with his bodily birth," but that the spiritual activity of these Maria Gebär-Mütter would call forth your "Christ within."[47]

A carpenter and believer of the movement stated:

> "That man should receive the Saviour and be completely ruled by Him.... and because the Christ child had a mother, this rebirth must take place through a female of the covenant."[48]

Martin Boos died in 1825 and Mailänder was born in 1843. Given this timeline and the atmosphere of the Kempten region which had been swept up by the Allgäu Revival Movement, it is impossible that Mailänder and Gabele did not grow up amongst immediate followers and personal friends of Martin Boos himself.

In many ways, Mailänder's Bund is a continuation of the Allgäu Revival Movement.

Here I provide *Statutes of our Covenant of Promise* for the first time.[49]

---

[47] Ibid., 26.

[48] German original: "Bei seinem Verhör in Konstanz gab der Zimmermann Justin MENDLER zu Protokoll: „Daß der Mensch den Heiland bekomme und dann ganz von ihm regiert werde ... und weil das Christ kindlein eine Mutter gehabt, müsse diese Wiedergeburt durch ein Weibsbild des Bundes erfolgen." In Hildebrand Dussler, *Johann Michael Feneberg und die Allgäuer Erweckungsbewegung Ein kirchengeschichtl. Beitr. aus d. Quellen zur Heimatkunde d. Allgäus* (Kempten (Allgäu): Verl. f. Heimatpflege, 1959), 139., cited in Hahn, "Ach, er ist ein armer Sünder."

[49] Wilhelm Hübbe-Schleiden, "Tagebuch von Wilhelm Hübbe Schleiden (Diaries)" (SUB Göttingen Cod. MS W Hübbe Schleiden 1013: 18 1896, September 22, 1895).

According to Conversations with Johannes.

The statues of our Covenant of Promise that each of us have are:[50]

Finding what is good for us and doing it. Letting go of what
we feel is harming us.
Keeping the church within ourselves.
The divine "I" fights against the animal-self-will within us. For
this we have to desire and strive for the good and ask for it. It
doesn't work with force, not even with "I want to be humble."
Even this grace must be requested.
You shouldn't want, think, and do whatever you most desire
whenever you feel the urge. Practice self-control and self-denial.
Give to others spiritual power from your own inner experience
and revelation. To do this, use the head, but it must come
from the heart.

Mailänder told Meyrink that he could never turn his back on
his students, that he must always lovingly support them. This
was once they had been accepted into the Bund because it was
impossible to demand discipleship with him according to his
Inner Word. Thus, many were not accepted. [51]

Another treat discovered was the home address of Gabele,
included for historical reference:

Address of Nikolaus Gabele: Hübbe-Schleiden's notebook from 1885

---

[50] In this instance, "Die Satzungen unseres Bundes der Verheißung Gottes."

[51] Karel Weinfurter, *Man's Highest Purpose: The Lost Word Regained* (Kila, Mont.:
Kessinger, 2010), 152.

Despite the long working days of labour Mailänder and Gabele underwent at the factory, we have to appreciate the beautiful environment in which the Bund der Verheißung found itself. Kempten is located right before Oberstdorf, a famous site today for fresh air and activities such as ski jumping and mountain hiking. Stunning mountain views are accessed via picturesque paths in this southernmost part of Germany, which immediately enters the towering Alps of Austria.

Franz Hartmann drew upon the scene for inspiration when penning his novel, *With the Adepts: An Adventure Among the Rosicrucians.*[52] Describing the mountains as sublime, with shining glaciers that glisten like vast mirrors in the rising of the sun, Hartmann says that he wandered into "one mysterious valley which had not yet been explored by me, and which led towards a high, bifurcated mountain peak, whose summit was said to be inaccessible." In his story, Hartmann accesses the inaccessible, but things shift gear when he meets a mysterious dwarf who escorts him to an adept residing in a hidden Rosicrucian colony.

Hartmann also appears to have sculpted parts of his novel after his contact with the Bund der Verheißung, for he writes in 1885 that, "In the heart of the Bavarian mountains I have found a society of real occultists, of practical workers, possessing a high moral character, and although they are illiterate and 'uneducated' people, yet they are well acquainted with the mysteries of the Hindu and Jewish religions, called the secret doctrine or Esoteric Philosophy." He attributes a range of Theosophical teachings to the Rosicrucian colony in his novel, like the acquisition of

---

[52] Hartmann begins describing his adventure as commencing in the village of Oberstdorf, writing, "I arrived at O., which was the place selected as a starting-point for my excursions into the mountains." In Franz Hartmann, *With the Adepts: An Adventure Among the Rosicrucians* (London.: W. rider, 1910).

psychic powers, but Prestel is honoured in the story through the transmutation of a silver piece into gold using a red powder.

Hartmann writes about his acceptance into the Bund, "I made the acquaintance of those people and went with them to the top of the mountain and looked into the spiritual Tibet or (as the Jews call it) Canaan. I saw with them the Promised Land, but like Moses was not yet able to enter it. When we went up there were six members in their society. When we came down that society numbered seven."[53]

I mention this here because Hartmann's acceptance into the Bund occurred in the mountains and therefore took place before Mailänder left Kempten to guide members of the Theosophical Society.

The location of Kempten, Oberstdorf and these mountains holds personal significance as this is the home of my partner and her family. As luck would have it, I found myself wandering the very same mountains where Hartmann and Mailänder took adventures and where I would soon have my own.

What brought Alois Mailänder out of this beautiful and humble setting in Kempten and caused him to accept a new role within the Theosophical Society? It doesn't appear to have been the seeking of fame as a mystic seer, exemplified by prohibiting his disciples from openly sharing his name. Roger Heil mentioned the change from his hard-working conditions at the Kempten factory to easier living and Franz Hartmann presented a ruling influence behind Mailänder's actions, writing, "They had repeatedly received offers of better situations, but refused them, saying that they were not permitted to change."[54]

---

[53] Franz Hartmann, *The Theosophist* 6, no. 12 (September 1885): 293.

[54] *The Theosophist* 6, no. 72 (1885): 29.

But change did come. Karl Weinfurter said it was the presiding force of the "Inner Word" that had previously prevented Mailänder from ever leaving Kempten until the time was right:

> They were both employed in a big weaving factory and were very poor indeed. One Saturday, when leaving the factory, they walked together home, and of a sudden the Leader informed his relation of his having given notice. To this his relation replied, "So did I." They were both induced to do so by their Inner Word. Though they did not know what they should live on, yet they obeyed the command without any objections, and did what they had been asked to do. But their uncertainty did not last long. The following day the Leader was already proprietor of a handsome country house, a gift of a rich lady, a pupil of his.[55]

Weinfurter never reveals the identity of this "rich lady" who snapped up Alois Mailänder, but we can now celebrate who she was and how she brought Mailänder into his role within the Theosophical Society.

Rosicrucian Teacher of the Theosophical Society

"Mailänder's abilities quickly became known to the leading occultists and theosophists around the 19th century," writes Roger Heil, a researcher on occult sects in Germany, adding, "One of them was the well-to-do Marie Gebhard from Elberfeld,

---

[55] Weinfurter's account confirms research by Birgit Liljestrom who in "Die Gebhard-L'Estranges - Eine Familie auf dem Weg zum Olymp" stated Mary Gebhard had already commissioned the renovation of the Bruderheim in Dreieichenhain prior to Mailänder's arrival to Elberfeld in 1886. See Weinfurter, *Man's Highest Purpose*, 153; Birgit Liljestrom, "On the Quest for Olympus: The Family Gebhard-L'Estrange - Pilgrims, Patrons and Founders, Part 1," *Farther Magazine* 2nd edition (2021).

wife of the manufacturer Arthur Gebhard. Once Mailänder was no longer able to cope with the hard work and had blood hemorrhaging, Marie Gebhard brought the entire family with Mailänder to Grotenbeck near Elberfeld, where they found easier work."[56]

In Elberfeld, Mailänder was welcomed by members of the very first Theosophical Lodge ever established in Germany, the Theosophische Societät Germania. This lodge was started by Mary Gebhard together with Gustav Meyrink and Franz Hartmann.[57] The group included Karl Kiesewetter and Wilhelm Hübbe Schleiden and was founded on July 27, 1884 at the Gebhards' Elberfeld property. Mary Gebhard was wife to Gustav Gebhard, owner of a silk factory and bank co-founder, allowing Mailänder and his brother-in-law, Nicholas Gabele, to easily continue employment in the same line of work in Elberfeld.

Given her status, Mary Gebhard was undoubtedly wealthy and could sponsor her spiritual teachers and, in so doing, select the best occult teachers the world had to offer. Mary Gebhard's previous teacher was none other than French occultist Eliphas Levi, who had also stayed with her at the same Elberfeld property in 1871. She was one of Levi's two known students. Karl R.H Frick asserted she was also the disciple of Yves Saint d'Alveydre.

---

[56] Elberfeld, Wuppertal is just a short drive away from my residence in Dortmund where I located the last Mailänder believers still active today in the nearby village of Wetter (who are esoteric followers of Jakob Lorber) in a sectarian Christian church. See Heil, "Okkultistische Sekte im Dreieichenhain der Jahrhundertwende."

[57] Meyrink and Kiesewetter were quite good friends. Meyrink's famous "Angel in the West Window" novel was actually first written by Carl Kiesewetter and titled "John Dee and the Angel from the Western Window,". See Karl Kiesewetter, *John Dee and the Angel from the Western Window* (Leipzig: Spohr, 1895).

Mailänder's arrival into the midst of the Gebhard circle was auspicious given recent events. The two scandals of the coulomb affair of September 1884 and then the Hodgson Report of 1885 had shaken the whole Theosophical Society, causing the group's loyalty to sway. Blavatsky's second visit to Elberfeld in the summer of 1886 did not instil trust in her within its members. As a result, the Theosophische Societät Germania lodge was closed on December 31, 1886, with a list of 13 active members.

It struck me to learn that Alois Mailänder's personal records showed he resettled from Kempten to this same Elberfeld property on December 29th of 1886.[58] This was just two days prior to the closing of the Theosophical lodge! Its closing must have been tied to Mailänder's arrival. It was clear to me that after the death of Eliphas Levi, Mary Gebhard and several Theosophists had found their new master.

The original plan for Mailänder to continue employment in Elberfeld changed, as Roger Heil recollects,

> Mailänder missed the mountains, and the Prussians did not suit him. Then Mrs. Gebhard decided to buy a farm in southern part of Frankfurt in Germany. She found this farm in Dreieichenhain. In the Solmische-WeiherStraße 22, a residential building, including lands belonging to the road contractor Wilhelm Gräser, was being auctioned off.[59] This Hainer Bürger

---

[58] The city archive in Kempten family records that Mailänder left Kempten in 1886. That document states Mailänder "Arrived to Kempten 1853, moved away from Kempten to Vohwinkel, Eberfeld 1886." The exact date of December-29-1886 comes from Mailänder's personal record. The document, which includes the date of Mailänder's marriage, was sent to me from Gernot Schmidt from Dreieichenhain city council who maintains Dreieichenhain archive records and is doing research on the history of the Mailänder Foundation, a charity Mailänder established to leave his wealth for an orphanage.

[59] Roger Heil writes, "Gasthaus "Zum Darmstädter Hof" Solmische-Weiher Strasse

carried out all orders in the nearby city of Frankfurt during the construction boom of the Wilhelminian period of wealth, so that he was able to build a most representative building in the style of historicism in the grove in 1880. When he died in 1890, his heirs had the property auctioned together with the inventory. Mrs. Gebhard bought the farm, probably also with the participation of other wealthy Theosophists, and gave it to the families of Mailänder and Gabele.

Alois Mailänder and Nicolaus Gabele no longer needed to do their strenuous work at the factory. They had found a permanent home, which they called henceforth "Bruderheim" (Brother-home). Here they received guests from all over the world and lived above all from their donations.[60]

Gernot Schmidt's archive material says Mailänder resettled in Dreieichenhain in 1890.

---

22. This building was built in 1880 by the builder Georg Gräser II in the historical style. Later it became the property of the freemason Nikolaus Gabele. The latter established a meeting room under the roof, called a temple by the Freemasons. In 1907, Richard Auth bought the house and established a restaurant with guest rooms there." The information that Gabele was a freemason could not be verified and may be based on speculation from Dreieichenhain locals who observed the comings and goings. See Gernot Schmidt and Roger Heil, *Feste Mauern, enge Gassen: Dreieichenhain in der Erinnerung*, Stadt und Landschaft Dreieich (Hayner Burg-Vlg, 1983); Gernot Schmidt, *Dreieichenhain Beiträge zur Geschichte von Burg und Stadt Hayn in der Dreieich* (Dreieich: Hayner Burg-Verlag, 1983).

[60] Roger Heil's research is excellent. Upon closer inspection, it appears he did not draw upon Meyrink's lecture on Mailänder "On the Transformation of the Blood," nor Hartmann's two books on Mailänder and Kerning but relied on local accounts from witnesses. See Heil, "Okkultistische Sekte im Dreieichenhainder Jahrhundertwende."

Picture of the guesthouse where many Theosophists stayed when visiting Alois Mailänder. The Gabele family became the owners of the hotel itself.[61]

---

[61] Schmidt and Heil, *Feste Mauern, enge Gassen*, 90. Permissions on images kindly granted by Roger Heil.

Mailänder and Gabele's Bruderheim that was bought by Mary Gebhard and financed also by several Theosophists including Carl Kellner.[62]

Another picture of the Bruderheim[63]

---

[62] Ibid., 84.

[63] Ibid.

The spiritual circle at the Bruderheim.
Mailander left with is wife, Nikolas Gabele right with his wife.
Unidentified male at the front right.[64]

I must credit Roger Heil's efforts as the primary work on Mailänder's participation in Theosophical circles. This volume combines facts and quotes from several sources to expand upon his findings. For completeness, I offer the following translation from Roger Heil's work.

Dreieichenhain Becomes a Center of Theosophy "Occult Sects in Dreieichenhain in the Last Hundred Years" Part Two, By Roger Heil, 1990

In the following years, all the leading Theosophists in the world, always wealthy citizens and aristocrats, made their pilgrimages

---

[64] Heil, Roger. "Okkultistische Sekte im Dreieichenhain der Jahrhundertwende." Landschaft Dreieich, 1990, 120–25. The unidentified male is usually identified as Wilhelm Hübbe-Schleiden. This figure is too old. It is possibly Carl du Prel.

to Dreieichenhain. They all wanted to become followers of Mailänder. Some of them already had earlier contact from during his Kempten period.

Anyone who wanted to become a student of Mailänder had to undergo an examination first. He led all those who wanted to find the way to Christ through him to the rose garden at the east of the house. When walking through the garden, Mailänder first questioned his inner voice. Only when he was ordered to take heart did he receive the pupil!

At the same time, many a high-ranking personality had difficulties with the manners of the simple weaver. This is seen in a letter to the colonial politician and Theosophist Dr. Wilhelm Hübbe-Schleiden where Mailander expresses with the following words: "Leadership is not so easy, and the so-called nobles and educated are so sensitive, my language will not please them, and it does not matter to me, whether a count or a servant, whoever they are that I lead, I demand obedience from them, and if they cannot obey, then they ought not to have ever demanded to be spiritually guided!"

Due to the loss of documents after the Second World War, only a few names of the high-ranking students have survived in addition to the already mentioned Hübbe-Schleiden and the Gebhard family, which was obviously often found in Dreieichenhain. Among them are the nobles Countess Spreti from Munich, the Austrian Countess Attems[65] and the Erbgraf zu Leiningen. Military figures, such as the Austrian Chief of Staff Scheuma[66] and the Colonel Olcott, Count Arienisches, as well as the recognized Art Nouveau painter and book illustrator Fidus (Hugo Höppener)[67] and the above-mentioned writer,

---

[65] Sophie Countess von Attems-Heiligenkreuz (1862-1937), née von Hartig, writer.

[66] Schemua, Blasius Edler von (1856-1920); Member of the Austrian General Staff.

[67] Erik Dilloo Heidger points out that Mailänder did not accept Fidus as a student.

editor and banker Gustav Meyrink (religious name Ruben-Juda). Mailänder was also closely connected with the founders of the Theosophical Society worldwide and in Germany. First and foremost is the most prominent occultist and one of the most dazzling figures of the 19ᵗʰ century, the Russian Helena Petrovna Blavatsky, who visited Dreieichenhain with her Indian friend Babaji.[68] Even the physician and mystical writer Dr. Franz Hartmann and many Czech occultists such as Karl Weinfurter were students of Mailänder![69]

Visitors of Mailänder spent the night in the former hotel Zu den Drei Eichen (Waldstrasse 2) of Hainer Mayor Wilhelm Eidam.[70] Guests of Mailänder were often to be found here, because almost daily the students, who had come from far away, sought his advice, through wagon transport from Langen or Sprendlingen railway stations, even in the winter months. Mailänder occupied an entire floor of the hotel, having many followers in England, who also spent the winter in Dreieichenhain because of the climate. The names of some of those Englishmen were: Mrs Dian, Mr. Thornton, Mr. Rauwie, and Mr. Finch.[71]

---

[68] Roger Heil seems to be mistaken there. Blavatsky left the Continent for London spring 1887, never to return.

[69] Driessen's diary is quoted in "Indisches Tagebuch," where he states they placed a Mahatma picture, painted by Schmiechen, at Mailänder's house in Dreiechenhain. Thus, Theosophy and Mailänder's Rosicrucian circle must really have been interwoven. Whilst important Theosophists made pilgrimages to Mailänder, our Alois Mailänder himself, and co, must have felt some connection to the movement. See Wilhelm Hübbe-Schleiden, *Indisches Tagebuch 1894/1896: Mit Anmerkungen und einer Einleitung herausgegeben von Norbert Klatt* (Göttingen: Norbert Klatt Verlag, 2009), 16 footnote #23.

[70] Roger Heil informed me that this hotel then belonged to the Gabele family of Mailander's circle.

[71] Mr. Finch, Gerard B. (1835-1913), was in 1887 the first President of the "London Blavatsky Lodge".

Through visits and recommendations, including occult sessions, Mailänder tried to guide his disciples to Christ. Here, Mailänder and Gabele, often with the family, as well as the visitors w e r e w i t h i n the so-called "temple", which was in the attic of the Bruderheim. The content of the sessions can no longer be reconstructed, but part of it has become known through the traditions of Gustav Meyrink. At a round table, so-called exercises of sentence mumbling "were performed!" Mailänder gave each participant simple sentences that they should speak to themselves. As a result of these concentration exercises, letter-shaped irritation symptoms on the skin became visible. From a table, the announced letters could be interpreted for prophecy. For example: A = Faith firmly, then it will get you; B = Only in spirit can one love God above everything; C = fight for my kingdom; D = I honour the pure bride.[72] These exercises were at the beginning of the training.

After the first visit to Dreieichenhain, the students received written instructions and did not need to come to the "Bruderheim" as often. Each student was given by posted letters other concentration exercises, which were replaced in due course by new ones. From time to time, the students had to share their mystical experiences, and then they received information from Mailänder. The reply dictated by Mailänder was written by Gabela, as he could write. Meyrink reports extensively on this type of remote correspondence, the training of which

---

[72] Franz Dornseiff in his 1922 "Das Alphabet in Mystik und Magie" mentions the manuscript owned by Meyrink, which outlined the meaning of letter irritations appearing on the skin. Dornseiff writes, "The following table is to be interpreted like this: "A" belief, then you will be exonerated. "B" One can love God above all only in the spirit. "C" fight for my kingdom. "D" I honour the pure bride etc. to "Z." The author was a weaver, illiterate, almost illiterate. The Ms. is a student suffix of Meyrink with the inscription "opened and received on October 23, 1892." See Franz Dornseiff, *Das Alphabet in Mystik und Magie* (B.G. Teubner, 1922); *Langener Zeitung*, September 24, 1890 to October 8, 1890.

incidentally began on October 23, 1892 in Dreieichenhain.[73]
END.

Looking at the names of these Theosophists, visitors came
from far and wide, even from English sections of the Theosophical
Society, to receive Mailänder's wisdom. Mailänder expressed
several times that he was so busy, he hardly had time to reply to
the many letters coming in, stating, "I am always surrounded by
visitors."[74]

Meyrink says that he met 54 of Mailänder's other students, and
in *Alois Mailänder: 44 Letters to Gustav Meyrink*, my friend Erik
Dilloo Heidger identifies 37 of these, drawing upon the writings
of Meyrink, Hartmann, Weinfurter and Hübbe Schleiden. It is
worthwhile to note that Meyrink included Friederich Eckstein
among the list, who was head of the Theosophical Society in
Vienna, and the entire group dedicated themselves to Mailänder's
Rosicrucian path. Furthermore, I would underscore that the
Ordo Templi Orientis founder Carl Kellner was Mailänder's
student according to Franz Hartmann, who writes, "Dr. Kellner
sought to increase his knowledge everywhere. He occupied
a high position in Freemasonry and was for several years a
member of a Rosicrucian Bund, which is mentioned in my book
Under the Adepts." In this book, he provides rich information
about Mailänder, with the "Bund" representing the Bund der
Verheißung.[75]

---

[73] Heil, "Okkultistische Sekte im Dreieichenhain der Jahrhundertwende." Thanks to
Roger Heil for granting photo permissions.

[74] April 19, 1903 letter to Meyrink in Mailänder, Dilloo-Heidger, and Allen, *44 Letters
to Gustav Meyrink (English Translation).*

[75] Orignal text: "Dr. Kellner suchte überall nach Vermehrung seines Wissens. Er nahm
eine hohe Stellung ein in der Freimaurerei und war mehrere Jahre hindurch Mitglied
eines Rosenkreuzerbundes, von dem in meinem Buche "Unter den Adepten" die Rede

The following photos prove Kellner and Eckstein were associated with this circle.

Back: Franz Gebhard, Frederick Eckstein, Nikolaus Gabele
Sitting: Alois Mailänder, unidentified man, 1890. 76

---

ist." In "Theosophische Rundschau - Deutsches Organ Der Theosoph," *Gesellschaft* XII. Jahrgang, no. 6 (1924).

[76] The photo is incorrectly thought to depict Gustav Gebhard. Wuppertal researcher Birgit Liljestrom identified the top left figure as Arthur Gebhard based on family photos in her "Die Gebhard-L'Estranges - Eine Familie auf dem Weg zum Olymp." The figure on the right bottom is not Wilhelm Hübbe-Schleiden, as is normally claimed, says Liljestrom. See Liljestrom, *Die Gebhard-L'Estranges - Eine Familie auf dem Weg zum Olymp.*

Left to right: Arthur Gebhard, Carl Kellner, Friederich Eckstein.
Credit: Josef Dvorak.[77]

---

[77] Carl Kellner (Mitte) mit Schülern bei Studium von Yoga-Texten. ©Josef Dvorak.
See Wolfgang Weihrauch, "Eine Reise Nach Wien: Bei Den Quellen Des O.T.O.:

Weinfurter's *Man's Highest Purpose* and Meyrink's lecture on the *Transfiguration of the Blood* (translated in this volume) both introduce the fact that Theosophists beyond Mary Gebhard's circle were also disciples under Mailänder, namely those of Prague with Gustav Meyrink and those of Vienna with Friederich Eckstein. Many details are not mentioned by Hartmann, and we cannot yet be certain of the specific dates that Eckstein came under Mailänder's guidance, although in 1886-1887 Franz Hartmann lived in Friedrich Eckstein's house for about one year. Meyrink introduced a veiled Eckstein through his riveting story that one "Professor K" nearly forgot to tell him that "a man lives in Vienna called XY. He and many other former Theosophists, both Germans and Englishmen, and even an Indian Brahman named Babajee are the disciples of a true Rosicrucian."[78]

Here, the identities of K and XY in Meyrink's account can safely be uncovered. The XY is none other than Friederich Eckstein and the K is one Oskar Korschelt (1853–1940).[79]

In *Transfiguration of the Blood*, Meyrink tells how he was firstly struck by the fact that he did not know of this, because "the

---

Interview Mit Josef Dvorak," *Flensburger Hefte*, no. 4 (1998): 184.

[78] Meyrink, "Die Verwandlung des Blutes," 12.

[79] My friend Christine Eike from AMORC Norway noted that in Meyrink's lecture on the "Transfiguration of the Blood" He names this person as "the K" or "Professor K" and lastly as "O.K." Meyrink writes "The then quick and seamless conversation with the strange gentleman revealed: he was called O. K., had been a professor or a chemistry teacher in Japan for a long time, had lived in Dresden for a long time and was a spiritist." Oskar Korschelt matches this description: He had studied chemistry in Dresden and Berlin, taught chemistry in Japan for many years and returned to Germany around 1885 where he moved to Zwittau which is near Dresden, aside from his name matching the "O.K." label. Professor Korschelt is also mentioned on September 25 by Hübbe-Schleiden in his diary of 1896. See Wilhelm Hübbe-Schleiden, "Tagebuch von Wilhelm Hübbe Schleiden (Diaries)" (SUB Göttingen Cod. MS W Hübbe Schleiden 1013: 18 1896, 1896).

mentioned X.Y. in Vienna had been a friend of mine for quite a long time," and secondly that occultists well known to him "were the disciples of an indicated Rosicrucian."

Then Meyrink states, "At last, in accordance with the prophecy of the inner circle of Theosophical Society, I had finally found the 'guru.'"[80] This item is of interest because during his years of attempting yogic practices, Anne Beasant had predicted Meyrink would discover a special guru to guide him on the path.

At the time, Meyrink was leader of the Blue Star Lodge of the Theosophical Society in Prague, so this new contact with Mailänder soon changed their orientation. Consisting of ten members, among its ranks were novelist Julius Zeyer and poet Emanuel Lesehrad. The Theosophical branch had arisen out of the group's dissatisfaction with its former séance-spiritualist experiments. Weinfurter describes the group as solemn, stating that zeal prevailed in their small circle. In their free hours, they met at a coffee house to exchange ideas, talk about books they read, and make propositions for different practices they could each apply themselves to. Leading up to their acceptance by Mailänder, Weinfurter states, "We presumed that for our further evolution we needed a Leader and tried everything possible to find one."[81]

Furthermore, Weinfurter writes, "We all perceived that our Viennese friends had been in touch with an Adept or a Leader. Of course, during our intercourse of several years, we had thought so, but nobody had ever mentioned it," and that, "they were clever enough not to prescribe anything."[82] Similarly, when Meyrink inquired with Eckstein in person during his Vienna

---

[80] Ibid., 12.

[81] Weinfurter, *Man's Highest Purpose*, 43.

[82] Ibid., 46–49.

visit about "Professor K's last words concerning the Rosicrucian guru, X.Y. quickly put his finger to his lips, telling me to be silent immediately." Apparently, Eckstein did not want any of this information divulged in the presence of G.R.S Mead, who was secretary of the Theosophical Movement of Adyar with Annie Beasant at that time.

Recalling that Meyrink was given the name "Ruben" in the Bund der Verheißung, this veiled reference becomes clear when Weinfurter writes, "Mr. R. soon afterwards left for Vienna to boast of his results to his friends in the Theosophical Society, who, as already stated, were advising us. But they received his communication with a grave and perplexed manner and told him that that practice was to be considered one of the most dangerous. He was not told more. Mr. R. returned home, but a few days afterwards he received a wire from Vienna with the following contents: 'Come at once, the way is open.'"[83]

Meyrink's response was to immediately depart for Vienna on the next train and, "The next day I told my friend X.Y. that I was ready to acknowledge the leadership of the Rosicrucian." And, because Meyrink says, "A few weeks later I drove to the location in Hessen, where the Rosicrucian lived" (Dreieichenhain is in Hessen), his first meeting with Mailänder would have first taken place in 1890 or just after.

---

[83] Meyrink was also given the title "Lord R" in the Prague Blue Star group when it also became a Martinist lodge under one Baron Adolf Leonhardi. See Karel Weinfurter, *History of Occultism*, 1932. Eventually, the great Count Saint Germaine of Blavatsky became associated with Alice Bailey's Rakoczy later in 1912. This occurs in Annie Beasant's "The Masters" which is twenty years after the true Master R (Meyrink) was known to have attended the Prague Theosophical lodge. Finally in 1925 Rakoczy is announced as one of the Mahatmas by C.W. Leadbeater in "Masters of the Path". "Both these sources are likely to be behind Ballard's own new construction of Saint Germaine."

However, Mailänder's Rosicrucian work contrasted with their enthusiasm, which typically sought out eastern methods, as Weinfurter expresses, "We then learnt that in fact some members of the Theosophical Society had a Leader. But it was a mystical Leader, and he led the Christian way. To us, who had been presuming that the only correct way was either the Indian Mystic or an occult training, it was a comedown."[84] However, this initial disappointment was clearly replaced with confidence and conviction in Mailänder's method, shown by the fact that when Meyrink departed from the group in 1904, the Prague lodge became entirely Rosicrucian and Christian in outlook under Weinfurter's leadership.

According to Roger Heil, Mailänder "devoted his best and final years to his students, he also always listened to the problems of his fellow citizens."[85] Mailänder, furthermore, had acquired wealth by donations from members of the Theosophical Society and Mary Gebhard bequeathed a certain sum to Mailänder and his household in her will. This money was managed and well invested so that from 1892, Mailänder could live on it and pay for the property upkeep until his death. Before Mailänder passed, he used this to establish the Mailänder Foundation in Dreieichenhain. He left his money to an orphanage and, in 1938, the final portion was given to establishing the first kindergarten in the area.[86]

---

[84] Weinfurter, *Man's Highest Purpose*, 50.

[85] Heil, "Okkultistische Sekte im Dreieichenhain der Jahrhundertwende."

[86] Mailänder's attitude towards the donations he received is also somewhat revealed in his letters to Gustav Meyrink. Mailänder expresses that he does not wish to receive money or gifts from someone (Meyrink) who himself is struggling to make ends meet. Still, Meyrink gave donation to the "Bruderhaus." See Mailänder, Dilloo-Heidger, and Allen, *44 Letters to Gustav Meyrink (English Translation)*.

Roger Heil concludes that there was an "End of a Great Mystical Epoch" as "with Alois Mailänder's demise in January 1905, the flow of visitors soon dried up. In the following decades, although some supporters sought contact with the Gabele family, Nikolaus Gabele did not have the skills to fill the gap that had been created."[87]

Given the Prague, Vienna and German Theosophical circles were so committed to Mailänder and his Rosicrucian spiritual alchemy (for example, Meyrink says he spent thirteen years dedicatedly working on the method), it seems remarkable that Mailänder's name appears to have all but vanished from popular occult history. We envision that through the efforts of our team, Christine Eike, Erik Dilloo-Heidger and yours truly, Mailänder will instead hold the honoured place in occult history he deserves.

We cannot be certain if Mailänder himself would have wanted this attention and, naturally, the oaths of secrecy extracted from members of the Bund der Verheißung served the opposite purpose. Yet that silencing played a role in fading Mailänder's memory to a role of lesser significance instead of at the forefront of Theosophical and Rosicrucian literature. This similarly evaporated several possibly crucial facts, such as that members of the Theosophical Society addressed Mailänder by other titles, and not only as "J" or "Johannes." This opens an area of likely hot debate for occult historians, seeing Theosophists also addressed Mailänder with the other moniker of "M."

The implications become controversial as it forces one to consider a revision of other mentions of a "Master M" within the literature, including that made by the founder of Anthroposophy Rudolf Steiner, who referred to such a figure in his autobiography of 1907, known as the *Barr Document*. In this famous document,

---

[87] Ibid.

Steiner describes his first meeting with M, writing, "I did not meet the M. immediately, but first an emissary who was completely initiated into the secrets of plants and their effects, and into their connection with the cosmos and human nature."[88] Thanks to the invaluable work of Emil Bock, it has been determined with certainty that the identity of this messenger for M was one herb gatherer by the name of Felix Koguzki (1833-1909).[89] Officially, no Anthroposophist to date has provided clarification on the identity of M was, although it is accepted that he significantly impacted Steiner's work and this unknown figure was indeed a Rosicrucian teacher. I addressed this topic at great length in *The Rosicrucian Fraternities in the Wake of J.B Kerning and Alois Mailänder*.

The first evidence of Mailänder's other title was recorded by Karl Weinfurter in his book *Der Königsweg*:

> "The students of the German Master M. (named Mailänder), with Gustav Meyrink in the forefront, practiced according to his instruction only in the centre and not in all bodily organs, as Kerning prescribed."[90]

Note that the insertion of Mailänder's name in brackets within the original German text was made by Weinfurter's editor Erich Sopp, who wished to clarify from some informed decision. The original quote:

> Karel Weinfurter 'Der Königsweg' writes: "Es ist also die Frage: Welche Mantraübungen führen direkt zur Erweckung der

[88] Rudolf Steiner and Marie Steiner-Von Sivers, *Correspondence and Documents 1901-1925* (London: Steiner Press, 1988).

[89] Born in Vienna 1st August 1833. Died in Trumau in 1909. The years given on his gravestone. See Bock, *The Life and Times of Rudolf Steiner*, 1:15–18.

[90] Karel Weinfurter and Erich Sopp, *Der Königsweg: der goldene Pfad der praktischen Mystik* (Freiburg: Bauer, 1976).

Schlangenkraft? Antwort: Nur solche, die der Schüler im ganzen
Körper übt, also nicht nur ins Zentrum. Zum Beispiel die
Schüler des deutschen Meisters M. (namens Mailänder, Anm.
E. S.), mit Gustav Meyrink im Vordergrund, übten nach seiner
Anweisung nur ins Zentrum und nicht in alle körperlichen
Organe, wie es Kerning vorschreibt.

A second instance appears in a diary entry of the Theosophist
Clemens Driessen on September 26, 1891. In this entry, Driessen
discusses Hübbe-Schleiden's progress with Mailänder's training. It
mentions that Hübbe-Schleiden was not satisfied, but that:

"This too appears to me that he's in opposition to the approach
of the M(ailander), who is critical towards him, but perhaps
only as far as the mental images are concerned."[91]

Mailänder's name was again inserted by the editor. The
original quote:

"Dies tritt, scheint mir, auch darin zu Tage, dass er sich mit
dem M.[ailänder] in Widerspruch setzt, zu ihm sich kritisch
verhält – vielleicht allerdings nur was die intellektuellen
Vorstellungsbilder angeht."[92]

Another quote states that the "Christian Theosopher M" was
close to one of Kerning's disciples:

"It can be found in the book *The Burning Busch* of the Christian
theosophist Weinfurter, a friend of Meyrink's, both of whom,
after a long search, found the well-known Christian Theosopher
M., who was very close to Kerning or one of his disciples."[93]

---

[91] Hübbe-Schleiden was called "Brother Daniel" by Mailänder. See Bock, *The Life and Times of Rudolf Steiner*, 1:204.

[92] Hübbe-Schleiden, *Indisches Tagebuch 1894/1896*, 16.

[93] *Zentralblatt Für Okkultismus: Monatsschrift Zur Erforschung Der Gesamten Geheimwissenschaften* 25 (1932 1931): 133.

The original quote:

> "Sie ist zu finden in dem Buch „Der brennende Busch" des Christlichen Theosophen Weinfurter, eines Freundes und Mitstrebenden Meyrincks, die beide nach langem Suchen den bekannten christlichen Theosophen M. gefunden haben, der Kernning oder einem seiner Schüler sehr nahe stand."

Therefore, we can now safely state that "M" was another title for Alois Mailänder.

As a result, a large section of this book's sister volume titled *The Rosicrucian Fraternities in the Wake of J.B Kerning and Alois Mailänder* reviews any references to the M in Theosophical literature in a new light.

The Second Sight, Prophecy & Pentecost

Franz Hartmann captivatingly introduces Mailänder's seership ability thus: "A long time ago such a word had grown into my consciousness. It became more and more vivid and living in me, but to not a single soul in the world did I ever reveal that word, nor would I dare to reveal it now, and yet that illiterate worker pronounced that word and received me as one who was spiritually not a stranger to him."[94]

In this section, I would like to address the nature of Mailänder's seership abilities because his views towards other esoteric systems influenced my translation of his *Soul Teaching*. During the examination of what he set out to transmit regarding seership, coupled with his spiritual status as "Johannes," we must ask: was Mailänder a Rosicrucian prophet with his Inner Word, a charlatan, a medium, or something else?

---

[94] *The Theosophist*, 1885, 293; Franz Hartmann, "Practical Occultism in Germany," *The Theosophist* 8, no. 86 (November 1886): 83.

Samuel Robinson

Hübbe-Schleiden states, "Mailänder developed in himself and his disciples the ability of cognition of higher knowledge, divine wisdom…"[95] Meyrink also writes, "X.Y assured me that this certain Rosicrucian was a seer in the spiritual realm, sometimes even physical phenomena occurred around him."[96]

Because two statements insinuate some sort of spiritism was involved behind Mailänder's gift, I will give this issue its deserved attention. The first spiritism statement was proposed by Emil Bock and the second came from Meyrink, who recanted his initial assumption while providing vital information. Central to the doctrine of spiritism is the idea of the intervention of the dead, which raises some questions.

Emil Bock stated that the "Christian Saint John spoke from him" so it appears at least Bock believed some form of mediumship was at hand. However, Bock was mistaken on this point because Mailänder's spiritual name was Johannes; he signed his letters as Johannes and lived among his followers in the Bund der Verheißung as John. More importantly, we find traces among his students' records that he was treated as the very living and returned incarnation of the Biblical John himself, and not only in name.

For example, Franz Hartmann enthusiastically informed his correspondents far and wide that the "beloved disciple John is still living in the body on earth,"[97] showing a consideration of

---

[95] Hübbe-Schleiden, *Indisches Tagebuch 1894/1896*, 533.

[96] Meyrink, "Die Verwandlung des Blutes."

[97] Butler writes in 1888 that "there are many now, even among the professed Christians, who believe that the "beloved" disciple John is still living in the body on earth, and if Dr. Hartmann's book, called "Among the Rosicrucians," is to be believed…," He also mentions a "German Leader of the Templars" they are in contact with, which I am assuming is Percifal Braun as shown in my other work, *The Rosicrucian Fraternities in the Wake of J.B Kerning and Alois Mailander*. See Hiram Butler, ed., *The Esoteric* 2 (1888):

Mailänder quite different from Bock's notion that it was the voice John speaking through him. Meyrink similarly portrays "John the Evangelist" in his *The White Dominican* novel as being in possession of the keys to Kerning's masonic mysticism of the hand signs and that he has held these mysteries since the time of Christ.[98] As shown below, Mailänder advocated the reading of J.B Kerning's books within Bund der Verheißung. Meyrink affirms this "John" is the prophesized Biblical saint in referring to John 21:22, saying Christ asserted that John "would not die," and "of whom Jesus says he might tarry till He came." After completing his description of Kerning's finger signs practice, he adds, "Those are things that St. John knew of and knows of."[99][100]

The prophecies of the Cristian mystic Jane Lead expand upon this subject below.

Meyrink places Mailänder's seership ability in connection with spiritism in his *Transfiguration of the Blood*, writing that Mailänder, "had undergone strange experiences in the field of spiritualism but called it 'the preschool of the true knowledge,' which only could come from the heart when it began to speak. This speaking

---

63; Hiram Butler, ed., *The Esoteric* 8 (1894); Franz Hartmann, "The Correlation of Spiritual Forces," *The Esoteric* 10 (1896).

[98] Meyrink, *The White Dominican*, 57.

[99] Ibid., 61.

[100] Originally published in *Allgemeine Zeitung* Chemnitz, 1927 Meyrink's lecture Hochstapler der Mystik, (Imposters of the Occult Arts) describes his meeting of one "John the Evangelist" figure. Meyrink describes him as a swindler, yet this character described the blood miracle of the Church of the Holy Cross near Kempten, just like Mailander did. This John the Evangelist figure attempted to dupe Meyrink out of his money. Yet, like Mailander sent Meyrink a postcard. The information is conflicting because this figure was younger than Meyrink, had blond hair, spoke with "pure Saxony" accent, and dressed like a big city man. These details, especially the age, hair, and accent, do not describe Mailander. They appear to address someone impersonating Mailander.

of the heart he called the Inner Word. It awakened with time and was bestowed with 'Grace' in the Christian sense."[101] Therefore, Meyrink appears to simultaneously acknowledge the influence of spiritism and dismiss it by acknowledging God's grace behind that inspiration.

It becomes apparent that this later conclusion from Meyrink regarding the nature of Mailänder's seership evolved out of an earlier event whereby he accused Mailänder of some form of channelling. On September 12, 1902, Mailänder firmly replied to Meyrink that:

> "As for the other part of your letter, where you speak of 'Spiritism' and 'Christian Piety' and whether the exercises are of the Spirit. I would simply refer you to the *Soul Teaching* and God Teaching.[102] If you have even a little of God-knowledge in you, then you will soon find from which source these teachings come. I have not dealt with spiritualism or bigotry or magic."[103]

Meyrink must have accepted Mailänder's response to later write as he did of Mailänder's Inner Word, honoring Mailänder's lesson in his novel *The Green Face* with the following words:

> We are by no means spiritualists, as you might suppose, Mynheer; almost, I would say, the opposite, for we have nothing to do with the realm of the dead. Our aim is eternal life. Now there is a secret power in every name, and if we speak this name into our heart with closed lips, incessantly, until it constantly fills our being for day and night, we draw the spiritual power

---

[101] Meyrink, "Die Verwandlung des Blutes."

[102] Mailänder's "Gotteslehre" material is also mentioned in Hübbe-Schleiden notebooks but this item is missing today. See Hübbe-Schleiden, "Tagebuch von Wilhelm Hübbe Schleiden (Diaries)," 1896, fol. 47.

[103] Mailänder, Dilloo-Heidger, and Allen, *44 Letters to Gustav Meyrink (English Translation)*, 108.

into our blood, which, circulating in the veins, changes our body in time. This gradual transformation of our body - for it alone must be changed, the spirit in itself has been perfect since the beginning - manifests itself in all kinds of feelings, which are the harbingers of the state called "spiritual rebirth."

This statement should be read in conjunction with *Transfiguration of the Blood* at the end of this book. The above demonstrates that the lessons of his master remained dear to Meyrink for the rest of his life.

The cause of these spiritist accusations put to Mailänder likely stem from the group's interest in the ten volume *Great Gospel of John*, written by the Christian mystic Jakob Lorber, who claimed his books were the lost Fifth Gospel. These he recorded from 1840 onwards after hearing the voice of Christ inwardly dictate words to him. Lorber's books were read by members of the Bund der Verheißung.

More significant, however, is Mailänder's strange Pentecost event of 1895, recorded in the diary of Wilhelm Hübbe-Schleiden in some abbreviated note. The original German handwriting reads:

> Abends im Gasthof Gabriele (Frl. von Pott's) Aufzeichnungen der von Johannes & Salomon im Geistes Kreise gesprochenen Worte durchgearbeitet, insbesonders die Scenen im Heim vom 13. Mai 95, bei der Johannes diktierte, während er in der Wasserrinne unter der Pumpe lag, nur die Tage um Pfingsten vom 22. Mai – 4. Juni in Dippelshof."[104]

Translated into English, this reads:

In the evening at the inn Gabriele (Miss von Pott's), notes of the words spoken by Johannes & Salomon in the spiritual circle

---

[104] Wilhelm Hübbe-Schleiden, "Tagebuch von Wilhelm Hübbe Schleiden (Diaries)" (SUB Göttingen Cod. MS W Hübbe Schleiden 1013: 15 1896, 1896), 98.

worked through, in particular the scenes in the home on May 13, 1995, where Johannes dictated while he was lying in the gully under the pump, only the days around Pentecost from May 22nd to June 4th in Dippelshof."

The original diary notes were not perfectly set out in common language but were written down hastily. What we can make out from this entry is that Hübbe-Schleiden together with "Gabriele" (Crescentia Gabele) worked through some notes of a certain Miss von Pott, who was likely a foreign guest at that time.

The notes under consideration were recorded words spoken by Mailänder and Gabele in the "spiritual circle." The term "Geistes Kreise" refers to the spiritual circle of the Bund der Verheißung.[105] In this examination, they paid special attention to "scenes from the 13th of May" in the "Heim" where Mailänder made some pronouncements while he was "lying under the pump in the gully." This occurred in the days of Pentecost, from May the 22nd until the 4th of June, meaning it was a series of recordings.

Most likely, the ritual act of dictating messages under running water refers to some form of "water purification," which was popular in Mailänder's home region thanks to the work of Sebastian Kneipp. Famously known as the "Water Doctor" and "Herbalist Priest," Kneipp not only came from Kempten, but his parents worked as poor weavers at the very same factory where Franz Hartmann found Mailänder's spiritual community. Kneipp threw down the weaver's shuttle at age 21, becoming famous for his water cures and was later credited for having preserved a vast oral knowledge of herbal remedies.[106]

---

[105] Mailänder refers to the compound "Geistesnamen" which the hand-written note seems to reflect. Mailänder calls Meyrink in his letters quite often „Geistesbruder" or „Geistesfreund" Gabriele uses the terms "Geistesbruder" and "Geistesschwester."

[106] Sebastian Kneipp, *Meine Wasser-Kur* (Kempten, 1889), 2.

The 1895 Pentecost event must have been something remarkable because it is referred to three different times in the few surviving manuscripts. One mention from "Gabriele" to Meyrink that same year refers to this event as something spiritually extraordinary. Then from Hübbe-Schleiden's Indian diary, we learn that the secret of this event should have been withheld from him. By carefully examining the accounts of this Pentecost event, I believe the spiritist vs. prophecy question can be settled.

Here "Gabriele" (Crescentia Gabele) mentions the event in a letter to Meyrink dated June 11, 1895. We know she's referencing this same event because she reports on her time in Dippelshof during Pentecost, writing:

Dear G.br. Ruben!

With the permission of the leader, this time I am allowed to send you a rich treasure of words overflowing with strength, which you as well are allowed to communicate to our siblings in spirit (who are in your vicinity and are interested).

We spent a very great time (over Pentecost) in Dippelshof with Franz Gebhard. Many spiritual actions took place, so the cornucopia of grace was really poured out over all of us. The abundance of light that emanated there will certainly throw its rays also on our distant spiritual siblings. Over time, the darkness must be overcome, and the hour of salvation will come to all those who believe in the Redeemer... It would be best if you could once again personally communicate with the Leader, for those who drink from this fountain draw from the water of eternal life. It is bubbling more and more with power. You would be astonished by the change when you come back here because it is now grown significantly better and better.[107]

---

[107] This additional letter will appear in the second edition of Mailänder, Dilloo-Heidger,

Hübbe-Schleiden's diary (1896 nr. 15), on July 20, 1896, reports of the event:

> "I received a shock today through the information in a letter from Countess Spreti that she 'spent quite strange days in Dippelsdorf with Mailänder,' but that they were making a secret of it. Should the magical development of Johannes already be so far advanced that it is too high and strong for me as a way of mediation?"[108]

Given the notes recorded on that day were derived from dictations pronounced by Mailänder, this one extraordinary event could easily be taken for some form of channeling. I believe to do so would be a mistake since there are distinguishing points that set this event quite apart from spiritism, and which furthermore suggest Mailänder had undergone as spiritual transfiguration during those days.

Firstly, we must recall the context of Pentecost, during which the event took place.

Acts 2:1-4 describes a sound that came down from heaven like a rushing and filled all those present, and that tongues of fire consecrated them and "they were filled with the Holy Ghost, and began to speak with other tongues, as the Spirit gave them utterance." Acts 2:17 also states, "Even on my servants, both men

---

and Allen, *44 Letters to Gustav Meyrink (English Translation)*; Alois Mailänder, *Nachlass: Briefe und Karten von Alois Mailänder an Gustav Meyrink - BSB Meyrinkiana I.2. Gabriele an Ruben* (Bayerische Staatsbibliothek, 1893).

[108] Hübbe Schleiden misspells Dippelshof as Dippelsdorf. Dippelshof is near Dreieichenhain. Original: „Erhielt ich heute durch die Mitteilung in einem Briefe der Gräfin Spreti einen Schock, daß sie „in Dippelsdorf mit Mailänder ganz merkwürdige Tage verlebte," daß man aber daraus ein Geheimnis mache. Sollte die magische Entwicklung des Johannes schon so weit sein, daß sie für mich als Vermittelungsweg zu hoch & stark ist?" He means it will be too hard for him to teach or "convey" to others in terms of "mediation" because he saw himself as a future teacher. In Hübbe-Schleiden, *Indisches Tagebuch 1894/1896*, 448.

and women, I will pour out my Spirit in those days, and they will prophesy." Gabriele's letter similarly reported, "The cornucopia of *grace* was really *poured out* over all of us." Meyrink's earlier comment that Mailänder's Inner Word ideal was "bestowed with Grace in the Christian sense" comes to mind.[109]

Traditionally, Pentecost is a Christian holiday commemorating the descending of the Holy Spirit upon the followers of Jesus Christ, and Mailänder's dictations are aligned with this revelatory event. The Bible states that the messages received from the Holy Spirit by Christ's followers were indeed intelligible (Acts 2:11: "We hear them declaring the wonders of God in our own tongues!"), suggesting Mailänder's dictations had an altogether different intention, setting them quite apart from haunted spiritist communications.

Essentially, I believe Mailänder was practicing an enthusiastic pietist form of ecstatic Christian prophecy.

Mailänder's *Soul Teaching* lecture titled "Aus dem Geisterreich" or "From the Spirit Word" most likely comprises those dictated sentences recorded during that 1895 Pentecost event.[110]

Something else is also hinted at when Hübbe Schleiden writes, "Should the magical development of Johannes already be so far advanced that it is too high and strong for me to mediate?" This suggests a new change in Mailänder himself and Gabriele writes to Meyrink, "You would be astonished by the change when you come back here because it is now grown significantly better."

Therefore, it is likely Mailänder was transfigured during Pentecost into a higher spiritual state.

---

[109] Meyrink, "Die Verwandlung des Blutes."

[110] Although Hübbe-Schleiden inserted this title into the manuscript himself, along with the other titles, this suggest they are some form of recorded channelled sentences.

[111] Hübbe- Schleiden, *Indisches Tagebuch 1894/1896*, 448.

Furthermore, as shown below, the Bund der Verheißung adopted the writings of Jane Lead, which explain this Pentecostal event in light of Mailänder's Baptism of Fire.

Unfortunately, we do not have all the necessary pieces to draw a definitive conclusion. Almost certainly, the 1895 Pentecost event in Dippelshof caused the spiritist question to arise amongst Mailänder's pupils, as occurred with Meyrink and as expanded upon by Emil Bock. Actually, the notion that Mailander allowed the voice of John to speak through him as put forth by Bock cannot be supported seeing the original material does not contain any reference to this. On the other hand, we do have Hartmann and Meyrink both describing a reincarnated John figure.

Views on Theosophy and Blavatsky

Exploring Mailänder's ecstatic seership and Pentecostal revelations influenced how I would come to translate several related terminologies within the *Soul Teaching* material. I took special care to meaningfully translate the word "Hellsehen" when presenting Mailänder's lectures. In esoteric literature, this is often translated as "clairvoyance" in English. However, through my growing appreciation of Mailänder's voice, I came to believe it would be a mistake to apply "clairvoyance" to his mysticism.

This is mainly because clairvoyance is a loaded and distinguished term within Theosophy. Although Mailänder would join the Theosophists, in fact, Mailänder made several statements concerning Theosophists and their practices that set himself and his Rosicrucianism apart from then popular occult forms, making it deserving of independence.

In justification of my approach to avoid using the term "clairvoyance," I present this section to demonstrate Mailänder's views on Madam Blavatsky and the Theosophical Society itself.

For example, Emil Bock found that Mailänder's stated:

> To explain our position towards Indian Theosophy, I would only like to tell you that the teaching, as far as we know it, is a real and true one according to the understanding of us poor subjects. We have nothing to do with the leaders of it, for we do not seek the personalities, but only agree with the spirit that animates the Indian teaching. Mrs. Blavatsky as well as Colonel Olcott and the former envoy Dr. Hartmann are as much use to us as a Munich milkmaid who pushes the cart.[112]

Wilhelm Hübbe-Schleiden recorded the following on September 24, 1896:

> In the evening John's great chastisement speech. John declared the claim of the leaders at T.S. headquarters in London that they could leave their bodies in the astral to be a lie and swindle. "Nor does it need such dislocation. We have everything in us. It all comes into our own sphere. In reality, this going to the Master in the astral body does not exist. Our place of union is not with a Master, it is with God. We have to find the life force and freedom within ourselves. Once that is achieved, one becomes silent. The inner processes (inneren Vorgänge) are sacred. Afterwards, one will only speak of it against one's will and it cannot be avoided it at all. No one can help the other. Everyone has to find the Master within themselves. We become free through the Redeemer within us. And in that freedom we have everything to gain.[113]

---

[112] Bock, *Rudolf Steiner*, 185. My translation into English.

[113] "Abends Johannes große Strafrede Johannes erklärte die Behauptung der Leiter am T.S. Hauptquartier in London, daß sie im Astralischen ihren Leib verlassen könnten, für Lüge und Schwindel. „Es braucht auch keine Versetzung. Wir haben Alles in uns, Es kommt alles in unseren Kreis. Das im Astralkörper zum Meister Gehen gibt es in Wirklichkeit nicht. Unsere Vereinigungsstätte ist nicht der Aufenthaltsort eines Meisters, sondern Gott. Die Lebenskraft und Freiheit haben wir in uns selbst zu finden. Ist das erreicht, dann schweigt man. Die inneren Vorgänge sind einem heilig.

Then the next day of September 25, an instance occurred where Mailänder was possibly jealous of his students seeking out other teachers. At the same time, he introduced the important subject of not disclosing the sacred nature of the spiritual processes (Vorgänge), which Mailänder taught would occur in the body as manifestations of the Holy Spirit during mystical work. Hübbe-Schleiden records:

> You, like an old woman, let the English put all kinds of nonsense into your head. You ran to India to find a guide there. I did not accompany you there in spirit. For you went against my will. You held Franz Gebhard back for two years by saying: John is not enough for me; I am going to India. Once you betrayed a series of spiritual processes to Prof. Korschelt, to your and his detriment."[114]

The following day, September 26, 1896, Hübbe-Schleiden records:

> 26 Sept. Dreieichenhain. In the morning Johannes was again very pleasant and only emphasized great caution not to talk to anyone, even silently, about spiritual processes (geistige Vorgänge) on the spiritual path, but especially not to disclose and desecrate them to others who would mock them. John also

---

Reden wird man danach nur wider Willen und wenn man es gar nicht vermeiden kann (äußerlich oder innerlich gezwungen wird?). Niemand kann einem anderen helfen. Jeder hat den Meister in sich selbst zu finden. Wir werden frei durch den Erlöser in uns. Und in der Freiheit haben wir Alles zu erringen." 1896 September 25. In Hübbe-Schleiden, "Tagebuch von Wilhelm Hübbe Schleiden (Diaries)," 1896, 16.

[114] „25. September 1896: Strafrede Du läßt dir, wie ein altes Weib, von den Engländern ?? wem allen Unsinn aufbinden. Nach Indien bist du gelaufen, um dort einen Führer zu finden. Dahin habe ich dich im Geiste nicht begleitet. Denn du gingst gegen meinen Willen. Franz Gebhard hast du dadurch 2 Jahre zurückgehalten, daß du sagte.st: der Johannes kann mir nicht genügen; ich gehe nach Indien. - Einst hast du dem Prof. Korschelt eine Reihe geistiger Vorgänge verraten zu deinem und seinem Schaden. (Zeuge ??? Gäste ohne von den geistigen Vorgängen zu reden!)" In Ibid., 17.

rebukes the desire to meet and get to know other leaders. He claims to have the definite impression that she will be exposed as a fraud in the future.[115]

Considering the year and the previous day's mention of issues coming from England, it would appear Mailänder had Anne Beasant in mind regarding she who "will yet be exposed as a fraud in the future."

Altogether, Mailänder's views regarding the Theosophical Society were relatively negative.

Contrarily, Mailänder had a Mahatma picture hanging on the wall at his Bruderheim, although Mailänder's criticisms lead one to suspect this was merely a gift from Theosophists which held little importance to him.[116] Still, Franz Hartmann also remarked that, "I have learned a great deal in the company of these people. In other things I was able to give them instruction."[117] This implies Mailänder absorbed Theosophical ideas and made them his own, and he quite possibly did so whenever he encountered useful ideas. This is perhaps supported by his treatment of John Pordage's writing (shown below), while Hartmann's self-assessment is partly supported by the Bock quote above. At the same time, this must be read together with Mailänder's

---

[115] "26. Sept. Dreieichenhain Morgens war Johannes wieder sehr umgänglich und betonte nur große Vorsicht niemandem, selbst nicht stumm, auf dem Geisteswege über geistige Vorgänge zu plaudern, insbesondere aber diese nicht anderen gegenüber die darüber spotten werden, preiszugeben und zu entheiligen. Auch nur andere Führer anzusehen und kennen zu lernen, tadelt Johannes. Er behauptet den bestimmten Eindruck zu haben, daß sie künftig noch als Schwindlerin entlarvt werden wird. Abends im Heim musiziert. Brief an Paula." In Ibid.

[116] Driesen wrote in his diary in 1891: „Bei Mail.[änder] ein [Hermann] Schmiechen [(1855-?)] - Mahatma Bild. M.[eines] E.[rachtens] ein Idealkopf ohne besondere Bedeutung." In Hübbe-Schleiden, *Indisches Tagebuch 1894/1896*, n. 23.

[117] *The Theosophist*, 1885.

outspoken criticisms regarding Theosophical personalities. Here, I would recall Mailänder's scathing remarks regarding Hartmann's inner contradictions, as presented by Bock. Although Mailänder acknowledged Hartmann was clever, he viewed him as a pest who too frequently visited their home. Finally, when Hartmann left the Bund, Mailänder reports, "I thank God that he is releasing me from this person."[118] Even so, it could be their bond was not entirely broken, for Mailänder once wrote that he was not permitted to turn his back upon his students, and Hartmann later writes, "I remained in contact with their leader until he died."[119]

All considered, the evidence mounted so that in translating Mailänder's *Soul Teaching*, I would seek out his unique voice rather than applying borrowed Theosophical terms upon his teachings wherever possible. After all, we risk filling his mouth with words or slipping right past his message.

This issue of adopting loaded terms becomes clear when viewing Madam Blavatsky's interpretation of clairvoyance, which includes the ability of "seeing through the densest matter." This does not sound like Mailänder whatsoever. Building upon Blavatsky, other Theosophists like Leadbeater and Alice Bailey introduced a wider range of psychic notions to define the term. Besides, their approach hinges on practical occult exercises specifically aimed at awakening the faculty as the goal, whereas Mailänder's "Hellsehen" and Inner Word are comparatively gained through bestowed grace. Consequently, given the broader connotations and likely aggrandizement of said powers supposedly granted through Theosophical clairvoyance, I opted

---

[118] Bock, *The Life and Times of Rudolf Steiner*, 1:206.

[119] Ralph Shirley, ed., "Autobiography of Dr. Franz Hartmann," *The Occult Review* 7, no. 1 (January 1908): 30.

for the preferred translation of the "Second Sight."[120] This alternative term, coupled with "Seership," seemed far more suited to Mailänder's unsophisticated and direct approach.

The Spiritual Alchemy of the Bund der Verheißung

Meyrink introduces a key aspect of Mailänder's Rosicrucian teachings thus, "The doctrine of that Hessian simple man culminated in this: The soul of man lives in the body, not to leave it, as one who spins around to see that he has fallen into a dead end, but rather it is to transform the matter in which we are born!"[121]

Over the course of contemplating the meaning and core message of Mailänder's teachings, I have come to appreciate certain points within his approach. In this section, I will report on some of my conclusions. By reading this book, which contains Mailänder's *Soul Teaching*, in combination with Erik Dilloo-Heidger's *Alois Mailänder: 44 Letters to Gustav Meyrink*, you come to sense what can only be described as a fatherly kindness transmitted through his instructions, so that Mailänder, in acting through the Christian spirit of generosity, becomes a Rosicrucian guide who most definitely leads by example. His letters evidence his strength, trust, tolerance, great patience, and especially his willingness to reassure others during their sufferings and struggles. In doing so, he exhibits the qualities he wishes to instill. His guidance and teachings cannot be called mere lip service or

---

[120] "For we are brethren of the Rosie Crosse. We have the Mason Word and Second Sight." Thought to be the earliest reference to freemasonry. See Henry Adamson, *The Muses Threnodie, or, Mirthfull Mournings, on the Death of Master Gall* (Edinburgh: King Iames College, 1638).

[121] Meyrink, "Die Verwandlung des Blutes," fol. 15. See my English translation in Part VI of this book.

viewed as ideals without realization because he was a constant living embodiment of that teaching he proposed.

It is quite clear Mailänder saw no problem in teaching his students from afar through letters and in this we may have hope that his surviving written words may still rouse something in the spiritual seeker today. Although this book doubles as an academic resource, I would say that one must not only read Mailänder theologically. While detaching oneself from the material to view it objectively has its intellectual benefit, his words were written with the intention that we integrate these concepts through practice.

Mailänder wished for us to understand that the Word made Flesh is not an object of worship reserved for a departed and returning Christ. It is not out of bounds to us, nor the exclusive property of an externalized deity. Rather, by a process of inner communication, the Word may pierce through our levels of spirit, soul, and body, so that a perfect transmission of the Word of God may be brought forth as our own Inner Word.

Through his *Soul Teaching* and exercises Mailänder forms a chain of transmission of that divine expression so that it is emancipated to become our personal Inner Word through the gates of our mind, feeling, and will. It is through an inner alignment of these properties that our entire being may resonate with the Word until a perfect line is traced from above to below. It is a line with grace at its higher end and purity at the human end of the spectrum, and once this channel is opened, the Word is set free from its invisible realm and follows its inner path towards the heart center, which Mailänder so emphasized in his practical instructions.

Then, it is our heart that is the sensory organ, which acts as the inner interpreter, and gradually our intellectual mind may become sensitive enough to grasp those inner whispers that the soul recognizes as divine communication. At first, we catch the glimpse of a sense, then a whisper until it becomes louder. The result could be described as a process of inner dialogue, which Mailänder called the Inner Word.

It is a form of Gnosis. Yet, where Gnosis is transcendent, Mailänder's special emphasis on the importance of the physical body provides a bedrock upon which to ground our quintessential truth in reality.

We are not to transcend the body. We are not to pursue astral departures from the body to become as fleeting tourist in higher planes. We are to live with divine awareness here in reality.

In fact, the validity of any conception of attaining "Christ Consciousness" is thrown into question in light of Mailänder's spiritual alchemy and his Word made Flesh position, especially in view of his Baptism of Water, of Blood and of Fire in the spirit. Of these, Hartmann stated, "The first baptism, with the Water of Truth, means the attainment of spiritual knowledge, and corresponds to the first of the four noble truths taught by Buddha, 'Right Doctrine.'"[122] In other words, even attaining Christ Consciousness can only leave spiritual seekers short-changed without this bodily awareness of the Inner Word because it is a half-completed labor in the course of reaching Mailänder's next Baptisms of Blood and of Fire — all along the course of attaining what Rosicrucian practitioners largely call the Body of Glory. Mailänder essentially takes matters further, planting such roots in us that the physical body becomes the anchor of wisdom.

In practice, the realization of Mailänder's vision for the Word made Flesh is found in his emphasis on the spiritualization of the blood, which is achieved through a conditioning of the heart.

---

[122] Franz Hartmann, "What Is True Christianity," *Theosophical Siftings* 1, no. 4 (1888).

The Heart Practice

Mailänder includes two main phases in his operative method. The first phase is drawing down grace through prayer-like inward sentences. The second phase is recognizing the signs of progress, as gifted from the Holy Spirit, which spur us onto further steps of development and transfiguration.

Key statements from Mailänder's students best outline the first phase of his practice.

In his *Transfiguration of the Blood*, Meyrink introduces the use of these inner prayers:

> He instructed his numerous disciples by giving them sentences to inwardly whisper, sentences he received, as he said, through his inner voice for each student. By such inward whispering the speech of one's own heart soon awoke, besides a certain transformation of the body went with it, until at the end of the path the immortality of Christ was instilled in the disciple, and with it the eternal life.[123]

Karl Weinfurter now affirms the method and introduces Kerning:

> This leader prescribed his pupils' training by the practice of sentences, which he did not impart to them himself, but by order of his Inner Word. Each student had a different sentence to practise, and after a certain time the respective sentence was alternated with another. Thus it was with any pupil, but each of them had always a different practice. This depended upon the inner unfoldment of the student, and the progress was, according to his individuality, a slower or quicker one. It further depended on his diligence, that is his fervour and the time devoted to the daily practice prescribed. Each disciple had

---

[123] Meyrink, "Die Verwandlung des Blutes," 13.

to inform the leader of the mystical experiences, which were then explained to him, if the disciple was not in touch with some progressed students, who could expound them to him themselves.[124]

Weinfurter elaborates elsewhere:

Sometimes the leader imparts to the disciple, immediately on his acceptance, a certain spiritual lesson, usually a sentence to be repeated by the student in thought for at least half an hour daily in strict solitude. He has to think of its contents and vividly imagine what the sentence means. A mere mechanical repetition without concentrating one's thoughts on its meaning, would be but a loss of time and without any result. In our mystical school each student received his own lesson, it being quite different to the others. On the attainment of certain results, the lesson was individually altered, which used to happen in unequal periods, as the necessity arose. As each leader has to be a clairvoyant, he easily perceives the inner self of all his disciples and accordingly imparts to them right lessons. Besides, such lessons are prescribed for each student by the leader's Inner Word, that is the voice of the Holy Spirit, Who has realized Himself in the leader.

This description from Hartmann's *Magic: White & Black* is the most riveting of them all:

Let us compare with these statements one received from an unlearned person, who possesses the power to see interior truths. He says, "Sink your thoughts downward into the centre of your being, and you will find there a germ which, if continually nourished by pure and holy thoughts, will grow into a power that will extend and ramify through all parts of your body. Your hands and feet and your interior organs will become alive; a sun

---

[124] Weinfurter, *Man's Highest Purpose*, 154.

will appear within your heart and illuminate your whole being. In this light you will see the present, the past, and the future, and by its aid you will attain the true knowledge of self.[125]

Hartmann also recorded that the method:

> ...consists therefore in the sinking of one's own thoughts down to the centre of the heart, excluding all other thoughts, which do not serve the purpose in view, and giving it therein expression in a word, a letter or a sign. Gradually such a sign, letter or word may become alive within ourselves, we shall hear it with our interior ear, see it with the interior eye, and perceive it by the interior sense of feeling. [126]

This sinking into the heart may be connected to a strange sentence recorded by Hübbe Schleiden in his notebook, which comes from either Gabele or Mailänder, and reads, "The spiritual I (Ich) floats to a certain extent above the head of the human being, but the soul self has its centre in the pit of the heart."[127]

In general, the Theosophists called Mailänder's method of sentences "mantra" exercises. Weinfurter usefully adds that:

> "When the disciple has found his leader, he must usually promise to conform implicitly to the leader's advice and hints, and bind himself to practise every day for at least half an hour to the concentration training, as prescribed by the leader."[128]

---

[125] Hartmann, *Magic, White and Black,* 311.

[126] Hartmann, *The Theosophist,* September 1885, 293; Hartmann, "Practical Occultism in Germany," 83.

[127] The German: „Wo habe ich mir den Sitz Mittelpunkt der Seele zu denken? am Scheitel oder in der Herzgrube? Das geistige Ich schwebt zu (illegible) ielichermaß über dem Kopf des Menschen, das seelische aber hat seinen Mittelpunkt in der Herzgrube." In Hübbe-Schleiden, "Wilhelm Hübbe-Schleiden's Notebooks," 1884 1885, 15.

[128] Weinfurter, *Man's Highest Purpose,* 52.

As to what kind of sentences Mailänder's students had to internally whisper and submerge into their being, several examples appear within the 44 letters Meyrink received from his teacher.

Here are three of those examples:

Letter 10, 1st of August 1895:

> ... As far as your exercise is concerned, it has nothing to do with the outside business. It affects the interior. But as you have become superstitious against this exercise, so refrain from it, but so that it may have an effect inside after all, practice from now on:
>
> "Our Father, who is in heaven, sustain your servant."
>
> Do it with all your devotion, as best you can. The Lord will sustain you and be merciful to you in the greatest of misfortunes. Firmly believe and hope for that.

Letter 26, 21st of December 1899:

> Practice from now on:
>
> "In the name of God the Father, God the Son, and God the Holy Spirit. Amen."
>
> For which I wish you God's abundant blessing.

Letter 28, 8th of February 1900:

> ... You can add to the previous exercise, for a change this practice:
>
> "In the number twelve lies the all, and that may be subjected to us."
>
> For this I wish you further God's blessing.

See Erik Dilloo-Heidger's *Alois Mailänder: 44 Letters to Gustav Meyrink* for many more examples.

Having shared these, we must recall that the sentences recorded in Meyrink's letters, as provided by Mailänder to Meyrink for his spiritual practice, were only intended for Meyrink's own spiritual development. Each student received different sentences whereby Mailänder guided them individually according to the promptings he received from his Inner Word.

Furthermore, Mailänder was careful to make a distinction regarding those who have attained the Inner Word for their own spiritual guidance versus those who have been enabled to guide others.

For example, Weinfurter writes, "The leader in question had about himself some very progressed Mystics, to whom belonged also his wife and one of his relatives. The latter also possessed the Inner Word, but he could not be a leader, for his Inner Word only replied to questions concerning himself."[129] Then in a letter to Meyrink dated November 24, 1897, Mailänder wrote that one, "Pollak does not receive the spirit of self-knowledge from his revelations. He cannot help himself, let alone another. I believe that Pollak has received 'his own' spiritual revelation... since it is not a 'perfect gift' he cannot help anyone."

The Transmutation of the Blood

The result of ardently practicing these sentences is that an infusion of revitalizing spiritual forces is impressed upon the blood, allowing the gifts of the Holy Spirit to sink into the flesh and transmute it.

---

[129] Mailänder makes a difference between possessing the Inner Word and Perfect Word in his 44 letters to Meyrink. See Mailänder, Dilloo-Heidger, and Allen, *44 Letters to Gustav Meyrink (English Translation)*.

Mailänder's 26th statement of his *Soul Teaching* potently states, "In the outer man the blood is the will over the flesh, and in the inner man the Word of God is the power over flesh and blood."[130] Mailänder's 52nd statement says, "The seed is drawn and placed in the head, which impregnates the blood," so that our bodies become "capable of giving birth according to the will of the Spirit" for the glory of God.

The first phase came under Mailänder's Baptism of Water, which for him implied receiving spiritual impressions, guidance, sensations, and dreams. In my experience, the hair will stand up, a strong sensation of the crystallization of light will shiver around the head, and its tingling will wash down over the body from the head to the feet. In this work, the heart will stir up and this morale regeneration begins to complete the Baptism of Water when the heart's first intimate whispers directed towards the mind are enkindled. At this point, we enter a phase of tincturing the blood itself with the spiritual prayers submerging, even impressing into the blood, as we sink down into the body. Herein we enter a form of bodily awareness that suffuses the flesh with our devotion as we discover the profound meaning of the inner prayers. In short, profundity, devotion, and faith overflow to pervade our corporeality.

Franz Hartmann described the Baptism of the Blood very well:

> There is a certain class of practical Occultists, whose inner senses are opened to a great extent, and who have been taught by no one but the spirit within themselves and their own experience. They say that the Baptism of Blood means a penetration of the growing spiritual germ in man through the flesh, and

blood, and bones of the physical body, by which even the gross elements of the physical form are attenuated and purified, and that this process produces pains and sufferings typically represented by the suffering, crucifixion, and death of the man Jesus of Nazareth. They say that no one can be a true follower of Christ, or a real Christian, who has not undergone this Baptism of Blood, and experienced the pains of crucifixion, but that man, having passed through that occult process, becomes an adept, when only the highest baptism, or the last initiation, the Baptism of Fire, will be necessary to enter the highest attainable state (spiritual power), and to become a Son of Light.[131]

Meyrink's *Transfiguration of the Blood* is a testimony to this process and should be carefully read in conjunction with Hartmann's 1888 *What is True Christianity?* Both are included in this book.

Meyrink actually credits the inspiration behind his famous novels to this part of Mailänder's teaching, stating, "My apprenticeship also brought the change of my blood, which forced me to become a writer."[132]

Signs of Progression

Mailänder taught that the baptism, the foot-washing, the Lord's Supper, and the crucifixion itself are to be experienced in our own bodies. This provided something quite unique to Mailänder's method, owing to the manifestation of oracular signs that would appear to each student as indications from the Holy Spirit regarding their spiritual advancement. As such, these spiritual manifestations were oracular signatures, omens and expressions directly sent from the Holy Spirit to encourage progress. Certain

---

[131] Hartmann, "What Is True Christianity."

[132] Meyrink, "Die Verwandlung des Blutes," 13.

of these signs were typical to the method, and experienced by many, and yet others were unique to each student.

There were two main types of manifestations. Hartmann says:

> The guidance took place not so much by any external means or verbal advice, as by symbolic visions seen during dreams or in a state of meditation, or even by signs and letters appearing visibly upon the skin."

These signs that appeared on the skin Mailänder called crucifixion signs; indicative of the transfiguration of the blood. Hartmann adds that, "the soul expresses itself in forms and images, and if we learn to read these pictures correctly we may know the state of our interior condition and act so as to improve it accordingly. [133]

Meyrink similarly reports:

> I want to mention such a "process" here, which was that letters appeared on the skin. Each such letter had a definite meaning and indicated the stage of development of each person concerned. The layman might now easily lean towards a superficial opinion that it might have been a worthless rapture or the like. Such a view would be completely wrong![134]

These symbols were called the "Form Teaching" in the Bund der Verheißung and their activity in dreams, or when they appeared as skin wounds by his students, Mailänder called "spiritual processes" (geistige Vorgänge) to indicate that an active spiritual transfiguration was underway.[135]

---

[133] Shirley, "Autobiography of Dr. Franz Hartmann," 30.

[134] Meyrink, "Die Verwandlung des Blutes," 13.

[135] Emil Bock did not quite understand the teaching when he wrote, "In the circle around Alois Mailänder, an entire philosophy in signs was developed. They called the 'form teachings'. All letters, plants and animals had a specific pictorial value. Something like a primitive derivation from Jakob Boehme's Theosophy was cultivated by them." In Bock, *The Life and Times of Rudolf Steiner*, 1:183.

"In fact, the mystical death is connected with many interesting phenomena," writes Weinfurter.[136]

Weinfurter only hints at the existence of the Form Teaching in public, writing, "Some leaders possess their own manuscripts, circulating them, of course, only among their disciples, and which must not be shown to anybody else." Then, "If the leader entrusts the disciple with such a personal script, the student has to study it carefully and meditate over it for a longer time, asking the leader for explanations, should anything not be clear enough to him."[137]

That oracular signs appeared on the skin is extremely important in understanding how Mailänder expected we would undergo the foot-washing and crucifixion in our own bodies. The phase of the foot-washing indicated the Baptism of Water, which drew down spiritual sensations and symbols in dreams, while the Baptism of Blood was realized through bodily pains or signs and letters appearing on the skin.

For Mailänder, these signs were not merely signs of progress. They were symptoms, signposts, and indications that Mailänder interpreted to ascertain the requirement for each student's advancement. In this respect, Mailänder's prescribing of new and unique prayer sentences to each student was a remedial, and at the same time advancing, response to the oracular indications given by the Holy Spirit.

Karl Weinfurter clarifies this subject very well:

> Therefore the Spirit may evoke at any time on the human body, as well as within it, phenomena named the mystical stages, which may be perceived by other people too. Those phenomena

---

[136] Weinfurter, *Man's Highest Purpose*, 191.

[137] Ibid., 53.

are identical with any mystical practice, be it the silent one or that of letters, words, or sentences, or both alternately. The phenomena appear according to the student's progress. To those phenomena also belongs a certain kind of the metaphorical writing of letters, numbers, and whole sentences, appearing on the disciple's body, and perceivable by anybody else. Of course, no disciple will show them to sceptics or laymen, while he may do so to persons seriously interested in the Mystic. Nevertheless, those signs may be perceived by profane people when they have appeared on the student's body unexpectedly in the presence of others. The mentioned signs or stigmas (for that in fact they are) show the student the degree he has attained to on his way, or the promise of the progress to come. They may also prescribe the practice of letters appearing.[138]

Several examples of these oracular indications appear in the surviving material.

Mailänder, for example assures Meyrink in a letter dated 20th April 1894:

> "...and I am glad that you are so diligent in the exercise. The heat blisters you write about belong to the phase of Crucifixion and are assistants for advancement of the inner birth that is coming."[139]

---

[138] Ibid., 89.

[139] Weinfurter also writes in his "Royal Art," "The first important step on the way is noticeable through stigmatization. These can either be externally visible or just felt. It is a sign that the Holy Spirit is beginning to reveal itself in the disciple. Kerning writes that these "wounds of Christ" are openings through which the Holy Spirit enters and exits. Stigmatization is the first sign of "mystical death". Without them we do not know whether the student has followed the right path or not. The "mystical death" is the death of the "old Adam" and only the beginning of further transformations that only later show how mature the student is for further development. So stigmatization means only the lowest level of enlightenment." In Weinfurter and Sopp, *Der Königsweg.*

Hubbe-Schleiden also reports in his diary on the 22nd of September from Dreieichenhain:

"Kreuzigungsschmerzen im linken Fuß."[140]

I should also point out that Weinfurter further provided a "List of Symbols and Their Explanations" in his Mystical Primer, which is his expanded version of Mailänder's "Form Teaching" given in this book.

He writes:

> Symbols and their explanations: Introduction. In this list, which is not intended to be any dictionary or a list of general things, as is the case with the well-known dream books, only those symbols, signs and images are given through which the Holy Spirit speaks to his students in dreams, visions or through signs, which appear on the body. By combining or connecting the symbols listed here, the pupil can find explanations for all other symbols that are not listed here.

Adding:

> These symbols and their explanations are drawn from a book which has not been written down anywhere and which does not exist anywhere in the material world, namely from the Book of Life, which is completely hidden from everyone and yet so close - closer than the hand reaches.[141]

Weinfurter's book contains many such indicative spiritual processes (geistige Vorgänge):

> Another important meaning of the letter Heh is the gap or the slot. Here we really see the great depth of these symbols. Air

---

[140] "Crucifixion pains in the left foot." Hübbe-Schleiden, "Tagebuch von Wilhelm Hübbe Schleiden (Diaries)," 1896.

[141] Karel Weinfurter, *Mystische Fibel: Ein Handbuch Für Den Schüler Der Praktischen Mystik* (Sersheim: Osiris-Verlag, 1954).

or wind penetrates through every gap and through every slot. Those who have received strong stigmatization from advanced students often feel a wind blowing through the wounds of Christ. But the wind goes through every gap is nothing other than the wind of the Holy Spirit, and, therefore, as Kerning says, the third person of the divine Trinity penetrates through the wounds of Christ, namely that spirit which is true to man and gives eternal life.[142]

Regarding Kerning's connection to the signs of letters appearing on the skin, see below.

Whenever these manifestations appeared, each member of the Bund der Verheißung was expected to remain silent, to only communicate these to Mailänder and not to his other students.

Meyrink clarifies this subject, which is also reiterated by Hartmann:

> All the more strange that almost everybody over time experienced on themselves these event type "processes," the "J.," as we generally called the leader, considered so important. In visions or, mostly in dreams, but not only, also on the body. Even though no one knew beforehand what would happen! It was strictly forbidden for anyone to tell the other person what he was experiencing, for the reason that autosuggestion would be ruled out.[143]

Furthermore, Mailänder taught that relaying these blessings might profane them and cause the influence of the Holy Spirit to depart the student. Therefore, the nature of the processes was sacred and intimate.

---

[142] Ibid.

[143] Ibid., 14.

Theosopher Literary Influences on Alois Mailänder

Within the Bund der Verheißung, several books were circulated among members as recommend reading according to the instructions of Alois Mailänder. This is quite unusual because by most accounts, Mailänder was said to be illiterate and yet the following evidence reveals he not only examined but furthermore commented on the value of the content of books for his students. This raises the question of to what extent Mailänder truly was illiterate and how he came to appreciate the content of those books. My theory is that these books were read aloud during evening group sittings at the Bruderheim. No matter the case, the titles of these books provide great insight into the doctrines of the Bund der Verheißung.

Three main authors were read in Mailänder's circle: J.B Kerning, Jane Lead, and Jakob Lorber.

These three authors were strongly influential in the development of Mailänder's system of internal spiritual alchemy. Before examining their relevance, let us first overview the original references.

Wilhelm Hübbe-Schleiden writes in his notebook that:

> "J. Kerning 'Key to the spiritual world.' Johannes thinks J. Kerning's 'Road to Immortality' is better."[144]

One year later, in another notebook, *Hübbe-Schleiden comments that* Mailänder lost his copy of Kerning's *Road to Immortality* and that they should send a new one.[145]

---

[144] Hübbe-Schleiden, "Wilhelm Hübbe-Schleiden's Notebooks," 1884 1885, 26.

[145] Wilhelm Hübbe-Schleiden, "Wilhelm Hübbe-Schleiden's Notebooks" (SUB Göttingen, 1886/87 numbered Cod. MS Hübbe Schleiden 1012: 6, 1886 1887), 40.

Then Hübbe-Schleiden recorded a note on borrowing a book called *The Rebirth* from Nicolas Gabele along with the name of Jane Lead. However, the notebook entry runs like this:

"Kerning 'Key to the spiritual world' Stuttgart 1855 Scheible 12

Jane Leade . Rebirth of Man to be asked for at Gabele's on loan."[146]

In the above, there is some difficulty in understanding if the name "Jane Lead" should be associated with the book title after her name appears. I've added the full stop myself, where the original notebook simply has a wider space between. The original German reads, "Jane Lead Wiedergeburt des Menschen, bei Gabele leihweise zu erbitten." This book, the *Rebirth of Man*, could mean some title by Jane Lead, but nothing titled "Wiedergeburt" appears to have been published in her name. Most likely, it refers to the *Die Wiedergeburt das innere wahrhaftige Leben* by Kerning, published by Karl Kolb 1857.[147]

On 28 September 1895, Mailänder cryptically mentions another author in a letter to Meyrink:

"...at least I would be happy to meet you personally once again. I enclose here a brochure from theosophical books that are very important for reading. Dreitagsscene is very beautiful, as well as the explanations by the master of the Gospel according to John is of great importance to us." [148]

It is not obvious at first, however these are clear references to two items by the Christian mystic Jacob Lorber, who was often

---

[146] Hübbe-Schleiden, "Wilhelm Hübbe-Schleiden's Notebooks," 1884 1885, 14.

[147] Karl Kolb, *Die Wiedergeburt, das innere wahrhaftige Leben, oder Wie wird der Mensch selig?* (Lorch: Karl Rohm, 1919). And later circulated by Gustav Meyrink.

[148] Alois Mailänder, *Nachlass: Briefe und Karten von Alois Mailänder an Gustav Meyrink - BSB Meyrinkiana I.2. Johannes an Ruben* (Bayerische Staatsbibliothek, 1893).

called "the Theosophen Lorber," as if he was an extension of Jakob Boehme.

Mailänder specifically names one Dreitagsscene, which is the "Three-Day Scene" (titled *Three Days in the Temple* in English), recorded by Jakob Lorber in 1859-60. Then, Mailänder describes Lorber's *The Great Gospel of John*, recorded in 1851-64 in ten volumes. Therefore, when Mailänder describes "theosophical books" to Meyrink, he is referring to Lorber's catalogued writings.

Moreover, Lorber is also mentioned by Meyrink in his *Transfiguration of the Blood* in describing Mailänder's disciple K. (Oskar Korschelt), who highly recommended Lorber's writings. Meyrink revealed that these books were studied in a Rosicrucian context within the Bund der Verheißung.

Two more interesting volumes are also mentioned within the Bund der Verheißung.

In a letter from Crescentia Gabele to Meyrink on 25 June 1897, she mentions John Pordage:

> "I have this spring once again read through your Pordage and written down the important things for me, so that I now really want to send those books back to you ... In Pordage I found once again confirmed everything that our leader has taught and still teaches."[149]

Lastly, on 4 April 1899, Mailänder dictates a letter to Meyrink, stating:

> "I have received your letter and the two booklets, and I (and also Gabriele) say many thanks for this. By the way I have had these writings in my hands already for many years (as they are contained in the *Theosophical Shield*. This does not matter

---

[149] Mailänder, Dilloo-Heidger, and Allen, *44 Letters to Gustav Meyrink (English Translation)*.

though, as I always know how to use them for the hungry and thirsty ones."[150]

This Theosophical Shield is *Der grosse, wahre und theosophische geistliche Schild*, a seven-part anthology consisting of, among other things, the writings of Jane Lead.

Entire volumes could easily be written on each of the above-named authors. Some of their writings are still largely unknown, untranslated, or unpopular in today's mainstream western esoteric audience.

I have remedied this problem for the writings of J.B Kerning by translating his books to support an understanding of Mailänder and the sister volume of this book, *The Rosicrucian Fraternities in the Wake of Alois Mailänder and J.B Kerning*.

For our purposes, only a brief introduction to these authors is required to overview their influence on Mailänder. What these authors all had in common was that they all belonged to the Pietistic Behmist vein of Christian Theosophy. In viewing them individually, it becomes clear that Alois Mailänder amalgamated their doctrines and methods into a single harmonious system.

Jane Lead (1624-1704) was an English born Christian mystic who recorded her spiritual visions after witnessing the Virgin Sophia appear to her in April 1670 following her husband's death. She wrote,

> There came upon me an overshadowing bright cloud, and in the midst of it the figure of a Woman, most richly adorned with transparent Gold, her Hair hanging down, and her Face as the terrible Crystal for brightness, but her Countenance was sweet and mild. At which sight I was somewhat amazed, but immediately this Voice came

---

[150] Ibid.

saying, Behold I am God's Eternal Virgin-Wisdom, whom thou hast been enquiring after; I am to unseal the Treasures of God's deep Wisdom unto thee, and will be as Rebecca was unto Jacob, a true Natural Mother.[151]

Three days later, Lead beheld the same figure "with a Crown upon her Head, full of Majesty" holding a Golden Book closed with tree seals, inscribed "Herein lieth hidden the deep Wonders of Jehovah's Wisdom." Six days later, Wisdom assured her, "I will not fail to transfigure myself in thy mind…for I thy Glass for Divine Seeing shall evermore stand before thee."

Lead's experience of Virgin Wisdom would unfold over the rest of her life as she continued to record new messages from Sophia. During her life, she declared herself a "Bride of Christ."

In 1663, Jane Lead met the Christian mystic John Pordage and together they formed a small English Behmist group which would go on to name itself the Philadelphian Society in 1694.

Lead's writings formed the core of the group's spiritual goals and ideas. The group recognized the presence of the Holy Spirit in each person's soul and maintained Panentheistic views, observing the belief in the presence of God in all nature while maintaining that all creation exists within the omnipresence of the Heavenly Father.

J.B Kerning (1774-1851) was the pseudonym for the German born Johan Baptist Krebs, a mystical freemason. Kerning was a well-known musician and vocalist in Stuttgart, where he was also involved in several operas. On 12 August 1820, he was elevated to the degree of "Knight Apprentice" in the

---

[151] Jane Lead, *A Fountain of Gardens* (London: Printed, and sold by the Booksellers of London and Westminster, 1697).

Johannes lodge of Berlin, commencing his life-long passion with freemasonry. As a mystical Theosopher, Kerning takes the place in German mysticism that St. Martin claims in France.

His work at the opera lent him special influence in artistic circles, the members of which would access freemasonry through him. German masonic historians have noted his extensive influence between 1820 and 1850. Documents show he was honored by lodges in Frankfurt, Erlangen, Fürth, Bayreuth, Mannheim, Ulm, Basel, Berlin, Frankenthal, and Worms.

J.B Kerning founded the Johannes lodge, "Wilhelm zur aufgehenden Sonne" or "Lodge of the Rising Sun." He became its long-time master of the chair. From this center, he would issue his new esoteric freemasonry, seeking to teach the "essence of freemasonry" — first through realizing masonic lodge work and the symbolism of its tools as an inner experience, and second through teaching that the masonic quest for the "Lost Word" was symbolic of our true calling to seek out the rediscovery of the eternal Logos, a power which humankind had lost to posterity.

For Kerning, the physical body is extremely important. He does not believe in achieving regeneration without spiritual rebirth in the flesh. The masonic "columns represent the human body," and he teaches that the masonic pillars "J" and "B" stand for whole letter groups, where the J on the apprentice column is a Hebrew Yod representing vowels, while the "B" column of the second degree signifies consonants. He says the "letters are the tools to work with to open the entrance."

Kerning's spiritual explanation for objects of masonic ritual included perceiving the square as the "angular Alpha and the compass as the circled Omega, as they outline Nature, and

Christ himself is the rule stick." For Kerning, the square, compass, and rule embody how "IAO was treated in all mysteries and religions as the root of the name of God, and therefore this root could not be missing in our fraternity."[152] In practice, these letters are "thought" into the body.

The ideal of speech, as formed in the mouth, "has to pervade us everywhere, in order that our entire being may become speech in which the Word of God resounds."[153]

In his Rebirth, Kerning clarifies the awakening of the Word:

> Through perseverant exercise new tongues will eventually be formed in man and begin to talk within him. As soon as he is by himself, he will perceive audible thoughts within himself, being amazed by the liveliness of the Word urging him to utter these thoughts. The uttered thought will, however, firstly penetrate his heart again, in order to further shed light on the stirring, rousing, and moving of the Word.[154]

Although Kerning often writes "he" as if his system were reserved only for freemasons and males, this is explicitly not the case. On the contrary, he stated women tend to advance in his method quite quickly.[155]

---

[152] J. B. Kerning, *Briefe über die Königliche Kunst*, ed. Gottfried Buchner (Renatus Verlag Lorch, 1912).

[153] Hiram Butler, "Key to the Spriritual World (English Translation)," trans. C. Wieland, *The Esoteric* 1, no. 8 (February 1888): 276.

[154] Kolb, *Die Wiedergeburt* Statement 450.

[155] Kerning writes, "The female sex, in performing most duties, can in thought spell into themselves, and thanks to their finer nerve-systems they are much easier and quicker able to feel the letters in the feet. Young maidens of noble pedigree especially would learn the thing in a fabulously short time, and when this art of spelling will once be generally taught, then prophetesses will grow up amongst such maidens like

Jakob Lorber (1800-1864) was an Austrian mystic who reported that on March 15th, 1840, a spiritual experience shook him deeply, for early in that morning he heard a voice arising from the region of his heart. It clearly commanded, "Take up your pen and write!" The call of that day changed the direction of his life entirely, for thenceforth, Lorber would write down all he heard with his "Inner Ear," spending hours each day transcribing what the voice dictated.

In many ways, Lorber was the first spiritual "channeler" in western spirituality.

A pile of manuscripts grew over the next twenty-four years, although Lorber published nothing in his own lifetime. When the work was published after his death, it amounted to more than 20,000 manuscript pages becoming known as the *Neuoffenbarung*, or *New Revelation*, published in 25 volumes, including *The Great Gospel of John* in 10 volumes.

Lorber's biographer, Karl Gottfried Ritter von Leitner, described him as uncomplicated and harmless, from farmer stock. Lorber first sought to work as a teacher and eventually changed his profession to make use of his musical talent. He began playing violin as a concert soloist and reporting on opera and concert performances for provincial papers. Von Leitner also described Lorber as a poor man but generous as far as his means permitted.

Most important to our study, von Leitner draws a connection between Lorber and Kerning:

> Thus he felt drawn to reading works that corresponded to his deep inwardness. And now, as far as his earning of bread allowed him, he read many works by Justinus Kerner, Jung-Stilling, Swedenborg, Jakob Bohme, Johann

---

mushrooms from the earth." Ibid. Statement 189.

Tennhardt, and J.B Kerning, the latter being particularly dear to him.[156]

A continued hidden tradition of appreciating Kerning's writings by Lorber Friends may also be observed in the writings of Gottfried Mayerhofer (1807-1877) who belonged to Jakob Lorber's inner circle in Graz. Mayerhofer reported receiving the gift of hearing the Inner Word in 1870 and his works are considered part of the New Revelation together with Lorber's own writings. A letter he sent to his spiritual son, dated November 14, 1875, names four of Kerning books, namely *Key to the Spiritual World, Road to Immortality, The Rebirth* and *Faith*. He describes placing these books into the hands of his disciple and praises Kerning's message and methods. [157]

Jane Lead, Jakob Lorber and J.B Kerning all presented distinct approaches. Yet they shared similarities, which Mailänder undoubtedly noticed when unifying their methods into his new spiritual alchemy for the Bund der Verheißung. For Mailänder, in many respects, the methods of J.B Kerning provided the practical keys to Jane Lead's teachings. Yet, this is an over-simplification as the subject is quite complex. Let us briefly overview some of their ideas that were adopted into his system.

Firstly, there is the nature of Mailänder's persona as the returned Biblical John himself. Jakob Lorber and Jane Lead established precedents for Mailänder here because in his second book, *The Spiritual Son* (1846), Lorber states that Swedenborg

---

[156] Jakob Lorber and Karl Gottfried von Leitner, Briefe Jakob Lorbers: Urkunden und Bilder aus seinem Leben. (Bietigheim/Württemberg: Lorber-Verlag, 1931), 13.

[157] The title of his letter is "Aufklärungen über „Schlüssel zur Geisterwelt" und „Weg zur Unsterblichkeit" oder „Wiedergeboren" und „Glauben." 14. Nov. 1875. Gottfried Mayerhofer. *Geistesgaben 2* (Published by Klaus Kardelke. Books on Demand 2021), 208. The writings of Mayerhofer also show that he had read and gave commentary on sections of the Emerald Tablet of Hermes.

was the reincarnation of the Biblical prophet Daniel,[158] while Jane Lead published her prophecy stating that, "So now again the Spirit of John the Evangelist is to rise and be the Forerunner of the Ministration of the Love."[159] Consequently, the return of Biblical figures was not unfamiliar within the Lorber and Lead movements, paving the way for Mailänder to not only arise as John returned but to actually stand in the special position of fulfilling Jane Lead's prediction.

Now we'll overview the practices proposed by Jane Lead, J.B Kerning and Jakob Lorber in detail, viewing their similarities and deviations to consider how Mailänder successfully wove them together.

Of the three, Kerning is the most practical. He insisted on mentally thinking in short sentences, single words, and letters throughout the entire body, with a special emphasis on building a presence of bodily consciousness, working from the feet up. He also used the Lord's Prayer throughout the body.

For Kerning, "It is of importance that all the organs of the human body contain the Word. It is necessary that teeth, lips, tongues and palates are represented in all organs."[160] He adds, "The brain is full of life, and each and every organ is separated with its own lips, teeth, tongue and palate."[161]

On this matter, it appears Lorber tried to distinguish his method from J.B Kerning's, even refuting Kerning's often-repeated emphasis on the tongue and mouth.

---

[158] Jakob Lorber, *Die geistige Sonne Bd. 2* (Bietigheim Württ.: Neu-Salems-Verl., 1929), chap. 14. The writings of Mayerhofer also show that he had read and gave commentary on sections of the Emerald Tablet of Hermes.

[159] Jane Lead, *The Messenger of an Universal Peace: Or a Third Message to the Philadelphian Society* (London: Printed for the Booksellers of London and Westminster, 1698).

[160] J.B. Kerning and Richard Cloud, *Kerning's Testament*, 2017 Statement 40.

[161] Ibid. Statement 54.

In his *The Household of God*, Lorber writes, "However, the spirit does not dwell in the tongue, but alone in the heart. But this does not mean that someone with an awakened tongue has also an awakened spirit in his heart, for the tongue is a part of the head, being the foot and arm of the same."[162]

Lorber never described exact practical outlines like J.B Kerning did for his students. Instead, Lorber wrote of spiritual regeneration through the Inner Word, only cryptically hinting at practices.

For example, Lorber recorded this dictation from his inner voice:

> But now to Chanchah! Chanchah receives the garment with reverence, and as soon as she touches it, it gloriously embellishes her whole being. Standing there in her celestial attire, she weeps for joy and says: "Oh, friend, tell me your name that I may write it forever in my heart with glowing letters." The reply

---

[162] Although on the same page Lorber presents a Kerning teaching describing one figure named Gabriel who is told to "look at the signs in your hand… And the youth turned into a man and examined his hand and found twenty-five signs (the Alphabet; ed.) on the same, together with their names and their origin as well as their inner meaning. And all the others discovered similar signs within them." Something else happens in Lorber's writings which uncannily mirrors the secret practices of Kerning's, then unpublished, masonic ritual. In his "Three Days in the Temple" Lorber describes the boy Jesus as telling his audience to pay attention to the single words in the "old Hebrew tongue," breaking down the names "Jerusalem" and "Melchisedec" into syllables, rendering them as "Je (this is) Ruh or Ruha (the dwelling place) Sa (for the) Lem or Lehem (great King). Me or mei (of My) l'chi or lichi - read litzi (countenance or light) Sedek (seat)". When viewing the entire Sabithengrad ritual from J.B Kerning in this volumes sister book, I recommend keeping this part of Lorber's teachings in mind. The similarity raises the question of whether or not Lorber himself was initiated into Kerning's lodge or if he had had somehow obtained a copy of the ritual. Jakob Lorber, *The Household of God*, vol. 2 (Bietigheim: Lorber Verlag, 1995), chap. 57. Also a gospel also used by Mailänder. Jakob Lorber, *Die drei Tage im Tempel Durch das innere Wort empfangen und niedergeschrieben* (Bietigheim/Württbg: Lorber, 1952), chap. 19 Section 1-2.

comes to her from Christ, "What you want to do is already done. Probe your heart and you will find what you want to hear from Me."[163]

Lorber repeats that it is indeed Christ who writes in our hearts, for he recorded Christ, saying, "When I saw that his penitence was genuine I clearly wrote in a fiery script the following words into his heart: 'Mehuhed, rise in the face of My great mercy!'"[164] Christ also dictated to Lorber the instruction, "It is also for you necessary to hear reliable words from the sphere of honest nature, full of power, and write them into your hearts in order to see how true, just and faithful your holy eternal Father is."[165]

Jane Lead similarly describes a spiritual alchemy process for the "Day-star rising first in our hearts."[166]

Similar to Kerning, she outlines a "cutting off of the head," which Kerning executes by cutting the index finger across the neck. But instead of drawing the letters IAO, Jane Lead says that we must draw the name JEHOVA into our bodies and stamp it upon our foreheads, "to give all place for the Fixation of this Holy Being, which will nullify all other Beings, that so entirely I may possess the Great JEHOVAH as my Fountain, continually within to flow, for the washing away of the Impurities, and for the preparing a Body in which the Holy Ghost so Fixedly may dwell, as never out of it to depart away."

---

[163] Jakob Lorber, *Bischof Martin: die Entwicklung einer Seele im Jenseits*, 4th ed. (Bietigheim-Bissingen: Lorber-Verlag, 2003), chap. 95 sections 1-3.

[164] Jakob Lorber, *The Household of God*, vol. 1 (Bietigheim: Lorber Verlag, 1995), secs. 9–10.

[165] Ibid., vol. 1, chap. 35 section 2.

[166] Jane Lead, *The Enochian Walks with God* (Printed and sold by D. Edwards, 1694), 196.

Similar to Lorber's realization of the Inner Word, Jane Lead instructs that we are to "keep our Hearts all pure, and clearer reserved, to be the most Holy Sanctuary for the Priestly-Spirit to minister in, and to make ready a Holy separated place for GOD and CHRIST to manifest themselves in us."[167]

However, for both Lead and Mailänder, there is an intriguing Sophianic element at work. Jane Lead says you should enter "the deep Center of your Virginal Heart and feel the Impregnation by the Godhead,"[168] and Mailänder similarly describes the seed of impregnation entering from the head.[169]

Mailänder's practical method, at least, is closer to Lorber's than Kerning's in the initial phase, especially in its application of sentences practiced in a mantra-like fashion upon the heart. Still, Mailänder's emphasis on enlivening the limbs with the life of the soul and invigorating the feet and fingertips are indeed influences he draws from Kerning. The stigmatic letters that should appear on the skin is Mailänder's own extension of Kerning's alphabetic mysticism in combination with Jane Lead's teachings, as explained below.

Furthermore, Mailänder appears to have adopted his art of instructing disciples from Kerning's *Key to the Spiritual World.*[170] Weinfurter comes close to suggest Kerning was Mailänder's model for teaching when he writes, "The best examples of the guidance of the student by means of a leader are given by the

[167] Ibid., 201.

[168] Jane Lead, *The Resurrection of Life or the Royal Characteristics and Identifying Marks,* Reverse-Translation (Old German to English), 1705. The English original was lost. The 1705 German edition was translated back into English for today's readers.

[169] See Mailänder's Soul Teaching statement # 52 in Part III of this book.

[170] Kerning writes, "At length, the pupil thought he had arrived at the top of the ladder and said: "Examine me, chaplain, and see whether I have attained it." "You have, "replied the chaplain. " In Butler, "Key to the Spiritual World," 223.

great Mystic and clairvoyant, J. B. Kerning, in his works *The Way to Immortality* and *The Key to the Spiritual World*."[171] In the later, a character called the Chaplain inspects his student's progress and can somehow discern whether the disciple has attained it. His disciple works in isolation for months at a time and only returns at intervals for inspection and to receive further practical outlines on how to progress his body.

The laying of the hands is a known Christian healing method, but a teaching particular to Kerning is that we should practice the laying of the hands upon ourselves.[172] Mailänder's *Soul Teaching* statement 75 reads, "One should lay hands on oneself and erase all material pains for they inhibit the Divine Spirit. Therefore have courage!" Hübbe Schleiden (1885) also records him asking Mailänder or Gabele about physical pains and he receives the reply, "Think firmly by Will. Pay close attention to it. Place your hands on your head so that your fingers are spread out along the vortex."[173] Similarly, *Soul Teaching* 78 reads, "This is a form of strengthening the faith, for the same power that goes out from the fingertips is in all parts of the body, flowing in vitality, if we proclaim the Will in the Word."

Wilhelm Hübbe-Schleiden also compared Mailänder's teachings to Kerning, and furthermore he left evidence that Mailänder was somehow aware of the practical nature of Kerning's exercises.

This occurs in Hübbe-Schleiden 1896 diary where he left a draft letter for Paula Stryczek, his future adoptive daughter, after he tried to persuade her over a long period to become Mailänder's

---

[171] Weinfurter, *Man's Highest Purpose*, 54.

[172] Kerning, *Briefe über die Königliche Kunst.*

[173] It does not say if it's from Mailänder or Gabele. Hübbe-Schleiden, "Wilhelm Hübbe-Schleiden's Notebooks," 1884 1885, 16.

pupil. Mailänder had recently accepted her, which was a rarity as he accepted very few at the time.

In the letter, we also learn that Hübbe-Schleiden had already been teaching Paula the method of word sentences or meditations, but he did not wish Mailänder to know of this fact now that Paula had been accepted as his student. Instead, Hübbe-Schleiden tells her to leave his name out of it and to describe what she is doing as Kerning exercises.

The draft letter from 16 August 1896 reads:

> But my joy when I received and read it this morning was really great. Everything will be fine now. Just don't be lacking in zeal on the spiritual path. To greet and encourage you on the way, I am sending you the "Johannes" picture. I asked him to put his spirit name first on it. …. You also know that his present personality is only that of a factory worker who was also without any school education. Only now, since about 6-7 years, has he been freed from that slavery. I'll tell you a lot more about him later.
>
> Neither he nor I doubted that you would freely choose to follow him. But I, a foolish human being, awaited your real and frank "yes" with tension.
>
> First of all, I would now ask you to write me a short report on your previous word exercises and the encounters and experiences you have had from them on a special sheet of paper (like your normal letterhead, on which you always write to me). Please leave my name out there. It will suffice if you state the words you practiced in Kerning's fashion and what you felt afterwards, why you changed the word practice and why you finally gave up, had to give up practicing it. In particular, mention where you had pain, what kind of pain it was (in the hands and feet, right?) And what other pain you felt. Didn't you sometimes

hear voices, animal voices, when such animals weren't in audible vicinity? Have you also seen apparitions or felt anything else, or also perceived smells in your mind, or tasted what you did not have from experience? It doesn't need to be too detailed, because if it were to have the right value, I would have to ask those matters from you; otherwise the probability is too great that you will emphasize the unimportant, unfavourable astral perceptions and overlook the spiritual processes that matter, but are often hardly noticeable. But let's just get started, the other things will soon be found in oral personal intercourse. I would then like to send your report to Mailänder very soon and ask him to give you an exercise now so start working right now.[174]

According to his diary, Hübbe-Schleiden sent the letter the following day.

Then on the 23rd of August 1896, he drafts another letter of interest to Paula:

Today I am sending you this enclosed letters from Johannes, which especially concerns you. I ask you to take a copy of it and then send it back to me and memorize every word exactly

... The path is now open to you in the finest way like a garden path through lovely terrain. How fast you can advance depends entirely on your conscientiousness and devotion, in short on your goodwill.

Today, first of all, the main thing: You probably know how you have to practice the word given to you. It is important that the thought or the feeling, the longing, should be connected with the repetition of the word. Think slowly and consciously or speak the word tonelessly into your interior, not upwards, into the head, but downwards, towards the heart or the pit of the heart.

---

[174] Hübbe-Schleiden, "Tagebuch von Wilhelm Hübbe Schleiden (Diaries)," 1896.

You should do this as often as you can, anytime, day or night, but with all seriousness. And since your occupation does not always, or not often at all, leave you the leisure to do so, it is good to set aside short time in the morning, at noon and in the evening when you can concentrate in your room undisturbed for this exercise, 10 or 15 minutes or half an hour.

This effort must not tire you too much, for it may be harder than you think. You could keep getting annoyed, and often have even ugly thoughts in between, especially when you concentrate yourself in practice. If that should be the case, you must not lose patience with yourself, but must, as soon as you become aware of the wandering of your thoughts, bring them back in full to the practice with complete calm and serenity.

You will also find peace of mind during the day or even at night if you repeat your exercise quite often and quite a lot with heartfelt concentration in between, even beside the practice times.

As for the effect of the exercise, you must by no means direct your attention to it during the exercise. That would distract you. The effects really only come at all then, and then best, the less you expect them. What Johannes writes with regard to your perceptions should not mean that your previous pains in your hands and feet are not the right thing. Rather, they are the natural and necessary beginning. This pain may also return.

If so, do not describe the type of pain exactly, where, and how, pressure or sting or whatever! And what you report later in this connection must of course be written on a separate sheet of paper, since I do not want to send your dear letters to me to Mailänder.

However, the feeling and hearing impressions you reported were, as you yourself know and felt, only annoying to you. First and foremost, a whole series of sensory perceptions in the skin, under the skin, in the limbs and otherwise must show up with you.

If you feel something new, or something old, for which you have not yet recognized the reason and cause, please mention it. You should also not misunderstand Johannes with regard to any auditory perceptions. Everything that comes from the astral world, as happened to you before, is an evil, what comes from the true spiritual world is all symbolic, but it is usually represented symbolically in animal voices or in some other way.[175]

The pains, feelings and impressions Paula should experience Mailänder called the "spiritual processes" (geistige Vorgänge). Weinfurter also explains how these were observed during Kerning practices as well:

Best is in the beginning to think the letters on the soles, proceeding then in time towards the toes, but always on the skin surface, when we finally reach the ankles. In the ankles there is a particular mystical centre. The student when reaching that centre will experience certain phenomena, provided he has practised thoroughly and not quickly. Until he has received the sign, he must not go on, but has to continue the practice up to the ankles. Having had certain signs, he can go on in his practice without precipitation up to the knees, these being the second mystical centre, the attainment of which has already effects on the whole body.[176]

Weinfurter gives another related example, whereby "the Mystic sees and hears around his head croaking ravens."[177] This corresponds to the alchemical "raven head." Kerning himself

---

[175] Ibid.

[176] Weinfurter, *Man's Highest Purpose*, 81.

[177] Ibid., 191.

writes that one might hear the sound of barking dogs, similar to the phenomena in Hübbe-Schleiden's description above.

All this evidence points to the fact that Kerning and Mailänder were quite inseparable.[178]

The same can be said of the relationship between Mailänder and Jane Lead as it becomes clear that Mailänder also adopted key ideas behind his Baptism of Blood and of Fire from her theosophy.

However, his concept of the Baptism of Water derives from Martin Boos and also from J.B Kerning, who wrote that one may "feel a cold shower running down his back, feeling the hairs stand on end and feel a strange breeze around him, so that one may well have undergone the baptism of John. After John, however, comes Christ, the inner life which baptises with fire, which begins in the feet and is not cold, but burns, consuming everything impure, sinful, and earthly."[179] This clearly matches Hartmann's below description from his 1888 lecture titled, "What is True Christianity," which elaborates on Mailänder's three baptisms.[180]

According to Mailänder, the Baptism of Blood follows the Baptism of Water, and a careful reading of Jane Lead reveals his likely sources of inspiration and particular books he had. However, Jane Lead's original outlines concerning the three baptisms are far more complex than Mailänder's, who appears to

---

[178] Austrian author Herbert Silberer (1882-1923) discusses the spiritual alchemy of Jane Lead at length and names Kerning twice in his "Problems of Mysticism and its Symbolism". Given his location he likely was related to Eckstein's Vienna circle. See Dr. Herbert Silberer, *Problems of Mysticism and Its Symbolism* (New York: Moffat, Yard and Company, 1917).

[179] Kerning, *Briefe über die Königliche Kunst* Statement 354.

[180] The names Mailänder and John are not named in Hartmann, "What Is True Christianity."

have drawn out their essence, and simplified them to their most elemental and practical form.

Lead describes the Baptism of Blood as a Virgin Tincture which flows in our veins during "transformation and transfiguration" to restore our bodies. Her initiatory stage of the Seventh Gate of Projection lays the foundation for what Meyrink would later describe in his *Transfiguration of the Blood*.[181]

The Baptism of Fire is also explicit in Jane Lead where Wisdom tells her, "I will descend in this fiery cloud into thee as a baptising fire."[182] Jane Lead clarifies it as manifestation of the Holy Ghost in an invisible flaming body which she says is described in the Book of Revelations as an angel standing in the sun.[183]

---

[181] On the Baptism of Blood, Lead writes of the "Virgin Tincture, as a warm Fireblood, doth flow in every vein, and a nourishing life is felt passing through every sense. This is that gift which the Virgin will bestow upon the fixed soul." Lead states that if we can attain the skill to stir up the precious gift from the "Tincturing Blood of the divine Virgin, we may be able to bring forth Matter, Form and Colour, according to the Quintessential Spirit, transferred from the highest Being," and that this projection "may be referred to these two heads, viz. *Transformation and Transfiguration.*" She says that the Virgin Tincture drives out the poisonous matter, restoring the "Body of fallen man." From her "In Jane Lead, *The Revelation of Revelations: The Compiled Works of Jane Lead* (Broken Bread Publishing, n.d.), 75.

[182] Ibid.

[183] In "Upon Ascension and Descension" Lead states that, "Bodily Death should overtake us, while upon this Ascending Ladder." Yet ascending to the heights with Christ is not the end of her system and neither is it for Mailänder. Lead introduces a glorification of the spiritual body at the apex of ascension before its fiery descent, writing, "Thus, we defined some part of the Glory that doth follow upon Ascension, through being fixed in the Body of the Holy Ghost, by whose glance of Light it is given us to see another Degree, how that the Ascended and Glorified, are again to Descend." This descending personage of Christ we attain or partake in is that fiery body of Christ returning in his Apocalyptic form, for Lead affirms, "Thou wilt with flaming ministering Spirits descend," consummating our perfection in the Baptism of Fire. Ibid., 52;182.

For Mailänder, this apparently occurred during his Pentecostal event of 1895 in Dippelshof.

Through a careful reading of Meyrink's *Transfiguration of the Blood* and his final typoscript, one can observe a profound connection between Mailänder's Baptism of Water, of Blood and of Fire to Jane Lead's outline of taking on, or advancing through, different forms of Christ for the spiritual transfiguration of our physical bodies in successive stages. For Jane Lead, we participate in the changing and renewed bodies of Christ in his upward and downward journey, which Jane Lead calls ascension and descension.[184]

In these stages, the initial broken and crucified body of Christ is the "first course" in the "Supper of God" at a symbolic furnished table whereupon we are to "daily feed upon a Crucified Christ." But then we are to depart from this state to "taste the Lord's Mystical Body," which is "risen from the dead,"[185-186] attaining that "transmuted Body, which is so restorative, as nothing of putrefaction shall more be known in the Soul's Properties," while

---

[184] Jane Lead, *The Heavenly Cloud Now Breaking: The Compiled Works of Jane Lead* (Broken Bread Publishing, n.d.), 44–52.

[185] "Christ the Lord presents himself in a Paradisical Body, and saith, Children, here I give my risen Body, as more powerful, strong, and pleasant, to feed upon: For you it is, who have not feared to encounter the Death. Oh, what less is this, but the Marriage Feast, where the Water is turned into Wine! And by the Governor of this Feast, ye are most earnestly called upon to eat of this transmuted Body." Ibid., 7–8.

[186] Elsewhere, she emphasizes the discarding of the suffering form of Christ: "Christ will not allow anyone to appear in his old Garment but wants to alter their Garments with a Radiance and Beauty of perfect Holiness, so that They may come into agreement with this lofty Condition whereto the LORD has called and redeemed them. Therefore, through the Impression and Manifestation of Himself in Them, He wants to make Them different." In the Preface of Lead, *The Resurrection of Life or the Royal Characteristics and Identifying Marks.*

we become glorified in our "Eagle-Body," which is "proper for Ascension."[187]

Mailänder remarkably presented these very same ideas, as Meyrink reported:

> There must be something from above that brings about the change," he said. He, of course, meant Jesus Christ with this "from above" statement, the resurrected Jesus Christ, who has overcome death and is around us every day, and not the form of the crucified Jesus. For those who only look at that crucified Christ, as practiced by Catholic monks, especially the Jesuits, and do not follow the living, risen one, would have their "bones broken" or would be left hanging with him on the cross. As an example, he liked to name Katharina Emmerich, the well-known stigmatized.[188]

Meyrink is largely considered a dedicated practitioner of Eastern mysticism, which makes his 1930 typoscript, presented at the end of this book, even more remarkable because not only does he regret having dedicated himself to tantric practices throughout his life, but he does a full one-eighty from his earlier rejection of Christ and concludes that he finally understands this lesson from Mailänder, stating:

> We are not to follow Christ but must take Him down from the cross!!! I am to crown the old man, whom I always see in the far distance, and dress him with purple and make him the ruler of my life. I see him now also crowned and clothed in purple. The more perfect he becomes, the sooner he will and can help me... "He will grow, but I will dwindle!!!" This is the meaning of the speech of the Baptist! Only now I realize that until now I had been severely wrong and the cause of all my suffering was

---

[187] Lead, *The Heavenly Cloud Now Breaking.*

[188] Meyrink, "Die Verwandlung des Blutes," 13.

that I did not know all this clearly but instead believed: "I" had to perfect myself, me and not Him!... It's just the other way around! So the old man is the Christos, and we have to untie him and make him mighty, only then can he do miracles. That working of miracles will pass into to us once the schizophrenia has been lifted away and we no longer concern ourselves with it. For example, the stigmatized Konnersreuth woman should try to spiritually untie the one she sees suffering, instead of always suffering with him! She but goes always around in circles.

Meyrink's statement regarding "the stigmatized Konnersreuth woman" is significant as it refers to Therese Neumann (1898-1962), a woman who suffered bleeding stigmatic wounds. Meyrink previously stated that Mailänder used to make an example of the then well-known, stigmatized Katharina Emmerich. Thus, not only does Meyrink come to the full realization of Mailänder's wisdom, but he actually emulates Mailänder by choosing another well-known stigmatized woman from his own lifetime to reconvey this lesson.

Therefore, I believe Mailänder successfully transmitted Jane Lead's outline of successive Christ forms.

Yet the cream of this discovery is Mailänder's understanding of Jane Lead's Baptism of Blood, which evokes the greatest appreciation of his system and testifies he understood Jane Lead like no other.

Aspects of J.B Kerning's teachings now come into play, which must be viewed in close consideration with Jane Lead's teachings to fully appreciate what Mailänder truly achieved in merging these systems.

Karl Weinfurter also confirms that Mailänder's method stemmed from J.B Kerning's teachings:

> The spiritual practice imparted by this leader was identical with that of J. B. Kerning, which may be found throughout

his works, but, of course, only by someone who is himself practising. To all others these things remain concealed. Any student practising must reveal these things to himself, that is they are revealed to him by the influence of the Holy Spirit. At the end of his life our leader announced that the time was approaching when the Spirit's realm would be easily opened to all those who intended to practise with a sincere heart. He further communicated to us that there is one practice, which may be carried through by everybody without a leader, and that everybody will be brought to the same goal as those practising the sentences imparted by him.[189]

For Mailänder, undergoing crucifixion was a major theme and Kerning previously wrote on this:

> From the day of the foot-washing to the crucifixion, all was written only for you. If we believe like children, blindly practising, then we shall rise from the dead. All that happened to our Master in those three days is to be our ideal. We must experience the passion of our Saviour, His scourging, the weight of the cross, and, in order to give place to the new man, exhaustion has to take place in all our limbs. Though the reason struggle against it, our senses rebel, even our whole nature revolt, we must suffer steadily to change the crown of thorns into one of life. He who does not use many words, but puts the few into action everywhere, thus raising his whole nature to the faculty of thinking, he treads the path towards victory and shall be glorified on the cross of life.[190]

Meyrink confirms Mailänder taught this specific Kerning approach in his *Transfiguration of the Blood*:

> "He said, 'Baptism, foot-washing, the Lord's Supper, and the crucifixion in its exact course, as recorded in the Gospels, all that

[189] Weinfurter, *Man's Highest Purpose*, 154.

[190] Butler, "Key to the Spriritual World," 104; Weinfurter, *Man's Highest Purpose*, 104.

had to be experienced literally on one's own body, otherwise it would remain only a theory, just something heard or read, and would only have the value of Christian edification.'"

Both Mailänder and Kerning state these Christ ordeals are to be experienced in our physical bodies. But how exactly? If this is not to be symbolic, how to enact it in corporeality? Flagellating ourselves to cause physical trauma, piercings or wounds is not at all implied. So the question begs, how should Kerning's method truly be realized in a bodily way? It was Jane Lead who provided the key to Mailänder's revised Kerning system and the following statements reveal how Mailänder perfected Kerning's art.

That key is reflected on the very same page of Jane Lead's 1698 work where she predicted that John the Evangelist would soon return. There she introduces the important concept of "Dying-Marks."[191] It becomes obvious that Mailänder also possessed a copy of the German edition of Jane Lead's *The Resurrection of Life or the Royal Charters and Identifying Marks*,[192] where she clarifies her subject.[193]

---

[191] "The first was the bearing the Dying-Mark or Crucifixion to the Degenerated Birth: in a most deep sense, deploring its Lapse and Apostasy from its original pure state, Renouncing the Earthly born Life and worldly Principle, quite sinking away by Abnegation and Annihilation here from being thus Buried with Christ in Death, we are taught to lie in the Passive Grave in Silence, till the Lord the Quickening Spirit shall descend to become a Life quickening Birth, whereby a new Creaturely Formation is brought forth, according to the Nature of the Divine Humanity of Christ: which will gradually spring and grow in every such one, till they come to be as full grown Trees of Life to replenish the New Earth and Heavens." Lead, *The Messenger of an Universal Peace: Or a Third Message to the Philadelphian Society.*

[192] "Die Auferstehung des Lebens: oder Das Königliche Merck und Kennzeichen, so denen aufgetruckt ist, Die mit Christo auferstanden sind." Lead, *The Resurrection of Life or the Royal Characteristics and Identifying Marks.*

[193] She writes, "Therefore let us consider that it is more honest and useful to bear the

Mailänder's ideal of crucifixion pains and the symbols that appear on the skin seem to be drawn from Lead's instructions that "it may be recognized as a true identifying Mark of a dying (to Self) Soul," whereby "a Person must conclude that the Perfecting and Accomplishment of this Dying is by steps gradually being granted," wherein "the Soul must become this Sin-Sacrifice in its own Person," and "bear the Marks and Signs of this dying Life." Lead further writes of "irrefutable Marks [Characteristics, Signs, Symbols which are impressed-imprinted on those Inhabitants of the Resurrected Flock of the Sheep-fold of Christ," and that "all People may see and read the Marks that they bear and know who are of the First Resurrection."

I have concluded that Lead's statements about the Dying Marks deeply influenced Mailänder's spiritual alchemy.

Lead does not describe how these Dying Marks should appear, but only that they, and the resurrection marks, may be seen and read, indicating their nature as symbolic characters. To the resurrection marks she also applies spiritual gifts of divine hearing, taste, smell etc., which perfectly matches J.B Kerning's description of those who have awakened the Word in their spiritual and physical being.

Mailänder's genius or insight provided the understanding that letter-shaped irritation symptoms should appear visibly on the skin in completion of Jane Lead's system. Where Jane Lead called them "Dying Marks," Mailänder called them "Crucifixion Signs" and his understanding was that these indicated the transfiguration

---

grinding Signs of Death rather than to bear the earthly Life," describing those who "were viewed under the dying-State Condition to which they were subjected, where they also went through many-fold Sufferings [Pains] and stood under heavy Servitude and painful Death-Woes to the Accomplishment of the Mystical and Spiritual Death." In Ibid.

of the blood whereby the soul's progress would express itself in forms and images. [194]

Therefore, between Kerning's emphasis on letters and Lead's Dying Marks, a perfect blend was established.

Still, Mailänder's genius did not stop there. He built upon these ideas by providing a register to his students in the Formenlehre (Form Teaching) so that they would possess a list of the oracular signs, symbols and letters, along with their meaning, enabling practitioners to effectively interpret their exhibited crucifixion signs.

In many ways, Jane Lead's spiritual alchemy was not fully realized until Mailänder developed it further. The same may be said for Kerning's spiritual alchemy, which was somewhat incomplete until Mailänder introduced key understandings from Jane Lead to complete Kerning's bodily crucifixion.

Spiritual genius or not, whatever else Mailänder may have been, he was a rather well-read illiterate.

---

[194] Shirley, "Autobiography of Dr. Franz Hartmann," 30.

Part Two

Franz Hartmann Introduces Alois Mailänder

Meeting Alois Mailänder

From the Occult Review of 1908:[195]

"I had become tired of "Theosophy," which, owing to the position which I occupied in the Society, consisted in defeating the attacks of its enemies, disputing with missionaries and quarrelling with psychic researchers. I longed for peace, for the solitude of the prairies of Texas, where one feels so strongly the presence of the Infinite, and for the sublimity of the peaks of the Rocky Mountains, that seems to lift us above the worthless things of this life and to bring us nearer to Heaven. I was almost ready to leave, when, owing to a concatenation of circumstances, too long to briefly explain, I made the acquaintance of an occultist who was the leader of a small body of real Rosicrucians. When he first entered my room I at once recognized his face as one which I had seen in a vision on the night of January 1, 1884, while lying half-awake on my couch

---

[195] Ibid.

at Adyar. It seemed to me at that time that a large serpent, the symbol of wisdom, was coiled up at the side of my bed, with its head erect, looking sternly at me. And that head was the head of the man I met, and I knew that a ray of wisdom would come to me by his aid.

I remained at Kempten, and he introduced me to his friends.[196] I attended their meetings, became one of his disciples and followed his instructions for many years. These people did not call themselves "Rosicrucians," but they were nevertheless such in fact. They were not learned people, but for the greater part weavers in a factory, where they had to work from early till late at a very poor salary. The two leaders were not even able to read or to write, and nevertheless they seemed to know the very mysteries contained in the books of the mystics and in the writings of H. P. Blavatsky. They knew these things, not from hearsay but by interior revelation, and their teaching did not consist in giving information of what other people had taught or even of what they had experienced themselves, but in showing the way to the direct perception of truth and preparing oneself to receive this revelation within. They rarely answered questions to satisfy curiosity, but they asked questions on which one had to meditate and find the answer oneself, and the guidance took place not so much by any external means or verbal advice, as by symbolic visions seen during dreams or in a state of meditation,

---

[196] The official Stadtarchiv Kempten sent records of Mailänder's whereabouts during the period, with his arrival and departure from Kempten, and the Dreieichenhain Stadtarchiv has a "Familienbogen" of Alois Mailänder's life credentials, both of which I obtained copies. They confirm: Date of birth: 25. March 1843, place of birth: Fidazhofen, Eschach, near to Ravensburg. Parents: Eggert Leonhart and Maria Anna, maiden name: Mailänder. He came to Kempten about 1853, he moved away from Kempten 1886 and went to Vohwinkel, Eberfeld, near to Wuppertal. Married at 21. May 1874 with Mailänder Karolina, maiden name: Gabele. Son: Mailänder Anton, birth 6. February, 1876, died 29. March 1877. See "Mailander SMF002318110516330 Kempten File" (Stadtarchiv Kempten, n.d.).

or even by signs and letters appearing visibly upon the skin, for the state of the soul expresses itself in forms and images, and if we learn to read these pictures correctly we may know the state of our interior condition and act so as to improve it accordingly, just as a gardener, who, by watching his plants, knows what he ought to cultivate and what cut away.

Thus a higher and more interior state of consciousness began gradually to dawn within my mind like the dawn that appears on the sky before the rising of the sun, revealing the beauties of a higher state of existence. I found that it is far more important to find the real Master and Guide within one's own soul than to seek to gratify one's curiosity to know all about the Masters in Tibet, and that it is far more valuable to help to create a heaven within one's own mind than to be informed of what is said to have taken place at the time when our world was created or how the old Lemurians and Atlanteans lived, however interesting and amusing and even instructive such information may be.

These Rosicrucians did not seek for notoriety, nor did they wish to catch members. They wished to remain unknown and avoided publicity. I remained in contact with their leader until he died, and many of the truths contained in the numerous books which I have written were made clear to me by his guidance.

To give a detailed account of the teachings thus received would require not only a long article but a whole book, and the mystic language in which many of these communications were given would be like some of the writings of Jacob Bohme, Jane Leade and others incomprehensible for many readers because such teachings deal with internal verities and not with outward facts known to everyone, and unless one has experienced the beauties of the higher and interior life they are beyond the grasp of the mortal mind. We all live a dream life, and we cannot know the reality unless we awaken to a consciousness of its existence in us."

The Rosicrucian Group

From Hartmann's "Under the Adepts:"

"Here it was completely different. Those of the "leaders," of whom I want to designate one with J. and the other with S, not only knew exactly what they were saying and understood it but lived according to the principles expressed by them. The family of S. was not altogether alien to me. My parents had been in touch with them some 20 years earlier. His mother was known among the initiates even then as a woman who possessed special occult powers, through which she healed the sick or aided possessed people and animals and did much good. Many curious stories could be told about her, similar to those described in Gorres, "Christian Mysticism," in the third volume, and even then, its descriptions there here seems superfluous to me in comparison.

The two (S. and J.) were also taught in their youth by a man named P , who was considered a Rosicrucian and Alchemist, whose occult talents suggest he and, like many Indian fakirs, was able to transfer the images of his imagination directly to others, thus making them see things that were not there externally. For example, he was once ambushed at night by a highwayman, but when the latter jumped at him, the perpetrator suddenly saw the scaffold of a hangman's gallows with its servants, who wanted to seize hold of him, causing him to run away as fast as he could while P. calmly went home. This P. also had the power to refine base metals, some samples are in my possession.

But all this could not explain the depth of the religious knowledge of these people, for it could have only come from their own inner intuition. Their knowledge could not be the result of logical reasoning, for that they lacked the necessary foundation of theoretical instruction, but if it is true that every human being is inwardly God and omniscient, then what other things should one need in order to penetrate deeper into the secrets of God than to approach him through a deeper and higher knowledge of God learned directly from the heart?

The practical occultism of these Rosicrucians was in fact nothing else than a method of promoting the growth of this higher consciousness. "The external, theoretical knowledge," said S. "is not to be despised. It is a tool for the seeker of truth. But the actual theosophy or self-knowledge is not that of being able to talk about evolutionary theories, rings or rounds, divisions and systems, about the states of the middle-regions or the sky, and other things that any other person has come to know or that one holds true whatever anyone, be it a human or a spirit, has said or written about it, but that one reaches one's own inward perception and self-knowledge of the secrets of God in the universe." "Our School" J. added, "is not a magazine for the preservation of scholarship, as necessary as it may seem to life in this world. Rather, we are concerned with the growth of the inner power of vision and the opening of the inner, spiritual senses, and much more about spiritualization and refinement than intellectual research on the outside, not external expressions and verbiage, but internal enlightenment and the Inner Word. When the word of God speaks in the heart, it is the language of truth, and if taught by this wisdom itself, no other instruction is needed. He who finds God in his heart, has all secrets revealed through Him. "But, "I could search for a long time," I interjected, "until I find a God in myself. I may

119

look into myself, as much as I want. I find in it nothing other than myself." "Good for the one," answered J., "who has found himself in truth, he has found God and has left the delusion of selfhood, which is the monster of your own imagination. Whoever wants to know the true self, which is God, does not have to seek it in the imagination, but in spirit and truth. In the prayers of Christians, it is said, "Our Father, who art in heaven." If we want to come to the Father, the Creator of all the phenomena, which men regard as "the Self," we must create within a heavenly space in which God can live and become manifest. This is practical theosophy."

I asked S. to give me a concise description of the method he followed, and he dictated to me: "Man is a ladder of spiritual development. It's like one who pulls the grass out of the ground. First, learn to recognize, you stand on your feet. Climb up this ladder, put on the steps, and you'll find that there are twelve, which summarize the body into a whole.[197] Enter from top to bottom into the centre, the heart. There you will find a germ to grow through the light of thought, and this growth extends to the senses, the spiritual ones, within you. Learn to eat from the tree of knowledge, and from the tree of life enjoy the fruit. Seek both in you, and when you know them and know your place, you have arrived at the top of the ladder. Then it is said, now learn to recognize the power, and this power overcomes death, and if this death loses its sting the cube of life will be found in the heart. It is a matter of forming a sun, an "I," which enlightens your entire being. In it you will see past, present and future. So your life is opened up and the new heaven opened,

---

[197] Mailänder taught twelve divisions of the body, unlike Kerning who taught seven. The division of twelve is based on the assignment of the twelve signs of the zodiac to the human body. Weinfurter, in his Man's Highest Purpose, presents Pisces, for example, at the feet. This division into twelve influenced the zodiac work of the Kerning 4.0 method. See Weinfurter, *Man's Highest Purpose*.

in which the perfect one will move. Ascend to the sea and learn to swim, like a swan which cannot sink, and you will reach the shores of the spiritual world within you.

I must confess that this language sounded as strange and incomprehensible to me as it probably will sound to most who read this, but in self-knowledge it is only so that the theory is only clearly understandable when it is confirmed by experience. This is why it took me many years before the deep meaning of these words was at least partly clear to me through inner experience, and I realized that the truth contained therein could not have been expressed more clearly. As little as a dead man can understand life can the spiritual life be understood if one is not awakened, and he who seeks to know spiritual powers must not look for them with his head, but must do it with his heart and seize the soul. For this, however, possession of the soul force is required. The training often requires many years of practice.

When man realizes the power of God within himself, as part of his own self, when he can inwardly distinguish right and wrong, eternal from transience, and can stand firm on the side of the eternal; only then it can be said he stands on his own feet. Then he can begin to climb up the ladder and "It is as if one pulls the grass out of the earth," i.e. in his consciousness he gradually rises from the physical to the spiritual, from the spiritual to the divine. The learned world has for a long time tried in vain to penetrate into the secrets of the Rosicrucians, and finally settled the case with the usual catchphrases of fraud and superstition, but even if these secrets were announced from rooftops, they would remain forever secret to all those who do not experience it for themselves.

Accordingly, instructions in this Rosicrucian family did not consist in answering idle questions for the satisfaction of anyone's thirst for knowledge, nor in any contemplation of the imagination through spectacular phrases, but it was in the reception of a heavenly food, and by the manner of answering questions put to him the student gave that proof which testified his own progress in the knowledge of himself. School scholars and theorists also attended these meetings for a while, but they did not understand how to grasp the heavenly manna, and they soon returned to the fleshpots of the Egyptians, i.e. to the logical conclusions, speculations and proof that are created for the blind. A scientific knowledge of the nature of mental powers is only possible if one owns these powers. What would be the use of any scholarly theories about the nature of intelligence or thought to a person if he himself was an idiot, and had no intelligence and no ability to conceive? What use are all philosophical speculations about the nature of the soul and immortality, if we do not feel that we ourselves have souls that carry the germ of immortality in our being?

But to go back to my memoirs, there is nothing more to be said other than that I first got to know the theories among the Theosophists in India and then, later, the practical methods I learned with the Rosicrucians in Germany, and that it was the latter circumstance which induced me to stay in Europe. In India it was mainly a question of getting to know the different religious systems, of comparing them with each other, and of discovering the truth that underlies all these systems in a roundabout way. Among the Rosicrucians I was shown the way to directly and personally seize the Spirit of Truth for myself. There in India it was about a theoretical knowledge of the yogic philosophy, but here in Europe it is about the doing of yoga, in the actual work of union itself. Both are necessary, for without the right theory the exercise is difficult, and without the exercise the best theory has no real value."

The Rosicrucian Method

From Hartmann's "Practical Occultism in Germany," 1885.[198]

Before leaving India I promised to inform you if I should find out anything in regard to any existing society of German Occultists, that is to say, such students as are not merely contented to philosophise and revel in theories; but who have arrived at the knowledge of the truth by a direct recognition of the same and are employing the result of their knowledge to some useful purpose. I am happy to say that my research has been successful. In the heart of the Bavarian mountains I have found a society of real occultists, of practical workers, possessing a high moral character, and although they are illiterate and "uneducated" people, yet they are well acquainted with the mysteries of the Hindu and Jewish religions, called the secret doctrine or Esoteric Philosophy.

They have received hardly an ordinary school education and the one whom they call their leader, is unable to read or write. They have never read "Esoteric Buddhism," still they know much that is identical with it. They know nothing of the Yoga philosophy, still they practice it. They know nothing of Kant and Schelling and Schopenhauer, still their system is the essence of those philosophers. They are poor people, working in a factory at two marks (one Rupee) a day, and still they are in possession of powers that no amount of money can buy.

I had heard years ago of these people. I was told that they were queer people and did not go to church. They were said to be very good, but probably very much deluded. They had repeatedly received offers of better situations, but refused them,

[198] Hartmann, "Practical Occultism in Germany." *The Theosophists*, vol 6, n72, September 1885. The original was also published in English.

saying that they were not permitted to change. Who prevented them was a mystery.

I made the acquaintance of those people and went with them to the top of the mountain and looked into the spiritual Tibet or (as the Jews call it) Canaan. I saw with them the promised land, but like Moses was not yet able to enter it. When we went up there were six members in their society. When we came down that society numbered seven.

I might tell you of many things that happen when the members of that society meet together. I might tell you of astral bells, of perfumes pervading the room without any perceivable source, of pairs of living eyes appearing in the air or out the walls, of a light appearing on the head of the speaker, but they pay little attention to such incidents, and as for myself I have, in consequence of former experiences, long ceased to be astonished at anything in regard to such phenomena. But there is one thing which interested me more, and of this I will tell you; but before doing so I must say a few words in regard to secret societies.

A long time ago such a word had grown into my consciousness. It became more and more vivid and living in me, but to not a single soul in the world did I ever reveal that word, nor would I dare to reveal it now, and yet that illiterate worker pronounced that word and received me as one who was spiritually not a stranger to him.

I have learned a great deal in the company of these people. In other things I was able to give them instruction. They practise the process of materialising thought in themselves and are sometimes able to project it objectively. They have their transcendental senses of touch, vision, hearing, taste and smell developed to a certain extent. They practice the process of development by spiritual aspiration and inspiration. They do not fall into trances but speak things far above what they have learned in the ordinary way, and when they meet, they have all only one thought, and while one begins a sentence, each one of the others is able to finish what the first began to say.

They do not believe in immortality in the ordinary sense. They say that nothing is immortal but the Word (Logos), and to become immortal man must develop the Word in himself. They look upon the majority of mankind not as men but as material out of which men may be made. They say that they will make men and they are preparing themselves to acquire full powers before they attempt the great work. They say that when they are fully prepared the Old Ones who have been saved up from the beginning will come out of their retirement and cooperate with them.

When I asked them about the process of their development, they gave a description, of which I will translate a few passages:

"Man passes through a spiral evolution, which appears like the steps of a ladder. Learn to understand that your strength is rooted in your feet. Descend from the arch of the temple (the head) to the foot of the stairs, and rise slowly up to the centre (the heart). There you will find a seed that will begin to germinate through the influence of a light created by thought. It will grow and its growth will penetrate into your senses. Learn to eat of the tree of knowledge. Look for it not in the exterior world but in your interior, and when you attain real knowledge by direct perception of the truth, you will have gained immortality. The cube of life will then find its place in your heart. A sun will appear that will illuminate your interior and in its light the past, the future and the present will appear as one and be revealed to you. Your life will then be your own. The door of eternity will be open, and a new heaven will appear."

"If you desire immortality you must materialise the Word in yourself by the fiat spoken through your will. In the light of your heart you will find the Word and the Word is the spirit of truth, the radiation of "Father" and "Son," the result of thought and expression."

The only power by which this process may be accomplished is the power of thought, and thought only becomes active, powerful, and manifest, if it is expressed through the Word. The whole of the universe with all its forms, the form of man included, is according to the assertions of all the sages and illuminated seers a product of the thought (or active Imagination) of the Great First and Supreme Cause, having found expression through His Word (or active Will,) through the action of which it became manifest or revealed. If the counterpart of the Universal Supreme Cause, resting within the centre of the soul of man, awakens to a consciousness of its own existence and powers, it will begin its immortal career as a self-conscious entity, all-powerful and all-wise, whose final destiny is far beyond the limits of our intellectual speculation. It must, however, be remembered that mortal man with all his power of thought, cannot at his pleasure, awaken the divine spiritual germ to consciousness, unless that germ chooses to awaken. The finite cannot control the infinite and cause it to obey its commands. It can only prepare the conditions under which the Eternal One may act. It can only prepare the temple for the residence of the god. It rests with the god, whether or not he chooses to enter.

Practical occultism or Yoga consists therefore in the sinking of one's own thoughts down to the centre of the heart, excluding all other thoughts, which do not serve the purpose in view, and giving it therein expression in a word, a letter or a sign. Gradually such a sign, letter or word may become alive within ourselves, we shall hear it with our interior ear, see it with the interior eye, and perceive it by the interior sense of feeling. Other interior senses will be opened, and certain manifestations of an interior power will take place, of which it would not be wise to speak, and the reason why they should not be mentioned is not that we wish to appear mysterious or to withhold any knowledge from others, but because an untimely knowledge of such effects would act injuriously upon the imagination of those who desire to obtain their results. They might fancy they possessed them, and their fancy would distract their attention and would thereby prevent the accomplishment of their object.

And now we come to one of the most important points regarding this subject. The power of the Word if it attains spiritual life is only comprehended by few, and it is not at all immaterial what thought, sign or word we choose, for by the action of the living Word those elements in the human constitution which correspond to its meaning become endowed with life, and if they are such as ought to be kept in subjection, they may become rebellious and destroy reason as well as the health of the body. No man's constitution is exactly like that of another, and an exercise which may be good and useful for one, may be evil and injurious for another. The beginner therefore requires the guidance of a spiritual instructor, an illuminated practical occultist, or in other words an Adept, to instruct him and give him the password and sign, until he has his own interior senses opened, and when he may receive further, instruction by his own spiritual ego or Master.

In India the common word used for the practice of Yoga is AUM. How far this word may be useful for all beginners, I am unable to state. In Europe the letters I. A. O. and afterwards the other vowels and consonants are sometimes practised for the same purpose, until they are seen, felt and heard.[199] They then form the key word, to other mysteries, but I do not know whether any one has ever succeeded in attaining a high degree of development by following such general rules and without having any guide to give him special instructions.

There are few who can see the necessity of such instruction, few whose Karma affords them an opportunity to obtain it, and fewer still who having obtained such instructions, have the energy and determination to carry them out to the end. And yet without this practical work how little can we accomplish. Only those can enjoy eternal life, who have come into possession of it by the process of spiritual regeneration. The spiritual life belongs to the spirit alone and is independent of the life which acts in the body. With the first divine and interior thought, penetrating the whole of the interior I and rendering us able to feel the truth, even as from afar, the germ is deposited for the future regenerated spiritual man. If this germ is continually supplied with appropriate food by a continuous flow of thought and good-will, it may become self-conscious and develop. "Then the new man may grow and the old one die, for the new one has seen the light and begins to love it." Without this regeneration we shall, at the time when the soul separates itself from the body, again enter the state of the formless, to begin the struggle for self-consciousness and individuality in some future incarnation, ennobled perhaps by merits acquired during the past or weighted by new evil Karma while those who have attained spiritual self-consciousness and self- knowledge will be free from the bonds of matter.

But in this practice of Yoga the student receives a certain word or sentence, which exactly suits his condition, and if he seriously applies himself to this work, letting his thought continually

---

[199] This shows a Kerning element, although Mailänder was observing Kerning's method.

dwell upon this word, unwelcome and inappropriate thoughts will soon cease to be attracted to him, the evil elements of his soul will die off, and if he attains the power of inner vision, he may even see the processes going on in the organization of his soul and witness the decomposition and putrefaction of its evil parts and excrescences, in the same manner as we may see a wart or a cancer on the physical body decay and drop off; until at last when all these evil parts have perished, there will be nothing left to attract such evil thoughts, which, like birds of prey, assemble where the odour of a carcass attracts them, and instead of animal elementals, the powers of light will surround the purified soul, in whose centre rests eternal life, peace and happiness."

An Interview with Mailänder

From Hartmann's "A German Adept," 1886.[200]

His figure was youthful and strong, his face expressed knowledge and happiness, his eyes seemed to penetrate into the innermost depths of my soul. I had suffered all day from a severe neuralgic pain in my face, he touched the place with his finger and the pain was gone and did not return either the next day or afterwards. I expressed my surprise to see him so much changed from what he appeared in his physical body, and he said:

"The form which you see now represents my inner self. That which you saw yesterday and which you will see tomorrow, is only an illusion. Material forms grow old in corruption, the

---

[200] *The Theosophist*, May 1886. Page 534. This interview is probably not a very reliable account of what Mailander said. Hartmann states in his introduction that he gives "the salient points as far as I can remember them," and there are several notions presented that appear too Theosophical and philosophical, and at the same time are similar to Hartmann's other writings. However, parts of the interview are clearly ideas from Mailander as well. The original article was also published in English.

spirit grows old in wisdom." Of the conversation that followed I will give the salient points as far as I can remember them. They treat of great mysteries, but there is no necessity to keep them secret, because only those who are wise will understand them. The sceptic who possesses not the inner light that shines into the heart, will not recognize the truths which they contain.

What is God? "God is the purest light, life and consciousness, radiating from itself, the cause of all power, sending continually its own active forces into its own productions and raising them into higher states of existence, and thus forming a living chain, in which everything is strength, life and power.

How can we know God? "By becoming the recipients of his wisdom."

How can we accomplish this? "We can accomplish nothing, because we have no powers of our own; but God may accomplish it through our instrumentality, if we become free of our own will and of the bonds of self and are prepared to obey and to fulfil the will of God."

Where can we find God? "In the centre of our own heart." *Then God is not everywhere?* "God is everywhere present, but he is not everywhere equally manifest. A superior power requires a superior form for its manifestation."

What is the origin of God? "The first cause of all causes can have no other cause but itself, it is self-existent, eternal and not limited by relative time and space."

Why is God represented by a trinity in all religious systems? "Because a circle or sphere cannot exists without a centre, a radius and a periphery, but the center may be incomprehensible, the radius infinite and the periphery without any conceivable limits."

What is the origin of evil? "The origin of good is beyond our conception of time. The origin of evil is within time. The potency of evil existed from eternity, but evil itself was caused by a deviation from good. Evil is therefore not a cause but only an effect."

Which is the true religion? "The one which supplies the knowledge of self."

Can man obtain self-knowledge by intellectual labour alone? "The brain is in the cupola of the temple, but the seat of life is in the inner sanctuary in the heart. Man thinks through the brain and feels through the heart. The one is the necessary complement of the other."

What is, the object of man's life? To free himself of everything that does not essentially belong to his being, so that his soul may be filled with the light of wisdom that comes from God."

What is the final object of man's existence? "The attainment of the highest possible happiness by the attainment of the highest Good."

How can the highest Good be attained? "By the attraction of love for the good."

How can we obtain a love for the good? "By a knowledge of evil, which will cause us to flee from evil and to seek refuge in good. If the soul is penetrated by a love for the good, the inner senses of man will be opened and he will know the truth."

What do you mean by "inner senses?" "I mean a spiritual power of seeing, hearing, feeling, smelling and tasting; a power of direct perception of which the vulgar have no conception and the learned do not even know the existence, unless they can experience it through the purity of their own hearts. Such a perception is not ordinary clairvoyance, which is a faculty that may lead into error as much as physical sight, but it is a recognition of the truth through becoming one with the truth."

Is it possible that by this spiritual perception a man may obtain knowledge of exterior things, such as cannot be found in the ordinary way? "Certainly. He who assimilates his soul with the harmony of the universe, will see everything in the universe as if it were existing in himself."

Why do our modern scientists not possess this power? "Because they cling to illusions, they mistake effects for causes, creation for the Creative power, the external appearance for the internal truth. The fundaments of modern science rest upon a superstitious belief that things are actually what they appear to be. Science deals with opinions, wisdom is the knowledge of the truth. Science is attained through the senses and from the exterior. Wisdom is attained in the interior and comes from God."

Do you mean to say that the truth is too high for the scientists? "No. The truth is not too high for the scientists, but the scientists are usually too high for the truth. The truth is too simple for those who love that which is complicated. They love to revel in systems that are the creations of their own phantasy, and they desire nothing but that which can be fitted into their systems."

Who are the true Adepts? "Those who have no other desire but to love the divinity in humanity and who possess the true knowledge of all."

Who are the false Adepts? "Those who attempt to mystify the people, who denounce the religious sentiment of man, boast of their own knowledge, quarrel about opinions and are opposed to marriage. The true adept knows that he has no life, no strength and power of his own, but that it is the power of God in himself that accomplishes everything through him. The false adept seeks for the source of power in his own self. He seeks the cause of phenomena in places where such causes do not exist. He is like a man who examines a lamp post to find out how the gas is prepared. The true adept knows the real and attributes little importance to the phenomenal. He does not quarrel about opinions nor fight for the truth, but he knows and teaches the truth. He recognizes the sacredness of the marriage tie and knows the divine power that is generated by true union of the souls of man and woman. He does not boast of his attainments nor pretend to be in the possession of secrets which are not accessible to others, but he is opposed to darkness, frank, open and willing to assist all who desire to come out of the shadow into the light."

F. Hartmann, M. D.

Part Three

The Soul & Form Teachings
of Alois Mailänder

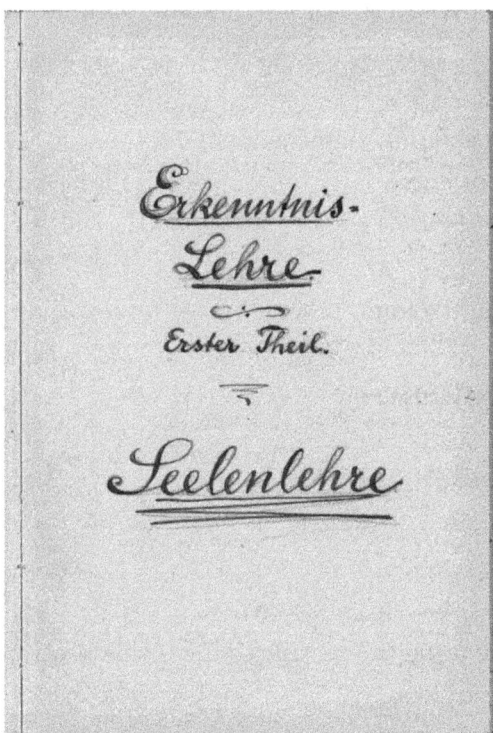

Erkenntnis-
Lehre
Erster Theil.

Seelenlehre

The Soul Teaching

1.
How do you think with the eye?
Through every form you see.
How do you think with the ear?
Through everything you hear.
How do you think with your nose?
Through everything you smell.
How do you think with the palate?
Through everything you taste.
How do you think with feeling?
Through all the revelations you perceive with feeling.

2.
How do the exterior stigmata open?
Through gentleness.

3.
What is Mount Zion?
True faith.
What is New Jerusalem?
Wisdom.
What is the marriage of the lamb?
Virtue.

4.
We can only bring the outside to the inside if we are imbued
with the fire of love.

5.

Man is created from God for the sake of the **Word**, from nature
for the sake of the **Spirit**.

For the sake of witnessing God we are made of the elements.

6.

The greatest thing in heaven is the Father revealed.

The smallest thing in the world is the seed,

which our heavenly Father has placed in us,

our God given talent.

7.

Firstly: From revelation comes faith.

Second: From faith comes will.

Third: From feeling comes fear.

Fourth: From fear comes conscience.

Fifth: From conscience comes reason.

Sixth: Out of reason comes spiritual insight.

8.

In the head is thought.

In the mouth is the Word, the center of all forces.

And in the heart is the revelation.

In the sense of feeling is the spirit of revelation, and the mind
its servant.

How does thought come into being?

In feeling.

9.

How do you think with your fingers?

If you but consider the inner forces with your fingers.

The hand is strong, yet the inner forces are even stronger.

10.

We love each other by having free will.

In Jesus' name we pray in love.

The antithesis of love is hatred, from which wickedness springs.

11.

How should we live?

In spiritual faith.

How do you arrive at home?

With a firm will.

12.

You shall believe in one God alone and not serve idols.

You shall only believe in **that** God who is in you and

who reveals Himself to you.

13.

How can you serve the Creator?

Through the prayer of Our Father.

One should not ask for this or that, but what is stated in the

Lord's Prayer contains all the right requests.

14.

How do we know what is on the inside?

Through love of the divine spirit within oneself.

Rise to the heights!
Hope raises us up!

15.
What is spiritual freedom?
When man pacifies the desires and passions of his own body.

16.
What is the I?
It is the strength. It is trust in God.
The inner man reveals the Self.
It advances through realization.

17.
What is the main force of man?
The force emanating from the fingertips.

18.
Christ says: I am the way, the truth, and the life.
Whoever draws from his inner teaching finds the spiritual life.

19.
The love of the woman leads us to our goal.
And this woman is our outer self.
And this self is our nobility (That is to say, our good will).

20.
Man is a triune being: First in cause. Second in effect.
Third inaccomplishment.

21.
Through self-will comes rebelliousness,
and through it the bad temper in man.

22.
Man stands on his feet, and this means life.
And what is life?
Love.
In the heart is hope, and what is this hope?
The fear of God.
In the head is order, and what is order?
The truth.

23.
What is the inner man?
Patience.
And what is patience?
The end of all struggle.

24.
The resurrection is in meekness,
and therein the Eternal One speaks:
"This is your reward, for it is the highest and greatest virtue of
man."

25.
How do you keep thoughts in check?
By looking at all outer things as a passageway
and not taking it all in.

26.
What is the will?
A power inherent in man.
And where does it reside?
In life, and life is in the blood. In the outer man the blood is
the will over the flesh, and in the inner man the Word of God
is the power over flesh and blood.

27.
With what does a man carry out his outer deeds?
With the hands and in them is the judgment
of good and evil actions.

28.
Thought is the light in man.

29.
The marks we bear on the body
are the first signposts of the spirit.

30.
The soul is the Word,
And my innermost soul is the thought,
And the recognition of both is the revelation.

31.
What you sow you reap.

32.
What is the power of the Inner Word?
The truth.

And how do we recognize the truth?
By bringing the Word to life in feeling.

33.
How are we brought to life?
By practicing the Word and learning to obey
the commandments of God.

34.
What is the soul?
The feeling.
What is its power?
The thought.
And what is its revelation?
The Word.
And where does it reside?
In the heart.

35.
Everything is seized by time.
And what is time?
Movement.
And what is movement?
Blood.
And what is the power of movement?
The truth.

36.
The soul shall endure by its power,
and its power is the air,

and by sound or tone it is manifested
in the ear of the outward man.

37.
The nourishment of the soul is done through the eye,
through its observation of forms.

38.
The body is connected with the soul by the Word,
the soul with the spirit by thought.
The spirit or power of thought is the breath.

39.
What spiritual quality penetrates the marrow and bones?
It is the faith which God gives.
What is the spiritual life of faith?
The Word of God.

40.
What is the power of the Word of God outwardly?
The deeds he can accomplish.

41.
How does one obtain mental power?
The same is already laid within us from birth.
How do we recognize it?
By the calling of our inner drives and tendencies.
For example, by our drive to heal the sick, teach the ignorant,
help through the second sight etc.

The power of these gifts is the spirit of love,
in which they creatively move.

42.
How is matter and spirit different?
The first is an external, visible creative force.
The second is an invisible operating force.

43.
What is the feeling of life coming out of the inner man?
It is surety.

44.
Thoughts, words, and revelation are united in action by the
inner impulse towards the divine.

45.
The rebirth gives the soul the power to rise into higher spheres.

46.
The foundation of man is faith.
The first stage: inner feeling.
The second stage: inner knowledge.
The third stage: inner love.

47.
We should not indulge in guesses, false feelings, and fantasies,
for they are seldom truth, because they come from our outer
spirit, whereby we become depressed and restless within.
We must learn to rise above these, as well as the whimsical
dreams that plague us.

Thus, the black flag held with its dark shadow under our feet becomes the basis for the new and free spiritual life.

48.
The first step:
One must learn to walk from feeling, meaning: to be dead to the sensuous exterior.
Second step:
Knowledge lifts us up, because we recognize the revelation of feeling as our spiritual guide in truth.
Third step:
Having the inner love for the Spirit of God within.

49.
What is the cause?
It is the faith that awakens in us.
What is the effect?
It is the love that awakens in us.
What is the result?
The newly awakened inner life.

50.
The past, present and future are within man.
How do we **live** in the future?
Through thought.
How do we **see** into the future?
Through feeling.
How do we **create** the future?
Through words.

51.
Hope is a consuming fire for those who do not persevere in it.

52.
The Goddess Fluda will give birth through the head,
that is, when the seed is drawn and placed in the head,
which impregnates the blood of both the man and the woman,
because both their bodies are female and capable of giving birth
according to the will of the Spirit,
for the glory and honour of our God.[201]

53.
Why is love greater and stronger than faith and hope?[202]
It is because love overcomes these two forces.
How is this possible?
Because faith and hope are only inward operating forces.
But love is a conquering, insurmountable force,
working both inwardly and outwardly.
Through this only can we help our fellow humans
in hardship, illness, and danger.

54.
What is the inner strength of faith?
It is hope.
Meaning everything we desire in coming into the Spirit.
These inner desires are the foundation of the cross
and lift it up ever higher.

---

[201] The word "Same" used for "Seed" can also mean "sperm" as an alternative translation.
[202] 1 Corinthians 13

55.
How do you see from afar?
By a firm will.

56.
And what is the power that makes the mind see from afar?
It works through our own faith.

57.
How do you honour your neighbour?
By doing good works for him.

58.
How do you honour yourself?
By keeping one's limbs away from evil deeds.

59.
The thought goes out of the heart.
It permeates the person like a circle from top to bottom
and goes back to the center of the heart.
As Light the thought enters the heart.
As shadow it goes out from the heart again.
The shadow is the evidence of Light
in the guise of the various forms it takes.

60.
What is darkness?
The person who has no knowledge of God.

61.
What is blindness?
It is when the spirit visibly reveals itself
and people do not recognize it.

62.
What is wisdom?
The open Book of Nature.

63.
What is the Will o' the Wisps?[203]
The wrong thoughts in the inner person,
when he imagines that it is this or that, and it is not.
This appears outwardly whenever we think evil of our
neighbour and yet do not know him or her.
The Will o' the Wisps are also those who pretend to be
teachers, but who themselves have nothing from God,
other than from books and their outer intellect.

64.
When we praise and thank the Creator in prayer out of our
emotional instincts, we do so not in our intellect but in His
language, where the acceptance of the request resides.

65.
What is an act of perjury against God?
If we promise Him in our hearts to do evil no more,
yet we do it again.

---

[203] False lights or spiritual apparitions.

This holds true also if we have a calling from the Spirit, where we gladly take what is good, but shrink away from the sacrifice we should make, especially in obedience.

66.
The Redeemer is man himself through the power of action in self-love in its higher sense.

67.
The seed is in the head, the root is the feet, and in the heart as the center is the ripe fruit.

68.
How does God love man?
For that purpose man needs his feet, just as in nature the root is found deep in the earth and absorbs all powers: the sun, moon, stars, planets, rain, and air.
Like a container, they find a root which draws them into the earth.
So it is with man, whereby, all the forces must descend in order to rise again, purified by the Spirit, through the love of God.

69.
We see the thought of God with our eyes through forms.

70.
The seat of thought in man has three series of steps:
First, in feeling, in one who walks in spirit.

Second, when man has progressed further, in the heart, through the Word, where he is witness. A perfect Word is given to him through thought, so on the second level the seat of thought is in the Word.

Third, the thought has its seat in action, for a perfect man carries out everything he thinks with his limbs. Here on the third level the thought is visible; on the second level it is audible, and on the first level it is perceptible.

71.
How should you believe in God?
In the hope that you can get what you believe in and achieve it.

72.
How is man to love himself?
Through perseverance.

73.
By what means or basis ought we to believe in God?
First: the revealed creation that we see, which leads us to think.
Second: to listen to and bring to life the Holy Scripture or the manifest Word of Jesus.
Third: man must learn to believe in himself. This is the hardest thing, because we must form a bridge from the visible to the invisible. Only a faithful disciple of the wisdom of God can accomplish it.

74.
What is faith?
A great power.
But the power that emanates from man is power in effect,

for when the person beside him has faith, the power comes into effect upon him and brings about an evident blessing, namely that he is helped. With an unbeliever, however, it goes back to the former and cannot help.

75.
How should one love oneself?
Through an accomplishing faith.
How are you supposed to do that?
One should lay hands upon oneself and erase all material pains for they inhibit the Divine Spirit. Therefore, have courage! Learn to feel the power, the great power that is laid in you and in every person.
It is God's gift of love, which you may only receive if you have the will and the faith.
The Eternal One says: "I do not want you to endure material suffering. Make My love a balm and coat your wounds. For he who loves himself sanctifies his body and limbs through his own power and My strength."

76.
How is faith to be considered?
As a spiritual life.
Spiritual death makes us alive, and in the material life the living dead.

77.
All of God's gifts we perceive through the senses in our head. But there is one thing we cannot perceive with our senses: The control we have over the whole body, that power and authority which we possess in our head.

The blood, however, must give birth to a new body, but this new shoot would be lifeless and exposed to the storm. It is only through the mastery of thought that it can be transformed over and over into something new.

78.
This is a form of strengthening the faith, for the same power that goes out from the fingertips is in all parts of the body, flowing in vitality, if we proclaim the Will in the Word.

79.
Blessed are the people of the earth who unite their spirit with the Spirit of God.

80.
How does soul reach another at a distance?
This happens through air, water, and sound.
Air is the power of the connection between two souls. Water is a pregnant coagulated air from which the form of the person emerges with whom we wish to connect so we can recognize him. Sound is the life of the whole, namely the Word, which is sent to us.

81.
What are secret forces of nature?
An invisible force.
How do we recognize it?
From revelations within and without us.
Where do we find them?
They are born in us, but they are lifeless unless we animate them.

What do we call them by name?
Faith and Will are two. The third is Revelation.
Have faith as much as you can. And do not forget the Will.
My strength is in you; where you feel life, my strength is.

From the Spiritual Realm

(Title added by Hübbe-Schleiden)

82.
I heard soft music.
A voice spoke: "You still can't pray?"
I sank to my knees, not speaking words;
only holy feelings filled me.
Now I recognized that I was lifted up from the earth
into the higher spheres.
And without understanding this!

83.
Does one egg look like another?
I say: No, one is big and the other small.

84.
"I Am that I Am."
I will send my spirit also.
Rejoice, at last. But know ye who I am?
The Spirit of Truth.

85.
My Will is so strong, my Word so mighty.
They must unite like fire, oil, and water.

86.
A pair of doves sway as they embrace.
The male begetter and female birther.

87.
We have recognized God as a force within us; but it is not God, but an outpouring of Him, and is subject to us according to our will, good or bad.

88.
Why is it that people cannot comprehend the spirit?
It is because they have no truth left in them.

89.
My very Soul is the way to the Lord.
I am earth, my feelings are driving forces.
Air and water refresh me.

90.
My mind with His mind, my Word with His Word.
Oh, fill my soul with His soul.
And where is the entrance?
I have found it.

91.
"Yes, you found it because I elected you.
Millions have gone round and round and never found the place.
Eagle's wing I call you!
On high mountains you have climbed.

Behold before you the breadth of the sea.

I counsel you to stay away from it for the time being.

The moon's rays shine brightly to and fro.

The flames are so strong.

There's a thrill in my arms.

Life is in you!

Oh, you earthbound creature, feel with me.

These sounds you hear, is it not my love call?

Remember me, I am on your side and invigorate you by my power.

92.

Tulips burst open themselves.

The iron will harden.

The ice, it's so weak.

But what about our hearts?

93.

Consider that even precious stones cannot be consumed by fire, and why?

Because they are alive.

Our hearts must be too.

94.

There is no I in evil.

That is why it is, and it isn't.

Nor can it create. It is limited to effect.

Note: Hubbe-Schleiden thought "I counsel you to stay away from it" means the world).

95.

I love a starry sky as the goddess swims upon the surface of the sea.
In love great, in flesh small, that is how you must be.
Keep your heart pure and always be gentle.
In the greatest heights is the seed.
In its greatest depths the flower and in the centre the sweet fruit.
Therefore, be gentle and pure within yourselves.

96.

We are born in the light.
In it I seek my duty.
The light has chosen me to be with it in eternity.

97.

There shines a bright star in the deepest darkness.
And its dazzling life moves my hands in gladness.

98.

There is also a dark point at the highest summit,
in which my soul is bathed that it may soon recover.

99.

Alive are your limbs. Dead is your bone.
How do I find my home again in the beloved precious spirit
realm!

100.

When my marrow has melted and your bone become soft,
then you will find me again, and what is mine will become
as yours.

101.
Often my limbs tremble in fear and anxiety.
Then again a little voice calls out to me:
"Insecurity weakens your limbs."
So I stand firmly on the big stone, upon which is written:
"I, Jesje [Jesse?], am united with the light!"

102.
In the heavens they are at home with those no longer with us.
On earth they are shadows and do not know that they are.
They want to stop the sweet rays of sunshine from the East,
for they are well aware of it, and yet they do not know that for
them they are but poisonous arrows by which they shall perish.

103.
If you want to draw near to me in spirit and in truth, you must
not have any thoughts in mind, not even a ready word.
It is done through feeling alone.

104.
You are to breathe the spiritual ether, not crude air.

105.
I call out to you:
In comfort you shall live, in courage you shall not die!
You must learn to rise to higher feelings in order to achieve the
desired goal.

106.
How do you start?
In the stillness of one's self.

107.
The Eternal One speaks:
"When I speak to you, I have no need of your thoughts.
You need only to fulfil my Word, in doing your duty.
But if you wish to speak with me, you must firmly formulate
what you will say.
Then I will grant your request, for I Am Charity.

108.
Roses and forget-me-nots I scattered for you on the path, but
thistles and thorns you have sown for yourselves for otherwise
you would have become my subjects.

109.
I will say one thing about the position of your servant.
He gives you much refined gold.
But no one can yet bear it.
Therefore he still labours in your employment.
Have mercy on him, for like you, he also wishes to warm
himself in my sun.

110.
You the first one I raised, as was my duty.
Therefore, you shall be called the Elohim because I am eternal
in your name.

111.
You also who give grace are a faithful soul.
Therefore, remain united with your servant, for he will lead you

to clear summits, where his spirit is united with yours, and you will walk together into the highest spheres where three are forever united with two!

112.
The transfiguration on the mountain is the fire of love towards your neighbour.
It transcends everything, and in it we sacrifice everything out of love, even our lives if we must, and this transcending leads us to an intercourse with blessed spirits.

113.
What shadows darken our eyes the most?
Ingratitude.

114.
How is man to master his blood?
By faith in the Word of God which He reveals through the mouth of His servants.
We have to believe in this Word, even if it is not fulfilled according to our intentions.
Give the glory to God, His will be done in everything!

115.
The clouds are lifted up by the storm, great and small, the smallest fish rise mightily.
But the torrent will split them in two down the middle.

116.

To be alive is a power, the will has brought it forth,
because the will itself is power.

117.

What is it that you saw that touched you with a tender hand?
Also his voice spoke out, and you heard:
"I languish in a dark shadowy land.
But thou hast known me, and shalt raise me up in the
brightness of Light."

118.

The feet are the roots, in the head the seed and in the center
the ripe fruit in the heart.
What is that ripe fruit?
The voice we hear within ourselves.

119.

Why cannot we see the Father?
Because we are not children of God, but children of the world.

120.

The first number is the Word, the second number is life.
Why is the number two life? Because without the form of the
body, the Word of God would be dead.

121.

Blood is motion; and the will shall be the master.
He who cannot arrest the motion has no spiritual will.

122.

What is the will?

The revelation of thought and Word.

(It is an invisible spirit, as long as it is not awakened).

How does this spirit become awake?

Through our passions for good or evil.

123.

The outer man should become the foundation of the inner man, that is to say, we must bring the outer received Word of God within us and believe firmly, for this faith is the foundation of the inner man, through which the outer comes in and the inner comes out.

124.

All forms of heaven and earth will fade away.

But the Word cannot fade away because it is perfection.

Let us humbly draw Words from the forms.

For it is forms that teach us.

125.

We are to be chaste in the fear of God.

How shall we fear God?

By doing what He wants. Then we have wisdom.

126.

In the hands is the action, and in the arms the power of spiritual will.

127.
What is the shadow of light?
The shapes we see.
If we have no light in us, we live in darkness and this is death.

128.
The blood must animate the thought.
With the light you must light a fire, and this is the passion.
This must form a chain, and this chain in turn leads to the light.

129.
There's a cloud of fog on the highest peaks we have to break through.
How can this happen?
Through hope.
Storms and battles strengthen faith.
A word of truth makes your sick soul healthy.

130.
In the revelation you have guidance in the ways of your own rebirth.

131.
What is third to faith and love?
Hope.
And it unites with knowledge.
From this a visible light comes forth.

132.
How can thought shine as a light in the heart?
Through the Word.

133.
When do we have oil in the lamp?
When we can sacrifice ourselves for the love of God.

134.
With which sickle will we cut the ripe fruit?
With the spiritual name given to us and faith is the fruit.

135.
And what is the power of faith?
The promise.

136.
How can you talk to me in an earnest way?
In need.

137.
Will and power are the spirit of thought.
The two stand facing each other and await union.
What is thought?
The Creator in the natural world. The body is the witness
of this Creator and the spiritual power from above are the
sensations. The realization of everything is within its motion
through its growth and advancement.

138.
Man's feet must be equal to ore.
The knees must have steel joints.
The stomach must be like a wildfire.
The pit of the heart a shining sun.

The hips golden vessels where I pour out my wine
(Passion, Life, Love, Faith and Virtue).

139.
What are the roses that bloom in the human heart?
Wisdom.

140.
What is the head that contains the seed?
Knowledge.

141.
What fires flow from the heart?
The fires of emotion, and they reveal themselves through the
Word.

142.
To help ourselves, above all else, we must stand on our feet
and have the firm belief that God's power is at work in us and
through that power we can help ourselves.
Faith is the yardstick. If it is great, we can conquer great evil.
If it is small, we can be of little help.
What one is able to believe, each person knows best for himself.
But in order to help one's neighbour, we must be imbued with
love, but with a divine love. Not love of the flesh, but of the
Spirit, which brings forth only good things. Nor should it be
done for gain or greed, but out of compassion and mercy.

143.
But what is the spirit of man?

A unit made up of three things:
1. The supernatural.
2. The natural.
3. The unnatural.[204]

144.

What is its substance?

All the elements of life that we attract. The supernatural is what the materialists cannot comprehend because it is divine. The natural is what one possesses and recognizes. The unnatural is when one denies what one has because one does not recognize it.

145.

The foundation or beginning of the spirit must be in the invisible God.

What are the elements the spirit requires for its development?
1. Words for conception.
2. Forms for guidance.
3. Numbers to build it up.

146.

How can you explain the spirit?

Through visions within yourself.

You must see spirit in your own light.

What is the greatest joy of the spirit?

When we are cheerful in heart.

What is the totality of the spirit?

The number three.

What is the mystique of the Spirit?

---

[204] The other meaning of widernatürlich is "perverse."

Its sudden inspiration from God.
What is the shadow of the spirit?
Sorrow, grief and pain.

147.
The human being is spiritually generating and giving birth in himself. God and spirit are connected with the human body.

148.
What is the spirit without the body?
A life.
What is the virtue of the spirit?
That it is a light which enlivens all that it enters.
What is the spirit's first commandment?
To put on a body equal to itself.[205]
What is the shining star of the spirit?
The soul.
What is the life of the spirit?
The eye.
When is the spirit certain for us, without deception?
When we perceive it in ourselves and in our body.
What is the gravity of the spirit?
The body.
Why?
Because the passion of the body is master of mind and soul.
In most cases, they must succumb.
How is it that the spirit does not always succumb?
Because it follows the inner voice that exhorts to goodness.

---

[205] Corinthians 12:12-31

149.
What is the gravity of the soul?
The material senses.
The **first** law of man is revelation, which he must have.
The **second** law is that man should be able to project his
soul wherever he wants.
The **third** law is that man should be able to communicate
and speak with the good spirits.
The **fourth**, man must be able to accomplish what he must,
even if it is completely against his character.

150.
What fire burns beneath the feet of man?
The fire of faith because it is a painful cross.
What fire animates man's knees from outside?
The truth.
Why?
Because only through this can man stand firm.
What fire animates the human heart from the outside?
The passions.
What fire animates the human head from outside?
Light, that is to say, everything we see.

151.
What is the circle that man forms?
A circle of light, for the sake of his thought.
How far does it extend?
Across all that is visible and invisible in creation.
How can man recognize the invisible in this circle?
Through Inner Sight.

152.

How can the spiritual name refer to the soul?

By the Baptism of Fire.

The soul is life, and the spiritual name is the power to stir it.

How must this stirring come about?

Through the spirit of thought.

153.

What spirit comes in and out of a person?

The mental spirit.

We have to learn to fix it because it cannot give birth outside of us but only within us.

154.

And when the stigmata open, what spirit will come through them into us?

A spirit of power that nothing material can withstand.

155.

Why is man formed upon the cross?

Because every man comes into this world to have faith and to know God, and through its powers one learns to love God in truth and does not shrink from the pain of birth.

156.

Loyalty and honour, what kind of spirits are these?

Loyalty is the power of love and raises it to the highest level.

Honour is the power of faith and makes you true.

157.
What is the most secret gate of man?
The fullness of his body. Into this the Lord shall enter.
But as long as no one wants to be a servant, it cannot be.

158.
What is Jesus in us?
The rays the light gives forth.
Within Jesus works as the form and the soul as the Word for our guidance.[206]
Only from the Word of the soul can Christ come forth.

159.
And when the Son of God is drawn to us, what is the soul in the inner man?
An everlasting light seeing from eternity to eternity.
Why?
Because the second sight resides in the Word.

160.
What then is the Father in us?
A Word that speaks from our feelings.
From what feeling?
From the feeling of faith.
And where does this lead to?
To the truth!
And where does this lead to?
To the conviction of faith.

---

[206] Here the word "form" means also "mould."

161.

If we live in the skies, what should we do there?

Keep silent.

Why?

Because Great Nature speaks to us through a thousand miracles, which should be food for the observer.

And where does this food lead to? [What is it for?]²⁰⁷

For the strengthening of the mental spirit.

162.

Everything unites in me. Do you know who I am?

The Word that you see in yourselves as form.

163.

What is the Principle according to the spirit?

An invisible being.

What is the All according to spirit?

A body in itself.

What is the above according to spirit?

The Word of Life.

What is the doings according to the spirit?

A foolishness before the world.

What is below according to the spirit?

Life.

What is the power according to the spirit?

Obedience.

What is virtue according to the spirit?

Suffering.

---

²⁰⁷ The words in brackets were added by Hübbe-Scleiden as an alternative reading.

164.

What is the binding agent between life and the dream?
The mind.
What is the dream?
A continuation of daily life.
How should one understand the dream?
According to the feeling it evokes.

165.

Who is a Father of Wisdom?
The one who draws it to himself.
Who is a Son of Virtue?
The one who cultivates it.
Who is a child trusting in God?
The one who is truly humble.
Who is a Daughter of Love?
The one who is chaste in life.
Who is a Hero of Faith?
The one who submits to the will of God.

166.

Which of the stars breaks up the clouds in our head?
The peace within ourselves.

67.

Behold the colours, who brings them forth?
The sun.

And the fruit of the field, who brings it forth?
The earth.
Behold the rivers of water, who brings them forth?
The air.
Behold the firmament of heaven, who brings it forth?
The fire.

168.
What does it mean to observe?
I live in the Light according to the degree of my realization.

169.
What is the meaning of me and you?
When the soul is separated from the body through death.

170.
The meaning of the kiss:
I seal my words so they are of eternal truth.

171.
Where man thinks, there is also the soul.
Why?
Because the form of thought is the soul.
The soul realizes the activity of the senses and presents it to us
in images as truth, whether false or not.
It is a diligent judge and yet our servant. It is the mirror of man,
through which we can see our thoughts, and which reflects the
sensual in us for our own perception.

172.

What is the soul?

The first revelation of Godhead, because it is an outflow of Godhead.

How can the soul be recognized?

By the human senses. Outwardly and inwardly by its desires. Upward by its Word and downward by the deed it performs.

What is over here and there?

The soul's will.

What effects does the soul have?

The divine.

What is its power?

A natural one in man, since the body must be its foundation.

173.

What are the characteristics of the soul?

1. Firstly, that it is immortal.

2. Secondly, that it can put itself outside our body.

3. Thirdly, that it can appear in visible form.

174.

How can the spirit connect with the soul?

With the body. The same is the power of the soul.

Without this the soul has no evident life.

175.

How should one approach the soul?

In the spirit.

In which way?

In the spirit of the light.
Without this the soul remains obscure for us.

176.
What is the language of the soul?
The thought.
The garment of the soul is the light.
The feet of the soul are the truth. Its knees are virtue. Its hips
are wisdom. Its loins are gentleness, and its heart is pure love.
Its hands faith, and its head is the thought of God.

177.
How can the soul leave the body?
On the wings of thought.
The eye of the soul is man himself because it reveals itself in
feeling, in dreams and in images.

178.
In which sphere does the soul move?
Only in spheres of light.

179.
What is the jewel of the soul?
Wisdom.

180.
What are the inner senses of the soul?
First sounds, the vocalization, and beautiful sounds.
After this it is to hear the Word of Life.

181.

What is the fire of the soul?

The blood.

Why?

Because it is physical motion, and thus food for the soul.

182.

What is the thorn of the soul by which it can sting itself?

The carnal presence.

183.

How can one first penetrate the sphere of the soul?

Through hearing.

How must the inner nature work on the soul?

Through the food of the spirit.

Man must learn to strip material thought from himself in order to become completely one with the soul. This can only happen in higher feeling. Not only be our thought, but light and soul...

184.

What is the splendour of the soul?

The song that we hear within us.

It sings praises to the eternal Father. Blessed are those who hear it! The sounds are sighs of the soul, and these sounds are words with which we learn to sympathize.

185.

What is the Word of the soul?

Our heart, through the feelings which govern it.

186.
What is the mouth of the soul?
The eye.

187.
The soul also has virtues, namely:
1. That it imparts the character of the Father.
2. That it is infinite.
3. That in all things it is obedient.

188.
What is the anguish of the soul?
That we have no love for it, while it lets everything happen to itself out of love.

189.
How does the soul declare its love?
Through revelation.

190.
What are the rays of the soul?
The shapes that show themselves on our body.

191.
The soul also has wings with which it soars into the heights and the depths.
That is our feeling.
How does the soul emerge from the clouds?
Through our body itself.

192.
How does it respond to the light?
Through the opening of stigmata.
The soul is like a butterfly but the wings are still bound to it.
This bond is the self-created cross, which seeks too often to
draw us down, and thereby also the soul.
The soul is the fragrance of the Lord because it carries out His will.
If man quells his own will, he is free.

193.
The soul has a high and a low flight but in the center is its rest,
that is to say, in a reborn human heart.

194.
If I think my soul on a high mountain, it is the singing sounds
that lift it up, and if I think it in the depths, it is the cry of pain
that springs from my breast. The soul is in man that it may be
revealed and lead us through life, on this place of penance.
But due to unbelief, many do not know that they have a soul.

195.
The truth is the golden rope with which we draw up the soul
from the depths.
I have also put a lamp for it. It must become evident between
me and you.
There is a cross on the high mountain too because when faith
has risen to the highest the body must sink into the grave,
meaning into its passions.

The soul can only walk on feet through the Word, and become visible for us through virtue, felt through practice, and heard through divine thoughts, and work toward the Most High by the power of truth, which must be revealed near and far.

196.
Seeing, hearing, feeling, and doing.
These are the powers of the soul.
But what is its language without our will?
The light of the deity.
The heaviest burden on the soul is the sensuous desire of the flesh.
The path of the soul is bliss.

197.
The bird has for its flight the air, the swan the water, the snake its belly, man his work on the earth. The animals have holes in the earth for protection and safety. But man digs deep into the earth for his own destruction.
The animal, does it not have a free will according to the principle of nature? And you poor children of men, have you no will [dominion] over yourselves?
So hear what the worm speaks unto you:
"I came out of this opening because I want to; crawl also into this hole with your will, if you can. And yet shall you be masters of this world?"
The grace of God is the light that enlivens the great universe, and in man the soul that receives all things.

198.

The devotion of the soul is that it calls the dead to life in man.
The prayer of the soul is to awaken the dead, to conquer evil by
the power of the Word.

199.

What is the highest level of the soul?
Faith. Only through this can it work in us.

200.

The soul can also be compared to a bird because it takes
nourishment from the mind and brings it into the flesh.
The soul is also to be compared to a crown because it is the
perfect truth in itself.

201.

What level of soul explores everything?
It is by our own revelation.

202.

The soul's righteousness is that it is truth to every man, even to
those who do not seek it.
But few recognize it because they lack love.

203.

What is the foundation on which the soul stands?
The spiritual gifts.

204.
If we call the soul, with what power must we think?
With steadfast faith.

205.
When is the soul in its most beautiful bloom?
When it gives off its fragrance in man.

206.
What is the shadow of the free soul?
Pure light.

207.
What is movement to the soul?
Our own Word.

208.
We know what the sound is.
What are the tones that we hear so often?
The language of the spirits that has been set free in us.
How can we understand them?
By listening to the holy devotion they teach us.
With our love we work on the inner being.
And being released from our own will, this spirit works on our body.

209.
We find equality in visible nature. Nor can the earth demand sun and rain.

Light, you Holy Light, you have penetrated our body!
Inner life, you have become light!
From without I receive you because you have become manifest.
For every one of us bears witness to you.

210.
Oh, great God!
That thy light is the life we feel within us.
Praise and thanks be to thee! Eternal Father, your love is as great
as your wisdom.
No one is capable of fully knowing it, and your grace flows
through all people, good and bad.
Grant light to our souls through your thoughts, Oh Lord, and a
Word of the Spirit will be our revelation.
And when the air blows, it strengthens the soul. It must rise
again as the image of the Eternal.

211.
Lord, frighten my soul that it may become more humble and
rule over my flesh and blood.

212.
My child, if you want to be clever, love your soul well and
believe that you can be obedient to it.
Soul, you are so beautiful. How your mouth is so sweet,
a fragrance of the Lord.
Lord in the heart, you are movement without pain.
Love like molten ore.

213.
Lord, your shoots are wonderful!
For our trees bear fruit and in them plants bloom, day and
night without end!

214.
I will coat my soul with oil, that it may burn, and its smoke
may be a thanksgiving offering unto the Lord.
I would gladly offer my own blood, but my enemies hinder
such sacrifice.
Therefore! Soul! Soul! Penetrate thou these unclean embers!

215.
The soul can only be shackled to the body by material thought
as a slave to it. Its revelation in the Word can then only be an
imperfect revelation.
The soul of man is life at birth.
When man is fully conscious it is freedom of will.
But when man seeks the spirit, it is thought, word, and feeling.
But when man is in spirit, the soul is the Lord in nature.
In these transformations of the soul the thought always remains
a child. The man who cannot connect the soul with the spirit,
their soul will again escape from him in death as breath

216.
Everything has its time, but for the soul time is eternity.

217.
How do you put wings to the word that it is effective
everywhere?
Through love.

218.
How is one to love the thought?
Through the life it brings forth.

219.
How shall we honour our feeling?
In innocent joys.

220.
If the soul is our life, how shall we crown it?
With good will.

221.
How are we to hope for the soul?
Through gratitude.

222.
How do we recognize the wisdom of the soul?
Through the light of thought within ourselves.

223.
How do we cause the soul the greatest pain?
If we do not obey her voice in battle, wrath, tribulation,
and distress.
Therefore, dear ones, in the commotion master the moment.
Hear the good voice within you. It is the soul that guides you.
If you obey, you may prosper on earth.

224.
What is the struggle of the soul?
Our material mind.

225.

Through what do we crucify the soul?

Through doubt.

Through what do we martyr the soul?

Through lies.

226.

What four points unite the soul?

1. Love.
2. Hope.
3. Faith.
4. Knowledge.

He who lacks this is like a wild beast that tears itself apart.

227.

How shall we glorify the soul?

By believing its Word from within.

Then we can also glorify God outwardly with deeds.

228.

How can we love the soul?

With the knowledge of spiritual thinking.

229.

In which people is the soul dead?

In those who have no spiritual Word to reflect.

In which one is the soul alive?

With the one who lets the Word come to speech.

230.
By what do we try the soul most?
By our wanting. For what we have is too little for us. We do not see it and do not want to recognize it, because it is truth. But that which we do not have, we would like to possess in our perversity.

231.
What is the star through which our soul first shines?
Premonitions and dreams.

232.
When have we won the victory of the cross over the soul?
When blessed spirits, messengers of God, can speak to us face to face.

233.
The soul is a life and with this we must struggle.

234.
How shall we start the first fight?
With our own body.
How can the body conquer its life?
Through the new inner senses that open up to it.
What is meant by conquering life?
To overcome everything that is wrong, which clings to us from material birth.
On the wings of the air the messengers glide in and out of the human being.

What are the messengers?
Created angels directing God's commands for the guidance of man.

235.
What are these spirits that we hear and feel but cannot see?
These are serving spirits, but not by our will, but by God's will.
They are free guides.
And from where do they come?
From the soul of the person which has become the Word.
These guides, therefore, are created by ourselves, like images of a dream.

236.
What must be the Word that brings forth living forms?
Love for eternity.

237.
How does the soul gain its due?
When man is in the bloom of his strength, that is to say, when man allows it free will.

238.
If the soul can command our will, what effect does it produce?
A power in the body with which you can do everything.

239.
How does one recognize the will of the soul?
Through the love that drives us to do good and to refrain from evil.

240.

Soul, you my goal, to the cross you lead me!

Soul, my confidence, I bow before thee!

Soul, you my playmate. You will be my message!

My soul, your breath governs my feet, and your tongue licks the tops of the mountains!

Soul, you great gate to He that is pure the fire of love.

Soul, you massive house in which my actions shall dwell.

Soul, you my hope. You bring me salvation!

Soul, you my life. In motion I arise in you.

Soul, my soul, to be united with you is my golden scale.

Soul, you comfort all who see your flowers!

To the soul, depth is melancholy and height its peace.

241.

When does the soul implore God most strongly?

When we are most cheerful.

How does the soul rage in itself?

When we have to see and hear cruelty.

When does the soul rejoice in itself?

When we obey its voice.

242.

Movement is the spirit of the will.

Mortify your flesh with the Spirit of Truth!

From the spirit of obedience the faith rises in strength.

From what must the spirit of faith arise?

From the glorious dawn from the east, from the grace of the Father.[208]

---

[208] Mailänder uses the term "Morgenrot" for the rising dawn of the east.

243.
From what does the spirit of patience arise?
From motion.
And where does it lead to?
To the clear mind

244.
What is spiritual food?
Wisdom.
And its spirit?
The Word of the Soul.
The one who has faith in God stands on a high mountain,
and righteousness is his strength.

245.
What the heaviest part of the soul?
Good will.

246.
And what force pulls up the soul most strongly?
Love for it.

247.
By what yardstick should the soul be measured?
The mind.

248.
What is outpouring of the soul?
The testimony we give of Godhead.

249.
How should one speak to the soul?
Through the forms revealed to us.

250.
Where is the seat of all thoughts?
In faith.
Where is the seat of all wisdom?
In feeling.
Where is the seat of all knowledge?
In the mind.
Where is the seat of all love?
In Revelation.

251.
What are the joys of life?
Dreams.
But joys of the spirit are everlasting. Of these I will testify.

252.
In nature there is a center, which draws everything to itself.
This center is the human heart, and the circles that enclose the
center are our feelings, which come from the inner forces.
How must the center work on the circles?
Through the light of thought, although a center is only
conceivable in nature. Besides, there is none because God would
not be God for us. By the word "nature" we must understand
the spirit of truthfulness in all that we see and receive.

253.
Nature forms a square that is invisible to the ordinary eye.
It binds and unbinds.
The solution is only conceivable in an enclosed space, or
otherwise stated: within the inner sense.
If a circuit moves, it is a wheel, and this is a circular.
The soul life is the driving force of this universe, meaning that
feeling and soul are bound to each other.

254.
He who recognizes the truth in himself spreads a seed that bears
fruit a thousand times over.
[Fruit means: reward].

255.
The second sight transfigures the mind.
[And transfiguration means: to recognize the truth]

256.
He who has faith also has the second sight.
From the same it comes forth.

257.
Power of the will, what do you bring forth?
Thoughts and feelings.

258.
Lightning flashes of thought are sudden effects in the mind and
come out of feeling.
Feelings after the mind are joy, pain, devotion, and love, etc.

259.
Man's premonitions of the spirit is an inner knowledge without the second sight.

260.
But where do the true feelings come from?
From the Inner Words of God.
How do you recognize this Word?
Through the mind.
What is spiritual mind?
The knowledge of invisible forces.
What are the invisible forces?
Everything not material, which comes from feeling.

261.
Man can recognize spiritual truth in his hands and feet, as in his body through what he feels in it, as also through the face and through touch.
Many weaknesses lead to greatest strength.
Many sufferings crown the head of man.
The boundaries of man are the spirit world.

262.
The inner sense of man is a revelation, the source of which is Godhead and leads us to perfection.

263.
The best way to perceive the inner sense is to listen to holy feelings, that is to say, to live silently in oneself and in the faith that God is with us in everything we do.

264.
How should we foster the inner meaning?
Through practicing the good.
What is good?
All we have to do.

265.
The inner sense is the spiritual being which strives to manifest itself in us.
What does it mean to die in spirit?
To go through transfiguration according to the law of nature from the one state into the other.

266.
When circles are formed on the human body, what is the center?
Life.
And when circles are formed inside a human being, what is the center there?
Light.
And when circles are formed in the innermost parts of a human being, what is the center there?
Love.

267.
What is the soul of truth?
Pure revelation.
What powers are subject to truth?
All that embrace the spiritual self and through this spiritual self the powers of all revelatory gifts come forth.

268.

The stone with seven eyes which Joshua laid is abandoned and will become manifest before all eyes.[209]

269.

How should man look into his inner being?
Through a fine glass, which he should have inside him.
Without this he will see only rough impressions of images.
What kind of looking glass is this?
True spiritual feelings.
This also relates to hearing, smelling and tasting.
Only by stripping away the passions can such feeling be refined.

270.

If there are nothing but words in the emotional circle, then what fire must be at the center?
The grace of God. For no man can deserve the love of God.
Rather, it is a gift of grace granted through the goodness of the Lord.

271.

When is the center of the soul truth?
When man can speak Words of Life.

272.

The center of the soul is the natural life.

---

[209] This refers to a passage from the prophet Zechariah: "For behold, the stone which I have set before Joshua, upon the one stone are seven eyes," (Zechariah 3:9). Interpreters assume that the John apocalypse in Rev. 5:6 refers to Zechariah as well. It reads, "And I beheld, and, lo, in the midst of the throne and of the four beasts, and in the midst of the elders, stood a Lamb as it had been slain, having seven horns and seven eyes, which are the seven Spirits of God sent forth into all the earth." (Revelation 5:6)

273.

When does man move in an orbit?

When he himself becomes the center, meaning when he comes to self-knowledge.

The center of all nature is God's visible truth.

274.

Where is the grave of the crucified one hidden?

In the Word of men.

275.

How does the soul separate itself from the material life?

Through the light of thought.

How does the soul separate itself from the material eye?

Through the second sight.

How does the soul separate itself from the feet?

Through balance.

How does the soul separate itself from material feeling?

Through pain.

How does the soul separate itself from the hands?

Through good actions.

276.

How does one measure the extent of a vision?[210]

By drawing it into yourself.

How does one withdraw from visions?

By knowing oneself.

---

[210] The word used for visions is "Gesicht" which means "face" but in old times meant vision or premonitions.

277
Where does the basic cause for the vision come from?
From the feeling.
How should one take measure in the vision?
One should realize that it is truth.

278.
What is power?
An operative fire.
What is the cause of power?
The light of thought.
Why must this power be?
Because without it there would be no spiritual life in man.
What is the peak of this power?
The living Word in yourselves.

279.
What is the purpose of the inner sense of taste?
It is the yardstick of the spiritual food that I give to man.
But one must first taste the bitter. Otherwise, one would
never recognize the sweet.

280.
What is the purpose of the inner sense of smell?
It is on the fragrant scents your soul will soar upwards.

281.
What is the goal of man?
To raise his soul from the bonds of the flesh.
What is the final destination of man?
That he becomes a true child of the Eternal Father.

282.

The breath is the life which draws the spirit Tarna to itself. (The power of forces).[211]

283.

What is the light of life?

The eye, because what you see evokes feelings within.

284.

What is natural?

Everything one understands.

285.

What does man still have within himself from his primordial beginning?

The feeling for beauty.

286.

What is the calling of the spiritual man?

To practice virtue. Doing this means to bestow the gifts he possesses by God's grace.

What is the goal of the spiritual man?

To unite the Three in One.

How can one accomplish this?

By thought. Thought can be united with the Word only by action. With thought the Word must be awakened, and with the Word the body and all nature must be defeated.

---

[211] Hübbe-Schleiden appears to use the brackets to describe the meaning of "Tarna."

287.

What is spiritual willpower of man?

The inner drive, and this drive is love.

Where does this spiritual will have its seat?

In man's feeling, and only through this drive can we find the way of rebirth.

288.

Faith is a secret invisible power.

But what is its real life?

1. The sufferings.

2. The humility.

3. The patience.

289.

For each one there remains a point towards which their eye is directed.

But the distant wanderer does not recognize it.

Blessed are those who have come near.

If I walk through these halls, I find the old again renewed.

290.

The legs must be penetrated by life.

291.

Without thistles no thorns.

First gather the thistle to the crown.

Only then the thorn can hurt you.

Your garments must be renewed.

For his blood has come upon us and causes much pain.
It is a sign of the covenant that I have made with you.

292.
In his footsteps you have followed the transfiguration.
Quietly my body trembles.
Not my will but your will rules.

293.
The **faith** is a branchless tree and towers high above.
You must make twelve steps in the same in order to climb
the height destined for you.
The **first** step is seed of promise.
The **second** step is nourishment.
The **third** is becoming natural as a human being.
The **fourth** is the cross as the foundation or pain in all the
limbs of the body, meaning to bear the crucifixion.
The **fifth** stage is the erection of the cross or transfiguration
of the mental spirit in man.
The **sixth** is the death of the serpent or resurrection.
The **seventh** stage is to be received by the beloved God as
righteous, or to come into the spirit according to power.
The **eighth** stage is the crown of life, or to receive the wisdom
of the messenger spirits.
The **ninth** stage is to be born again, or to pass from the
corruptible into the incorruptible.
The **tenth** stage is the open Book of Light in its first potency,
being the divine clarity.
The **eleventh** step is harmony or union.
The **twelfth** step is attaining to the universe or God.[212]

---

[212] These bold words are underlined in the original German handwriting.

294.

The **transfiguration** is seven-fold in:

1. Mortifying through life.
2. Making the dead alive.
3. Separating the light from the darkness.
4. Separating spirit from matter.
5. Making their spiritual will known.
6. Doing it justice.
7. Tying the love bond with the spiritual world.

295.

This is worship in Spirit and in Truth when one brings the conviction of revelation to the body.

296.

Those who have been transfigured display white garments through purification.

Meaning that low thoughts can no longer be active in them.

297.

The spiritual death breaks through the gates of the human shell and will be revealed in the servants and maidservants of the Lord.

298.

From this root goes out (the true) life.

299.

The true Lord's Supper is when man hears God's Word in his ear. No one else sees it. Yet still he obeys.

Then the Lord is his guest.

300.
He who the received **baptism** through Jesus shall wash his
hands clean and then he can also eat the finest honey.

301.
The **first** baptism is the attraction of Christ and the crucifixion.
Then we step into the Spirit of Truth.
The **second** baptism is the reception of the power of spirit
through accepting the Lord in the spiritual life.
The **third** baptism is the conception of the Holy Spirit,
which is the work of the spirit

302.
When the bones tremble, the marrow must rise and fall.

303.
Hurray! To the Children of Light!
A praise from the soul to those who climb the thorny path of
the mountain.

304.
In the material weakness of man, the soul utters its sighs.
In a sound it calls:
"You are not abandoned for me!"

305.
The soul treasured repository in the body is thought,
and the soul itself is the feeling.

Where does the light stream into the body?
Where there is life in it.
Why is there life where the soul reveals itself?
Because it is the truth.
What is the soul's truth?
The Good, as that of God.

306.

How does the soul become the power in the flesh?
Through the fire of love for God.
What is oneness with the soul?
The love, the revelation, the truth.
How does the Word become flesh?
Through the life of the soul.

307.

The true spiritual will is love and this leads us to our goal.

308.

What spirit will God pour out upon all flesh?
That of Wisdom.[213]

309.

How is man to recognize that his sins are not counted against him?
Through the spiritual nourishment of the Word and revelation, which we receive through His grace.

---

[213] Joel 2:28, referring to Acts 2:17

310.

How does one pray with the soul to God?

Through the thoughts.

311.

What is the light shining in darkness?

The seed of the mind as light.

312.

When is the human heart a true temple of God?

When we have become children.

313.

The blood of Christ is the spiritual life, for a living
faith brings forth the **<u>baptism of the blood.</u>**

What is the baptism of the blood?

All the pains that come forth in the flesh, as one seeks the spirit
in the ways of the law.

How can you speak to Me in My voice?

With your soul.

How can you turn your soul to this?

Through the **rebirth**.

What does the rebirth of the soul mean?

Seeing, hearing, feeling, smelling, tasting the divine.

314.

How can one achieve the ultimate with the soul?

When one dedicates the whole of one's life to that which one
strives to accomplish.

With what kind of life?
With the heartfelt life.

315.
When the Word has become power in man he recognizes it best through the inner sense. The stronger the perceptions, the greater the power of the Word in him.

316.
What is the stirring of the heart?
Hear the words of life!

317.
What is the great totality?
Man.

318.
If you want to think right, how must you do it?
Look for that and learn to recognize what you are thinking.
If you want to climb up, how must you climb?
Be upright within yourself.

319.
What is the straight path?
The spiritual power within us.

320.
What is a good foundation?
The faith of a newborn person.

321.
What lifts us up into the air?
Humbleness toward God.

322.
In the **square** is the truth of the soul.
The **soul** level is the human heart.

323.
What is the soul lyre?
The ear of man.

324.
Why is the **soul** to be compared to a little bird?
For the sake of its freedom.

325.
Why must the **soul** have natural forms for its revelation?
Because it is a Spirit of Truth.

326.
Why does the **soul** audibly manifest itself?
So that we may learn to recognize it.

327.
Which number has truth in it?
The number **four**.

328.
What is the foundation of truth?
The knowledge.

329.

What are the **necessities** to which truth is truth tied?

1. To revelation.

2. To the faith.

3. To hope.

4. To love.

330.

What are instincts of truth?

All inner perceptions we have.

331.

The banner or victory over truth is faith.

The Truth

332.

What spoils the truth in itself?

Exuberance.

333.

What is the strongest force of truth?

Love.

334.

Truth, where are you?

In the soul.

335.

What are fruits of truth?

Learning to know the beloved God.

336.
What is the position of truth?
Feeling.

337.
What is crowned by truth?
The people of spirit.

338.
What are the virtues of truth?
That they awaken and strengthen all the spiritual "I's" in us.

339.
What is the praise of truth?
That one recognizes God through the same.

340.
What is the glory of truth?
That it gives us ever new nourishment.

341.
What is the highest movement of truth?
That it animates us.

342.
What are the footsteps of truth?
That it brings us more and more knowledge.

343.
What is the love of truth?
That it brings us help.

344.
What is the seal of truth?
The soul in its revelation.

345.
What is the fire of truth?
That it works in miracles.

346.
What is the teaching of truth?
A manna against erring.

347.
What is the crown truth?
That it never leaves the one who possesses it.

348.
What are champion spirits of truth?
1. The mind.
2. The body.
3. The soul.

349.
What is boldness of truth?
All the evidence she gives us.

350.
What are characteristics of truth?
All forms that we see.

351.
What is the fervour of truth?
That it brings forth life.

352.
What is the fate of truth?
That it weds with Wisdom.

353.
What is the death of truth?
That it dissolves into pure light.

354.
What is the joy of truth?
That it possesses freedom in itself.

355.
What are sorrows of truth?
When one does not obey it.

356.
What is the breath of truth?
The power of God.

357.
The **spiritual name** opens the book of the inner being.
It is its main key.

358.
What is the **spiritual time**?
The faith that comes from the truth.

359.
What now is born is a ripe fruit and in it is a seed.
In truth lies the seed to Wisdom.
In Wisdom lies the seed to love.
In love lies the seed of freedom.

360.
What is my truth?
The conviction.
What is doing truth?
Walking in my laws.
What is the increase of truth?
Keeping my commandments.
What is the duty of truth?
Believing in it.
What is the basis of truth?
To be reasonable.
What is the Goddess of Truth?
Honora, being the testimony we give of her.
What is the curse of truth?
When one sins against her.
What is the greatest burden for truth?
When one tramples upon her.
What is the jubilation song of truth?
When one enjoys her.
What is the honeydew of truth?
The one to whom she is merciful.
What is the circle of truth?
The person who dons it as a garment.
What is the star of truth?

The feeling.
What is the sunlight of truth?
When you understand it.
What is the moonlight of truth?
The human body.
What is the mover of truth?
God himself.

361.
What is to be understood by the **renunciation of worldly pleasures?**
To be humble toward God and content with the lot that has been appointed to us.

362.
What is a **prophet** on this earth?
A guiding star by the will of God.

Seekers of Truth

363.
Silence and waiting is worth more than talking and acting quickly.

364.
Hope has never been destroyed unless one deceives oneself.

365.
Whoever can bear mockery and shame with patience will be honoured in heaven and sought by men on earth.

366.
Whoever wants to be wise in his speech always has stupidity in his center.

367.
Whoever can save wisdom in his mouth will never be impoverished.

368.
Whoever loves truth and practices virtue is an eyesore to the world.

369.
Those who often tell lies and deceive much are often the so-called respectable people.

370.
Outwardly so beautiful and inwardly so empty. People say, "What more can one want!"

371.
When the world declares that it loves you, it is usually misfortune that befalls you.

The Enigma of Truth

372.
Find me and I'll love you.

373.
Comfort yourself, then you look for me.

374.
If you live for me, I will serve you.

375.
If you simply shine for me, I will shine for you threefold.

376.
If you swear to me yes, I won't say no.

377.
If you seek my heart, it is yours.

378.
Behold all that I have, I give to thee.

379.
I am a sharp weapon. Whoever fights against me will lose.

380.
I judge rightly, and no evil can stand before me.

381.
I pass through many fires, and yet none can consume me.

382.
I always do what people do not like.
Why?

383.
If I am to your liking, then clothe me.
If you are to mine, I will call you.

384.

Do right and leave me not and I will be your match.

385.

What you have before your eyes that you may believe.
This is simply my art.

386.

Yes, if you go, you can find me because I am everywhere.
If you are sitting you can see me, but you have to know
where I am.

387.

My strength is not a power, and His strength is the strength
of all powers.

388.

My love is not love, and His love is eternal.
My desires are not desires, and His desires crush everything.

389.

He who does not know me does not find wisdom when it
jumps at his nose.

390.

He who exercises violence without my authority is an unfaithful
false servant.

391.

He who does not know me does not see me when I step on his
feet.

A Discourse on Feeling

392.
A tree: a natural feeling
Shelter: the feeling of protection
Dressing: the feeling of necessity.
Flowers: the feeling of joy.
Death: the feeling of fear.
Pictures: the feeling of beauty.
Sun: the feeling of warmth.

393.
How do we feel the inner man?
Through the benefits we receive.
How do we feel the inner animal?
In vain-self-love.

394.
Humility is the sense for knowledge.

395.
In the head is the feeling of the Word.
In hope is the feeling of faith.
In the promise is the feeling of hope.
In the heart is feeling of thought.
In the eye is the feeling of pain.
In obedience is the feeling of salvation.
In will is the feeling of freedom.
In freedom is the feeling of purity.
In virtue is the feeling of justice.

396.
In love we have the feeling of duty.
(That we are virtuous, when we feel the fear God,
and this is the same as to love God).
In truth we feel the wisdom.
In the number we feel the world.
With the animals we feel the servant.
We feel that we have gained a victory in the baptism
we have received.

397.
When do we feel the strength within us?
When we receive revelations.

398.
In the light we feel the Word.
In the senses we feel the spiritual world.
In struggles we feel our weaknesses.
In the gifts of the spirit we feel God himself.

399.
Among people in general there is the feeling of transitoriness.
In the whole of Nature we feel development or work.

400.
In the resurrection of the flesh we feel the light of God.

401.
When do we feel the light of day within us?
When we are master of our passions.

402.
What Holy Spirit do we receive in the **first baptism?**
The of the Light of God.
In the **second baptism** that of the life of God.
In the **third baptism** that of the love of God.

403.
Who generates the flowers in you?
The warmth.
What warmth?
That of love.
Who generates the animals in you?
Life.
What life?
The natural.
Who generates the stones in you?
Passion.
What passion?
The struggling.
Who generates the metals in you?
Pains.
What pains?
The sensuous.
Who generates the human potential in you?
Ingenuity.
What ingenuity?
The worldly.
Who generates the stars of heaven in you?
Order.
What order?
The mortal.

Who generates the election in you?
The Redeemer.
What Redeemer?
The Inner Word.
Who generates the whole earth in you?
Obedience.
What obedience?
The lawful.
Who generates the human being in you?
The seed.
What seed?
The one of our deeds.
Who generates the numbers in you?
Language.
What language?
That necessary for form.
Who generates God in you?
A force.
What force?
That of thought.
Who generates the spirit world within you?
The senses.
What senses?
The inner ones.
Who generates light in you?
Truth.
What truth?
The unerring.
Who generates the Word in you?
Feeling.

What feeling?
That of the will.

404.
What is the depth of hell?
The torments.
Who is bound in hell?
The wicked.

405.
How does one live within?
When one hears the Word of God within.

406.
What is the heavenly language?
The truth.

407.
How do you get into the interior?
Through the mind.

408.
What prayer strengthens man best?
To remain and live in faith.

409.
When has man been restored to his natural state?
When he recognizes himself.

410.
When have we ascended to heaven?

When obedience lifts us to heaven.
When righteousness lifts us up from the earth.

411.
Christ's blood is **spiritual** life for us, a strengthening wine.
What kind of spiritual life is it?
One of sacrificing oneself.

412.
When have we attained true repentance?
When we feel joy and light within ourselves.

413.
By what power do we defeat the false ego in the very germ
of its birth?
Through the Word.

414.
What we see on earth inside are images of our deeds.
The soul is the truth and leads us to the inner human being.
The soul is the natural guide in us, the childbearing woman.

415.
What is the key of David?
The living revelatory Word of God, our spiritual guide.
Where does he live?
In the head of man, meaning in the light of thought.
How can we come to him?
Through the practice of the Word, which is an everlasting prayer.

416.
How do we recognize the spiritual from the natural?
In the natural, the spiritual is an invisible working force.
In the spiritual, the natural is the revelation of our five senses.

417.
How do we recognize the human being in us?
By the truth that we see in ourselves and by wakeful dreaming.
(What enters in is the human nature and what comes out is the divine spiritual.)

418.
The right hand of the Lord is a key, a power that we can attract through divine thinking.
(With God's Word we also attract His power).

419.
All revelation that comes from the truth is called **Wisdom**.

420.
He who lives by his faith is a saint, being pure, and no one can strike him or rob him of his treasure.

421.
Every action springs from faith.

422.
How do you remove the sting from death?
By the grace of God.

423.
What is the key to the gospel?
The Holy Spirit.
(Patience is the key to purification and makes us pure).
What is the key to justice?
Love.
(Only the righteous can love God in truth).

424.
What are ghosts?
The outflow of a form.

425.
What is spiritual courage?
The foreknowledge of the various things that one
must accomplish.

426.
What is spiritual humility?
The satisfaction with what we have, both spiritual and material.
Spiritual humility is also the key to repentance in oneself.

427.
What is the purpose of the activity of the Word in us?
Learning to recognize the power of the Word in seeing.

428.
The key to feeling is our will.
The key to hearing is movement.
To smell submission, to taste the inner driving force.

429.

The power of the Word is greeted through seeing.
The power of the will is greeted through feeling.
The power of thought is greeted by hearing.
The power of submission is greeted by smelling.
The power of love is greeted by tasting.

430.

How do we attract Christ in the flesh?
Through spiritual truths.

431.

How does the glory of the Woman manifest itself?
By all manner of revelations which we receive.

432.

By what do we recognize the honour of the will?
By the evidence that we have.

433.

How do you honour the Woman?
Through love.
How do you honour freedom?
Through oneself.
How do you honour God?
Through knowledge.
How do you honour the Son of God?
Through the will to goodness.
How do you honour the Holy Spirit?
Through understanding.
How do you honour your own life?

Through the actions we perform.
How do you honour your neighbour?
By forgiving their faults.

434.
Where does the will dwell in man?
In reason.
Who is the leader of the will?
Man himself.

435.
Who is the master of the will?
The good or evil in oneself.
Who finds rest in the will?
The one who is subject to it.
Who finds unrest in the will?
The one who is the slave of his passions.

436.
Who lives in purity?
A Chosen One.
How high can purity raise one up?
As far as to the Living Word of God.
Who is pure?
The innocent.
Where does purity dwell?
In love.
Who seeks purity?
The real in us.
Who loves purity?
The one who can sacrifice himself.

437.
Come here, you risen ones, according to my words!
I say unto you, you shall come to my rest!

The Form Teaching

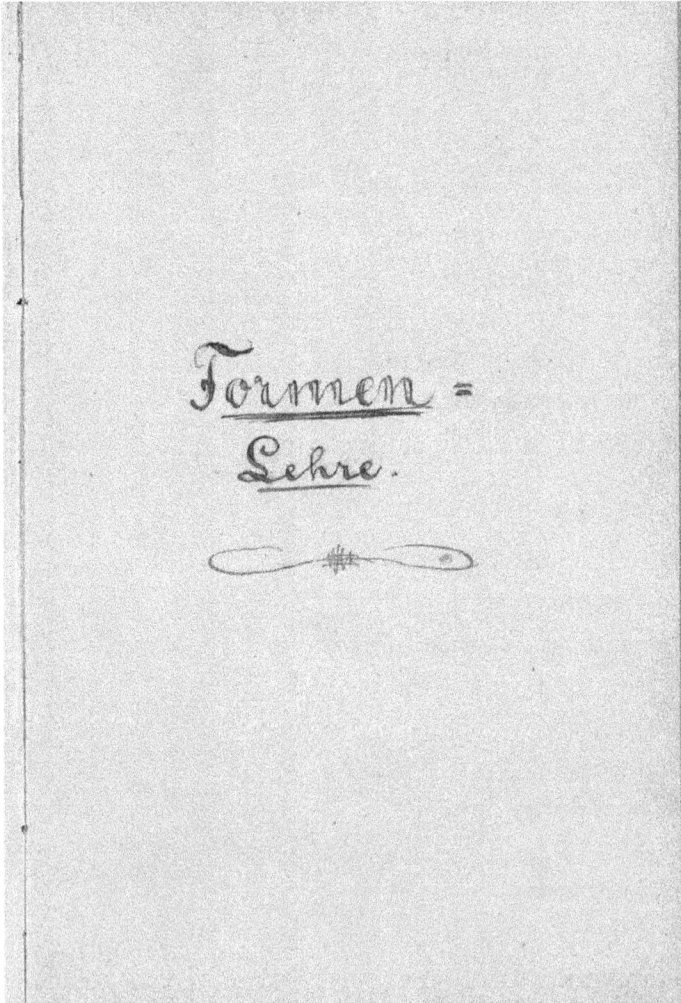

Buchstaben - und Zahlen-
Schlüssel.

(im Äussern.)

Letter and number keys (external)[214]

A. Believe firmly. It will lift you up.

B. Only in spirit one can love God above all.

C. Fight for your kingdom.

D. I honour the pure bride. I will testify to you.

E. I want to give you a clear mind.

F. Truth we foresee.

   I want to reveal myself to you.

G. You are still far behind in faith.

H. I disapprove of your values.

I. I will transfigure you.

J. - -

K. Be of good will! I will erect my throne in you.

L. Obedience to God. I will make you reborn.

M. I testify of God. You also testify of me.

N. The Spiritual Name. I will be strong in you.

O. Wisdom, that is the knowledge of God.

   Have fear of God!

P. I am coming soon.

Q. Your blood is cleansed.

   You are able to step forward.

R. Love your neighbour as yourself.

   Beware of useless words.

S. You are a spiritual child.

---

[214] It is called "External" because these signs appear on the skin, whereas the other forms are seen "in the Spirit."

T. I will connect with you.

Fight against your evil desires and passions.

U. The motion (blood) and creative power (revelation) causes the emanating effect.

I move to revelation in you.

V. To elevate the soul.

W. Patience! Be childlike!

X. I don't want you to torment yourself!

Y. The cup of joy, delight and bliss.

Z. Righteousness in faith.

Beware of evil acts!

1. <u>Death</u>: Let your external person perish.

2. <u>Life</u>: Resurrection in the spiritual.

3. Deity. Trinity.

4. Wisdom. Have fear of God.

5. Crucified. External pain caused by spiritual birth.

6. Fire or Spirit. Love.

7. Justice. Be just.

8. Devil or malice.

9. Sword or Word. Beware of error!

10. Battle. Be steadfast!

11. Light. Thought.

12. Rock or stone. <u>Perfection</u>.

Formen · Sprache
der
Erkenntnis.

(im Geiste.)

Form-language of knowledge (in the spirit)[215]

Anointing: You will attract inner forces of redemption.

Arrow: In lightning-fast movement: Eternity of the soul. It is subject to you.

Ash: You deserve punishment.

Axe: The moving life will become power in you.

Bag: full: Desire for temporal treasures.

Ball (blue): I'll pour my spirit upon you!

Ball (dark, grey): You will bear witness through the word.

Bell (see or hear): Have devotion!

Berries (black, like elderberries): The soul is in its revelation.

Berries (red): You are so fierce (violent, anger).

Bird: Your soul.

Blood: I move inside you.

Blue: See sky blue colour.

Book: A living one that opens by itself and turns the pages: Have love for the soul.

Book (open): You are passionate on the inside.

   (On the human body, like in a book, is written the stamp of the passion for good and evil).

Bread: Receive my word in you.

---

[215] In German this list follows the words according to the alphabetical order of the German spellings.

Bricks: Build!

Bridge: Fight for purity.

Candlelight (burning): Have trust in God!

Cat: You want to deny my spirit!

Chain (black, iron): You want to destroy yourself through your unbelief.

Chain (golden: promise): The sign of the covenant that God has made with us.

Chalice: You have to go through pain, labour and fears!

Chickens: Do your duty!

Child: Stay in humility!

Christ head: see "Son of Man."

Cleaver: The moving life will become a strength in you.

Clock (that tears itself apart): The temporal should have no value for you!

Clock: Be content in yourself!

> (A clock that works well is the symbol of inner contentment. Whoever has this in himself feels something incessant in him and these are spiritual joys and the awareness that his sins are forgiven).

Cloth: fluctuating, white: Greetings from higher spheres.

Clouds: Passions.

Cloves (red): I want to give you goodwill! (Love).

Coals (glowing): I want to purify you!

Colours: see also yellow and sky blue.

Compasses: Beg!

Cross in different light colours: Sacrifice yourself through self-denial!

Cross of iron, on the right side one hand, on the left one foot: Believe firmly!

   (With the firm belief you can call the soul).

Cross where there are written words: You will be the winner in faith!

Cross wooden: Shame, disgrace, mockery and scorn.

Cross, white: Be patient!

Crown of thorns: Curse of the world. Renounce all worldly joys.

Crown: Seek truth!

   (Truth is the crown of life, whoever recognizes it has wisdom and can explore the depths of the Godhead).

Darkness: Separation of the outside and the inside.

Dawn: seeing it: New life is beginning.

Dead people ascending: Strive in spiritual power!

Diadem: Show humility!

Diamonds: The thirst for truth should be quenched in you.

Dices: Gifts of the spirit.

Drum: Argue for faith.

Ears of wheat: The thankful receives God's blessing.

Egg: You will be rewarded.

Excrement: see feces.

Eyes: The measure or the seeing (second sight).

Feces (human feces): Excretion of the evil principle.

Feet with open stigmata: Believe in a better "I"!

Feet: (are the root of man): The driving force of faith is alive in you.

Female: see Woman.

Fir branches: You are a chosen one:

Fire: Receive God's word!

Firewood: see or carry: You should sacrifice yourself!

Fish: Learn to be silent.

Five: The senses.

> (Man crucifies himself with the sensual when he is subject to his senses, not they to him.)

Flags: Victory signs.

> Black flag: Life.
>
> Blue flag: Spiritual dreams
>
> Green flag: Divination.
>
> Red flag: Eternity.
>
> White flag: Revelation.
>
> White-red flag: Spiritual death.
>
> Yellow flag: I promise you.

Forest: You are a chosen one!

Forests (green ones, gates and groves): I am subject to you. I want to serve you.

Funeral procession: Sadness, tribulation.

Gates: I am subject to you. I want to serve you. See also forests.

Glass balls, white with brightly shining fire: Have hope in the spiritual.

Gold: Free your soul from external plagues! (The soul is purified like gold in the fire of faith).

Golden sparks, playing around: I am gracious to you! (See also light sparks)

Grapes: The will of the spirit speaks: I want to, I really wish to be strong in you.

Groves: see forests.

Hammer: Knock! Believe!

Hand: Have power!

> (According to the spirit, the hand is the power, to which all contraries must yield).

Hand (waving): Spirits are ready to serve you.

Headband: The redemption.

Heart (iron): Be patient!

Heart: Have divine feelings!

Honey: Don't let yourself be seduced!

Horse: Be humble!

Human excrement: see feces.

Human hair: I want to honour you!

Iron (glowing): I want to purify you.

Iron (round piece): You are causing yourself unnecessary suffering.

Key (a man's height, iron one): The Spirit of Prophecy as the power of all forces in you.

Key: Inner forces are awake!

King (with a golden crown): The power has entered you!

Knife, open: Beware of arguments! See also "razor".

Ladder: Power of Wisdom.

Lance: You have penetrated from death into life.

Laurel wreath: Strive for perfection!

Leaves (arid on the earth): You are in the withering away of the material.

Letter with a red seal: Good news.

Lightning (in the face or with open eyes): The forces of the sky move the human body. Bouquet of flowers: present and future in joy.

> (In the flower we see the reflection of the driving force of nature, inside and outside).

Locomotive: Good will.

Lyre (golden): I speak to you.

Man (a handsome one, from whose mouth an animal emerges): Beware of men!

Moon: Give birth to the soul.

Naked persons: Be at one with yourself!

Oil: See words (Written words within us. All shapes form words):

On the steps of faith, love and hope we can penetrate into the depths, comb through flesh and soul.

Ox: Disbelief in you.

Palm branch: Victory over the inner nature.

Peacock or peacock feathers: Don't be haughty (proud) of what you have (or are!)

Pearls: Joys in the spiritual.

People: See persons, naked.

Persons (naked): Be united in yourself.

Pine cones: You are impatient!

Press: I want to seal you!

Rainbow: The omnipotence of God.

Razor: I want to purify you! See also "knife".

Rock crevices: Don't look back to the past.

Rock: The opposite of you.

> (He dissolves finally into his elements like the weathering rock).

Rod: I will chastise you.

Rooster: The dawn (morning red) of the East! The love of God becomes second sight in you.

Rose (red): I want to give you spiritual food!

Rose (white): Thank the Eternal One!

Ruin: See rock crevices and walls.

Saint Ilgen: Make the spirit free!

Scales: Be reasonable!

Scythe from the first to the second baptism: The harvest is here!

Scythe before the first baptism: You will have a problems!

> (A scythe going up and down, especially if it's quite rusty).

Scythe: Do justice! Inner justice.

> (Whoever wants to be righteous must obey what his faith demands; and that's hard. It is like having to cut piece by piece the meat off your bones. The sufferings are the life of faith, without them, faith is dead).

Sea: see water.

Sealing wax: Don't push your mind back inside you!

Senses: see five.

Shamrock: Kill the sensual love in you!

Ships: (Seeing them or sailing in them): Exhortation to perseverance. Be steadfast!

Signet ring: I give you.

Silver (round piece): Have wisdom, fear of God.

Sky (blue colour): Be happy!

Snake: Be cunning (wise) to keep the commandments of God.

Son of man: Be forgiving to your neighbour!

Sparks of light (blue): I give you the power of faith. See also "Golden sparks".

Spider: Strive for Purity!

Square (angular measure): Inner vision

Square golden: Your eye shall be light!

Squirrel: You do follies.

Stag: Immortality lives in you!

Starry sky (blue): Innocence. Be innocent!

Stigmata five: Refrain from evil acts!

Stigmata on feet: Believe in a better I.

Stigmata on hands: The life of the spirit is apparent in you.

Stigmata on the sides: Remain in patience!

Stigmata, open: You live in the revelation.

Stone, large, square: The spirit of prophecy, as a foundation for building.

Stones, small ones, hanging on strings: Hold on to your inner guide!

Straw: You worry unnecessarily.

Strawberries: Everything will be right.

Sun: Procreation is alive in you.

Swan: Stay in hope!

> (No matter how much it storms and waves, the swan cannot perish. So also with man when his hope is alive).

Sword: You are wrong! (Truth is born with pain).

T (the letter itself and seeing it spiritually inwardly): The Word has become flesh (life force) in you.

Tongs: Trust your leader in you!

Torch (burning): Be innocent in thought!

Tower: Search the human heart! (Faith stands in the heart like a tower).

Tree, with green leaves: Knowledge will become strength in you.

Trees, flowering: the soul in its growth.

Triangle with one eye or point in the middle: I want to give you second sight!

Triangle: Free spirit will. The measure of the mind.

- Depth: The head.
- Width: The acts.
- Height: Self-knowledge.

Trowel: Search!

Trumpets: Retribution.

Violets: Be gentle!

Wagons: Railway carriages or other wagons: Perverted desires and passions.

Walls (ruined or in disrepair): Don't look back on the past!

Wasteland (dead): Man remember who you are without the spiritual self.

Water flowing down from a mountain: Go into the depth!

Water (large amounts, or sea): The worldly stands in your way.

Weight: Watch that your actions are good.

Weights: Spiritual Truth.

Wheel: Step forward!

Whips: The evil principle which comes from annoyance. Watch over it!

Woman (a beautiful one from whose mouth an animal emerges): Beware of women!

Word: Be free in the soul.

Words (seen written or printed): The spirit speaks. You will become free and redeemed!

Words (painted in oil): You shall attain the Word and receive revelation!

(Words that are written in us. All forms shape words).

Wreath (crescent-shaped): Spiritual gifts

Wreath (round): Thoughts. Think!

Yardstick: Stay in order!

Yellow: Rejoice in the spirit of love!

The language of life of the inner self

Except for the first "I", these refer to human activity.

I in written or printed letters: Love of the noblest force.

I the common human me: The temporal, the animal.

I in white light: The natural (truth).

I in the fire light: The creative.

I in the sky-blue light: The source of life (the Word).

I black as night and dark: Passions in the material.

I in the sunshine: Self-knowledge.

I in humility: The bride, the testimony.

I pouring out water: The reminder to spiritual obedience. To sacrifice oneself.

The I of faith, deeds and justice: Is the revelation in man.

Addition: The language of the animal-I in us has become subservient to the natural human being.

Part Four

Recollections from Under the Adepts

The Hartmann Version of the Soul Teaching

Originally, this section was titled "Memorable Recollections" in Hartmann's book "Under the Adepts," which has never been translated into English until now. He claimed that this was a set of his old personal "diary notes" taken during his time under the instruction of a Rosicrucian, whom he does not name. I have given the entire series of his notes in full. These originally appeared in the second section of his "Under the Adepts."[216]

Memorable Recollections
Diary notes collected among the Rosicrucians and destined for the few who are capable of feeling and comprehending the truth contained herein.

1. Wisdom is a precious treasure known only to those who received it by the grace of God.

2. Despite all the many learned in the world, one has to become a child and learn letters through the art of living.

---
[216] Hartmann, "Unter den Adepten," 1900.

3. If you want to find the Philosopher's Stone, you must descend into the interior of the earth. Whoever wishes to understand this must first be ready to adopt higher feeling and thinking.

4. Lift up your soul to me. I want to show you wonderful things.

5. We can only bring the exterior into the interior if we are permeated by the spirit of love.

6. The elemental spirit comes from external nature. The mental spirit (being the spirit of love and justice) is from the angelic world. The third spirit is the light and this the divine thought.

7. Man is of God, for the sake of the Word, out of nature for the sake of the Spirit and out of the elements for the sake of witnessing all creation.

8. The air is water, the earth is fire, the sun is life, love is the spirit, light is thought, life is eternity.

9. The grace of God is self-knowledge.

10. What we see inside are the pictures of our actions.

11. Before man can control the organic processes of his body, he must first be able to control the emotions of his soul by the power of his mind, for the body is the expression of the soul. You have to go from the inside to the outside, not from the outside to the inside, because you have to be mentally developed in order to be able to perform spiritual things.

12. Excessive physical work tires the body. Yet work in the spiritual (Divine Spirit) can cause physical pain through the spirit that permeates the marrow and bones.

13. No one can approach the fire in which God dwells, because it is the spiritual Word. In itself, it must be kindled by the light, which itself becomes the fire (or words).

14. Just as rocks gradually disintegrate, dissolve, and transcend into another being, so it must be with the opposites in us.

15. Man crucifies himself through the sensual when he is subjected to it instead of subjugating it himself.

16. God gives us a spiritual name for our progress, so that we may remember our mission through it. This name should be a force for us in times of doubt and unbelief. It should raise us from the animal state and that of the material, and give us the state of consciousness that allows us to become a reflection of spirit.

17. "Love God over everything and your neighbour as yourself." How do you keep this commandment?

18. As the church bells call people to worship, the voice of the soul calls man to God.

19. Like the gold that is taken from the earth to be purified in fire, so too must the soul be drawn from the flesh to be purified in the fire of faith.

20. The crown of life is the knowledge of truth. It should grace the head of man. He who possesses it has truth and can explore the depths of deity.

21. The human heart is like a harp. If the strings are tuned correctly, there is perfect harmony.

22. The heart is an encasement of thought. Not in the head but only in the heart can the mind develop to sense divine feelings.

23. There are no keys that open the door by themselves. We have to apply our hands to use the keys. The action proves its strength.

24. No man can perish as long as hope lives in him.

25. If there was no mistake, there would be no struggles to overcome. So the truth must be born with pain.

26. Those who want to be righteous must do what their faith demands and this is difficult. Suffering is the life of faith. Without it, faith is dead.

27. A pure, innocent human heart can always see and feel the sky, and enter and leave it at will.

28. As a stream of water penetrates from the heights to the depths and destroys everything that is not sustainable, so too our spirit must penetrate into the deep chambers of hell and produce new flesh and powers.

29. If faith is alive in our hearts, it carries us over the high mountains and deep valleys. It flies over the wide seas and penetrates the thicket of the forests.

30. He who has inner contentment feels in himself the bliss, which has no end.

31. The passions are the clouds that hide the light.

32. All forms are words, but the soul-spirit is not a form. It is the Word (the power) of Life.

33. In the hands is the action to practice good things. The love of one's neighbour must be effected through the hands.

34. If you love God above all else, you must stand firm in everything that comes over you. But when we waver or fall, we realize that our love is not perfect.

35. We should endure everything with patience, whatever comes upon us, especially from our enemies, and seek not justice, but tolerate everything, even if the heart bleeds.

36. In a man striving for the divine, the lower influences also appear more strongly as a result of the energy thus awakened, because there are two poles that fight each other. But if you seriously think of your spiritual name in self-confidence, you will be astonished by its power, to which all the lower sensual thoughts must give way. Man must, as it were, awaken God to life, for God is conceivable only as power in us, and we must recognize Him in thought as primordial power, in feeling as efficacy, and in all our actions as creative power in revelation.

37. Being educated in the art of living is a task that every human being should set for themselves. The road to true life, to the higher spiritual light and to self-knowledge, is not easy and only succeeds in a steadfast courageous person. For light and darkness, as powerful contenders, meet each other in man.

38.   Anyone who has come to the resurrection in the spirit does not need to be reincarnated unless one voluntarily undertakes a mission for the world.

39.   Man can be regarded as the noblest creature because everyone has received a spark from the Primordial Mind, which is God. For this spark connects with God and with the spirit of the world, bringing it into harmony with the world soul. If you want to walk the path to immortality, then you must embody the idea of God in yourself by the word "Let it be!" It must be so through your actions.

40.   The right spiritual guide each person has to find within themselves is the spark of God in us and it can be perceived in all five senses when they are awakened and alive. Remember, the student has no power over the master. The guide resides within us in freedom and manifests itself in love and grace to the one who willingly submits to it. We must strive to come to the Spirit and to stay in it, and then not to step out of it during times of necessary trial.

41.   Do not worry about the past and do not worry about the future. The past has no value for the seeker of truth, and the future arises from the present. In the present, the divine spirit reveals itself in man as a light surrounded by the radiance of the spiritual sun.

42.   A person who endeavours to progress on the path of self-refinement is impeded on all sides by obstacles: from God, from nature, and from men, all of which are steel him for the spiritual path of self-knowledge and self-control. This is not easy nor everyone's calling. Many are called, but few

are chosen. The path is difficult, the dedication even harder, but without battle there is no victory. Therefore, never cease in your struggles to awaken the higher "I" in you to life in striving to reach the true spirit.

43. The spiritual path is not easy. One can penetrate into the truth, and one has already landed in it at the first revelation within. But to come to the source of truth requires years, for it is the very essence of the centre of the spiritual life. The triumphantly resurrected person can draw from it, but we still lie in a grave of our manifold passions..

44. Man's task is to rescue his true self and bring it up to where it belongs. Man's life on earth is short, and therefore it is his duty towards God and himself to realise the eternal in himself during this life, so that when he departs his soul may shine in the divine light.

45. The working of the Spirit of God in man is mysterious. Blessed is he to whom the golden rope of the redeeming power of grace is thrown, and who grasps it and allows himself to be pulled up by it through the goodness of the omnipotence of the Eternal.

46. Not everyone is ready to know the truth until he has gone through the secret school of life. The theory may be very beautiful but living in that truth for ourselves is our goal. The way to the light is only gradual and slow, but courageous persistence never retreats.

47. Spiritual revelations within us do not happen because we want or desire them, for our will is of this world and only inhibits the active spirit in us. But as soon as our will ceases

to want, the will of the spirit becomes manifest in us. Then a birthing occurs that is a useful revelation to us.

48. Man can only find the ultimate purpose of his destiny within himself. Where else could we find our rest than in our innermost being? In the innermost is the divine. The more we penetrate into it, the calmer we will become. The more you descend in yourself, the more spiritual power will increase you.

49. Where the material begins, we must fight with our will to drive out that which hinders us. But if we come to the interior, to the very threshold of the sanctuary, then our willing shall cease and we shall be free.

50. There are no disciples in the spiritual realm who do not put obstacles before themselves at some point; but it is precisely these that bring us to awareness and stimulate in us ever anew the desire for the higher.

51. Everyone has their own spiritual guide, but not everyone has the grace of God to perceive it in everything.

52. Whoever is in the battle of rebirth, should not look to the right or to the left, but wait until they have established a firm foundation on which it is no longer possible to fall when the storms come. He who stands firm can examine and learn everything by seeing it all as passing.

53. The word practice is a grace of God because only that which comes down from above can ascend again.

54. Truth is everything material that we see, touch, hear, etc. on the outside. But revelation is what we perceive inside in all five the senses and not what exists on the outside.

55. Spiritual obedience is when you fight as much as you can against self-will.

56. When the body is ill and attacked, the inner senses emerge stronger, because then the nerve-forces are weakened, and with it the will to live.

57. Where there is no temptation there can be no fight and no victory. Whoever has nothing to combat in himself is like a dead man who is never able to attain real life. Losing in such battles is not a disgrace, but it is a sign of weakness if one remains discouraged and does not rise again.

58. When the inner senses are awakened, through them we perceive the presence of the higher ego within us. Above all, it can do the greatest good work which anyone may accomplish in oneself, by elevating us to the light, and not letting the dark powers have power over us.

59. Anyone who is dissatisfied with what he has received makes himself unable to receive more. The greater a pure thanksgiving resounds to the throne of the Eternal, the clearer and brighter it becomes within us. He who is mentally grateful for the little things he has received will be granted something bigger.

60. There is a twofold "Inner Word," one true and one false. The false or deceitful Word comes forth through self-will, the true Word through self-denial. He who no longer want to remain merely in their lesser self, but let's God's will reign, will never go astray. Such a person is in true self-awareness and is purified in rest. Therefore, he also receives the true Word from God. The dissatisfied and agitated man

is always wrong, and therefore his Inner Word is wrong, and he deceives himself. Give glory to God alone and let him become truth within you. The true servant of God is chosen to be a witness of God in this World.

61.	The born-again man is begotten by the one who takes power in the world, power in will and achievement, in being and becoming. God begets himself in man and bears witness to himself in and through him. No one recognizes Deity but the one who captures Him in oneself. Love is the good, grace the truth, and man the temple in which God reveals his power and glory. Only through him alone can peace be had on earth.

62.	God states: "I am Eternal Love. He who holds himself to Me is My property, and whoever turns away from Me is lost." It cannot be otherwise, for the sake of freedom is to preserve the free will of man.

63.	Stay, O Lord, always in the Son of Man so that the resurrection in him will become power, strength, and glory. For in you alone the true life will celebrate its triumph in every single human being who embraces you with his whole spiritual being.

64.	Love states: I demand nothing from you except that in the maelstrom of the world, in the family, and under the effects of the various opposing forces, you always remember me. I am love, and anger is far from you. In love and wisdom I educate you. In patience I receive you. In grace I deliver you. In righteousness I raise you. Your desire is to be my will. In this alone I am master within you.

65. We started from God and in him is our home. If you want to come home, you have to yearn for it. Our home is the light, and those who aspire to the light will rejoice that a star is shining that announces their home. Take the view of a childlike perception, forget the evil in you, then love will be the power that animates you. The worm that nibbles in you is created by your own will. You are bound to him. Only the creature that rises to its Creator is free.

66. We can only bring the exterior into the interior when we are permeated by the fire of love.

67. The greatest in heaven is the manifest Father. The smallest thing in the world is the seed that Heavenly Father put in us.

68. Faith comes from revelation. The will comes from faith. Out of feeling comes the fear. Out of fear the awareness. From that awareness the intellect. And from the intellect the spiritual knowledge.

69. We love each other by having a spiritual free will. The counterpart of love is the hatred from which all malice springs.

70. Spiritual freedom is in fighting the desires and passions of one's own body. The spiritual life is in drawing instruction from within. The mind is restrained by seeing everything that is external as passing by and not getting attached.

71. The will is a power inherent in man. It has its seat in life and this in the blood. In the outer man, the blood is the will over the flesh, and in the inner (celestial) man, the Word of God is the power over the flesh and blood. The

power of this Word is the truth, and we recognize it by bringing the Word to life in our feelings. But this is done by practicing the prayer of the heart and learning to obey the commandments of God.

72. The soul is in feeling, its power is in thinking and its revelation the Word. The Word connects the body with the soul, the mind connects the soul with the spirit. The power of thinking is breath, and the power of the Word of God in man is manifested through the actions he can accomplish.

73. Matter is an external, visibly acting thing. Spirit an invisible force.

74. Thought, Word, and revelation become active through the innate instinct for the divine. Rebirth gives the soul the power to rise to higher spheres.

75. We should not indulge in forebodings, false feelings, dreams, and imaginings, for they are seldom truths, because they come from our external mind, whereby we become oppressed and uneasy in our inner being.

76. Past, present, and future lie in man. We live through the past through the mind, look into the future through feeling and act in the present through the Word.

77. Hope is a consuming fire for one who does not persist in it. It is the inward power of faith. Love is stronger than faith and hope because it transcends these two forces.

78. The thought goes out of the heart, penetrates man all around! It goes back again into the centre, into the heart.

As light the thought enters the heart and as shadow it goes out again. The shadow is the witness of the light and it shapes the different expressions of forms.

79. Darkness is when a person has no knowledge of God. Spiritual blindness is when the spirit manifests itself visibly and people do not recognize it. Wishers are those who (in religious matters) pretend to be teachers, but do not have their doctrine out of God, but from books, from hearsay or outrage.

80. It is insult against God if we promise him in our hearts not to do evil anymore but to do it again.

81. Just as in outer nature the roots of the trees stand deep in the earth and absorb all the forces of the sun, moon, stars, planets, rain and air and attract it as a container, so it is with man. All the heavenly impulses must go down to rise again, purified of the Spirit through the love of God. (Nothing ascends to the sky, which did not first come down from heaven.)

82. The seat of thought in man has three stages: in feeling, in the heart and in action. Its seat is in the feeling of a person (neophyte), who takes up the spiritual path; in the Word through the heart, where it is conceived in a man who has progressed further in the spiritual; in the action of a perfected man, who carries out what he thinks through his limbs.

83. One should believe in God in the hope that one receives and obtains what one believes. One basis of this belief is to learn to believe in oneself. This is the hardest thing because we have to conclude from the visible to the invisible. Only

a faithful disciple of wisdom can accomplish it. Another foundation of faith in God is the revealed creation that we see, which is there to lead our contemplation, and yet another is the doctrine, or the evident Word, that we must hear and receive within ourselves, make it come alive.

84.   Faith is a great power of action, but the power which emanates from a man who has the true faith is an agency, that is to say, it is transmitted through the works of the man who has faith and brings about a manifesting spiritual birth out of him. This is the agency of spiritual guidance.

85.   One should love oneself through an accomplishing faith. One should "lay the hands upon oneself," spiritually speaking, and eradicate all material pains, for they inhibit the divine spirit. Learn to feel the power, the greatness that is placed in you and in every human being. It is God's love gift that you should seize hold of, provided that you have the will, faith and courage.

86.   Faith is spiritual life. It makes the spiritually dead in us alive and in the materialist the living dead.

87.   In the head is the seat of power and it has authority to exercise dominion over the whole body. However, the blood must give birth to the body again. Otherwise, this sapling would be lifeless and abandoned to the storm if it were not transformed anew by the power of thought.

88.   The laying on of hands is a practice that has the purpose of strengthening faith, for the same power that emanates from the fingertips (in the case of an enlightened person) vividly emanates from all parts of the body when we

express the Word in the will. Blessed are the people who unite their spirit with God's spirit.

89. The soul of one person connects with the soul of another across the distance through "air, water and sound." The "air" is the power of the connection between the two souls, the "water" a pregnant thickened air, and from it emerges the form of the person with whom we wish to exchange, so that we may recognize him. The "sound" is the life of the whole, namely the words he speaks out to us.

90. The secret forces in nature we call faith, will and revelation. We recognize them from their manifested expressions. They are there but we have to liven it up from a stagnant birth. Believe as much as you can, but do not forget the will and its discernment.

91. We have recognized God as power in us. But this power is not God Himself, but an emanation from Him, and it is subject to us according to our will, be it good or evil.

92. People cannot grasp the divine because they themselves have no truth in them.

93. Evil has no "I" itself. That is why it is and is not. It cannot create anything either. It is limited to effect.

94. The Lord says: "If you want to approach Me in spirit and in truth, you must have no thought and no word ready. But only approach Me through the sole activity of feeling."

95. You should breathe the spiritual ether (love and knowledge). Not the raw animal air.

96. The brave do not die, but the doubter spoils the way.

97. All beginnings lie in the silence of oneself. Only then can one achieve the desired goal. The Eternal One says: "When I speak to you, I do not need your thoughts, but if you want to talk to Me, so put in thoughts that which you wish to speak, giving words in an internal way to Me. Then I will grant your request because I am love. I sprinkle roses and lilies on your path. You have sown the thorns yourself."

98. The transfiguration on the mountain is the fire of love towards man, which overcomes everything and in which we sacrifice everything out of love. This overcoming leads us to an intercourse with the blessed spirits.

99. Nothing obscures the spiritual eye more than ingratitude

100. Man overcomes his bleeding wounds by believing in the law of God, which is proclaimed to him through the mouth of the enlightened one. We should believe this Word, even if it does not come true according to our own meaning.

101. "Aliveness" is an electric force produced by the will. The will itself is this power.

102. We cannot see the Father when we are not the children of God but remain as children of the world.

103. The blood is movement. The will shall be the Lord. He who cannot inhibit the movement (the passions), has no will of the spirit.

104. The outer man shall become the foundation of the inner man, that is, we must receive the external divine power within us and fix it in us through faith, for this belief is the foundation of the inner man out of which the outer comes in and the inner comes out.

105. All forms of heaven and earth will pass, but the Word cannot pass away because it is perfection.

106. The forms we see are the shadows of light. If we have no light in us, we live in darkness and darkness is death.

107. We are to fear God by doing what he wants. Then we have wisdom.

108. In the hands is the action, and in the limbs the very power of the spiritual will.

109. A word of truth heals the sick soul.

110. The body is a witness of the creator (of mind) in nature. The power of the spirit is in the feelings of the senses.

111. To help yourself, you have to firmly stand on your feet and firmly believe that God's power is working in us, and that we can be helped through it. If the faith is great, then we can eliminate great evil. If it is small, we can only be helped a little. But in order to help one's neighbour, we must be penetrated by love, and that of a divine quality, not of the flesh, but of the Spirit of God, who brings only the good.

112. The spirit of man is composed of three properties: supernatural, natural and unnatural. Supernatural is what the materialists cannot understand. Natural is when man realizes his true nature. What is unnatural is when man denies the qualities he possess because he fails to recognize them. The unnatural human being must become natural before he can grasp the supernatural.

113. The light of the spirit is rest, contentment, blessedness. The shadow of the spirit is grief, worry, pain. The first

commandment of the spirit is that one should put on a body that is equal to it.

114. The gravity of the spirit lies in the body with its passions. The gravity of the soul lies in the material senses. We must learn to fix the spirit in ourselves, for we cannot bring forth a new birth on the outside, but on within ourselves. For this reason, we are in this material world. The Lord wishes to take shelter in our material sheath, but our self-will makes us resist, and as long as no one wants to surrender to Him, as the presence in our body, the true work cannot happen.

115. Man's power lies in his obedience. Whoever resigns to the will of God is a champion.

116. Peace in ourselves is a star that divides all the clouds in our heads.

117. Spiritual perception is when man lives in the light according to the degree of his knowledge.

118. As man thinks, so is his soul, because the soul is the form of thought. The soul performs the activity of the senses and presents them to us in images, just as they are, be they beautiful or ugly, true or false. The soul is man's mirror in which he sees his mental thoughts and his sensuous thoughts materialized and embodied.

119. The soul is the first revelation of deity because it is an outflowing of deity. The power of the soul is natural because the body must be its foundation. The characteristics of the soul are thus: First, that it is immortal. Second, that it can move outside the body. Third, that it can take form. The spirit can only connect with the soul through the body. It

is the power of the soul. Without it, the soul cannot have an open-hearted life. Without the light of the spirit, the soul remains in darkness for us. The states of the soul are recognized in the interior by one's desires.

120. The language of the soul is the thought. Its garment is the light of knowledge. Its head the divine thought. Its feet the truth. Its heart the love. And its adornment wisdom. The sting of the soul, or the spike by which one can create wounds for oneself, is the lust. Man has to learn to strip himself of material thoughts in order to become one with the soul. This can only happen in higher consciousness. It is not about becoming merely intellectually great in thought. There should only be more light and soul.

121. The soul speaks in our hearts through the feelings which prevail in it. It can be compared to a butterfly, but its wings, through which it penetrates into the height and depth, are still bound by our self-will. If this is suppressed, it is free. It is the "fragrance of the Lord" when it accomplishes its will.

122. The soul is in man, that it may be revealed and lead us through life on this place of worship. But for their unbelief, many do not know that they have a soul. Through the knowledge of the truth, the soul is drawn from the depths. The heaviest pressure that weighs on it is the sensual lust of the flesh.

123. The soul can only stand on its feet by the power of the Word. It becomes visible through virtue, perceptible through practice, audible through divine thoughts, and acts on one's neighbour through the power of truth,

which must be manifested near and far. Seeing, hearing, feeling and doing are the powers of the soul.

124. The grace of God is the light that animates the universe, and in man it is the light that enlightens the soul. Through the devotion of the soul, the spiritually dead in man is brought to life. Its highest level is faith. Only through this can it work in us. It takes nourishment from our thoughts and brings it into the flesh.

125. The soul can only be bound to the body by the material thought. It is then its slave and its perception wrong. The soul of man is life at birth. When it reaches full understanding, it is free will. In a spiritual man it is feeling, thought and Word, and in a perfected one it is the mastery of nature. For the man who does not connect the soul with the spirit will see it escape again in death. The opponent of the soul is our material mind. We cause it the biggest pain if we disobey the soul's voice. He who obeys it will fare well on earth.

126. Love, hope, faith and knowledge unite the soul. Those who do not have these powers are like a wild beast tearing itself apart. We crucify the soul through doubtfulness and torture it through lies. But if we believe its Word, we glorify it inwardly, and then we can also glorify God outwardly through deeds. In a person who has no consideration to these words, the soul is dead.

127. People try the soul by feeling inadequacies in life. What they have is too little for them and they never recognize it. What they do not have, they want to possess in perversity.

128. We have achieved the victory of the cross over the soul when the blessed spirits and messengers of God can speak to us face to face. We have to strip away everything that is attached to us from material birth. This opens up new inner senses in man.

129. Out of the spirit of obedience, faith rises mightily.

130. Mortify your flesh with the spirit of truth.

131. The soul is a life, with we have to struggle. The first fight is with your own body.

132. The food of spirit is wisdom.

133. The resignation of the soul is the testimony we give to deity.

134. The joys of life are dreams, but the divine pleasures of the Spirit are everlasting.

135. In nature is a center, which attracts everything to itself. This center is the human heart, and the circles (aura) that surround it are formed by the emanations of our feelings coming from the inner forces. Through the emanation of thought light may arise from the center to act on these circles, and the inner life expands. The light of God (Wisdom) is the life of the soul. His love is as great as his wisdom. No one can grasp it. His grace flows through all the limbs.

136. Through our love we work on the inside and free of our will, and this spirit, in turn, affects our body.

137. The reason the soul may rise is due to the spiritual gifts it has received.

138. The shadow of the free soul is pure light. Its desire is to redeem the dead and remove evil through the power of knowledge.

139. He who knows the truth in himself spreads out a seed which bears fruit a thousandfold.

140. He who has true faith also has the second sight, because it arises out of it. The second sight reveals itself through rising thoughts. "Transfiguration" means to recognize truth. Man's forebodings of the intellect give rise to an inward knowledge without the second sight. True inner feelings, however, come from the Word of God, which is recognized by the mind when it reflects upon it.

141. Many weaknesses eventually lead to greater strength. Many sufferings crown the head of man.

142. The inner sense of man is a revelation whose source is deity and leads to perfection. It is best to perceive the inner sense in listening to holy feelings, to be silent in oneself, and to live in the belief that God is with us in all that we do. Through the practice of exercising the good, this inner sense is encouraged in its growth. It is the newborn spirit man which strives to reveal itself in us.

143. Dying is changing, or passing from one state to another.

144. The outer is life, the inner light and the inmost the love. The spiritual ego produces its revelations through the powers that embrace it.

145. Man should look into his own inner being, as through a fine "looking glass" that he should have in himself. Without this, he sees only rough impressions of the perceived images.

Only by stripping away the passions can the feeling for what is true be refined to perceive in clarity.

146. The center of all nature is God's visible truth.

147. No man can earn the love of God. It is a gift of grace from the goodness of the Lord.

148. The purpose of man is to raise his soul from the bonds of the flesh so that he may become a true child of the eternal Father.

149. The spiritual willpower in man is an internal impulse, and this impulse is love. It has its seat in the emotions. Only through this drive can we get to the path of rebirth.

150. Faith is a secret and invisible force. Its active life is suffering, humility and patience.

151. Those who have been transfigured by purification wear "white vestments," meaning that low thoughts can no longer take effect in them.

152. The spirit is love leads us to the goal. Through the fiery love of God, the soul becomes a power in the flesh, and the Word flesh through the life of the soul. Through it enters the thought of God. Through the thought we perceive, as it springs from the heart, one prays to God with the soul.

153. The human heart is only a true temple of God when we become children of God.

154. The rebirth of the soul reveals itself through the opening of the inner senses, i.e. through divine seeing, divine hearing, feeling, smelling and tasting. Through the soul one can

accomplish the utmost, when one acts with the whole of one's emotional life on that which one wills to accomplish.

155. He who wishes to think rightly must learn to seek and recognise with all his soul what he wants to consider. He who wishes to climb upwards must be just in himself.

156. In height lives humility before God.

157. The foundation of truth is its knowledge. The fruit of it is the knowledge of God. The mirror of truth is the soul in its revelation. Truth is reality. True is everything that is real.

158. In truth lies the seed of wisdom, in wisdom the seed to love, in love the seed to freedom. The truth-breath is the power of God.

159. By "renunciation of worldly pleasures" one understands it to be humble before God and content with the material lot that has been destined for us.

160. Silence and waiting are worth more than talking and acting fast. If you want to be smart in your speeches, stupidity is always the focus.

161. So beautiful on the outside and so empty inside! Man of the world, what more can you want?

162. He who with patience can endure the injustice of the world is honoured in heaven and sought by men on earth.

163. Hope has never been to blame, unless you have cheated yourself.

164. The unbeliever is bound to death. The lack of faith drags him down to his own death and ever away from the divine.

165. You live inwardly by hearing the Word of God in you.

166. The prayer that strengthens the most is that act of remaining in faith and living in it.

167. Man becomes natural again by recognizing himself.

168. Obedience lifts us to the highest heaven, and justice lifts us up from the earth.

169. In true repentance we feel joy and ease in ourselves.

170. The true spiritual life springs from sacrificing oneself.

171. In the natural, the spiritual is an invisible force, and in the spiritual, the natural is the revelation of our five senses.

172. Wisdom is the revelation of the truth.

173. A "saint" is the one who lives according to his faith.

174. Man "takes away the sting of death" by the grace of God.

175. The key to the gospel is the Holy Spirit.

176. The key to justice is love. Only the righteous can love God in truth.

177. Spiritual humility is the absence of covetousness. It is contentment with what we have, both spiritually and materially. It is also the key to redemption.

178. God is honoured by our knowledge, and our own lives through the actions that we accomplish. Bur our neighbour is honored by the forgiveness of his mistakes.

179. Man's will dwells in his reason. The master of the will can bring good or evil in itself. The leader of the will is man himself.

180. Purity is innocence. Only one who can sacrifice himself lives in purity.

181. Our fervor is the animating life within us.

182. Man is free insofar as salvation lies within himself and he is willing to take hold of it. Nothing holds him back but his own disbelief.

183. Man only begins to live when he gives birth to himself.

184. For the man who realizes himself in truth, everything in the world has no real value. We should leave everything that is dark.

185. The greatest honour will be for the one who sacrifices himself.

186. The great path of struggle is one of love and renunciation.

187. True love is not desire but being. One arrives at this through selflessness.

188. In truth is love, in love is life, in life is light. This is the light of which we bear witness.

189. Power stops where violence begins.

190. The purpose of existence is to reach true knowledge and freedom.

191. Only that which we know is our own property.

192. By self-knowledge one defeats death.

193. Man's freedom is not in his thoughts, but in his actions.

194. True being is immortality. True self-consciousness springs from where we recognize the power of God and His revelation within us.

Part Five

Mailänder's Path According to Franz Hartmann

The Baptisms of Water, Blood & Fire

From *Theosophical Siftings* Volume 1, 1888:

"What is True Christianity?"
By Franz Hartmann M.D

Christianity is a religion. The word "religion" has evidently three distinct meanings.

1. In the first place, it signifies the practice of a certain kind of spiritual training by which the higher principles in the constitution of man are developed and re-united (bound back) to the divine source to which they belong. In this sense it is the same as Yogism (from Yog, to bind).

2. In the second aspect it implies the knowledge of the true relation existing between microcosmic man as a part of the All and the macrocosm of the spiritual and material Universe. In this sense it is a science.

3. In the third and common acceptation of the term, "religion" means a certain system of forms, ceremonies, and usages, by which some supposed external, deity is worshipped or propitiated, and his favour obtained, so that the sinner may escape the deserved punishment, and evade the law. In this sense it is a superstition.

To become a "Christian" of the third order it is merely necessary to submit to a certain ceremony called Baptism, whose mode of administration varies in the different sects; but it seems that to become a real Christian some other baptism is necessary, namely, the Baptism of the Water of Truth, the Baptism of Blood, and the Baptism of the Living Fire of the spirit.

The first baptism, with the Water of Truth, means the attainment of spiritual knowledge, and corresponds to the first of the four noble truths taught by Buddha, "Right Doctrine".

The second, or the Baptism of Blood, is commonly supposed to mean a shedding of blood by martyrdom in the defense of a belief in a historical Christ. But such a process would be a loss of blood, and not the inception of it, and could not properly be called a "baptism." The best way to obtain information in regard to this "Baptism of Blood" will be to ask those who have received it, or who are receiving it at present.

There is a certain class of practical Occultists, whose inner senses are opened to a great extent, and who have been taught by no one but the spirit within themselves and their own experience. They say that the Baptism of Blood means a penetration of the growing spiritual germ in man through the flesh, and blood, and bones of the physical body, by which even the gross elements of the physical form are attenuated and purified, (Compare the "Elixir of Life" in the Theosophist.) and that this process produces pains and sufferings typically represented by the suffering, crucifixion, and death of the man Jesus of Nazareth.

They say that no one can be a true follower of Christ, or a real Christian, who has not undergone this Baptism of Blood, and experienced the pains of crucifixion, ("That which was from the beginning", etc. John, Epistle I, i) but that man, having passed through that occult process, becomes an adept, when only the highest baptism, or the last initiation, the Baptism of Fire, will be necessary to enter the highest attainable state (spiritual power), and to become a Son of Light.

But, it is asked, what has Jesus of Nazareth to do with that process? How does the latter come to be typified by his suffering, and what is the rationale of it?

It is claimed that at the beginning of certain historical periods — when old religious truths are about to be forgotten, and the idolatry of form assumes the place of true religion — some great spirit (planetary) appears upon the earth, incarnated into a human form, and by his word and example impresses the old truths forcibly upon a number of receptive minds, to communicate to others, and thus lay the foundation of a new religious system, embodying old truths in a new form.

It is believed that the man Jesus of Nazareth was the mortal form in which such a spirit was embodied. The latter being no less than what I believe every planetary spirit to be an emanation from the Universal Logos or Word. (This has nothing to do with so-called "stigmatisation", the latter being merely the result of a strong imagination upon a weak body).

But what is the Logos? Or, to express it better, how can we form a conception of it? We can conceive of no other God, or supreme Good, but the one which lives within ourselves, and which is said to be the image of the Universal God reflected in the purified human soul, where it (He) may attain self-consciousness and the knowledge of self. The Universal God may be described as the incomprehensible centre from which proceed the elements of Love, Life, and Light in the various modes of manifestation on this different planes. The whole of Nature is a product of the Spirit of God, being poured out throughout the All by the power of the Word, which is the life or thought rendered active by will.

The same process which took place in the eternal Macrocosm of the Universe takes place in the inner world belonging to the Microcosm of man. "No one can come to the father but through the Son". That is to say, no God will take his seat in the interior temple of man, except through the power of the Word; in other words, by the concentration of thought and goodwill upon the divine germ which rests in the innermost centre of every human being. If we concentrate our love upon that centre of good, the divine germ will begin its active life, and the interior world gradually become illuminated by the Light of the Spirit. As this principle grows it will penetrate the soul and, through the soul, all the lower principles, even the physical body, throwing off the impurities of soul and body; and the more impurities there are present the greater will be the suffering, typically represented by Jesus, until finally the Baptism of Blood is completed, the soul purified, the animal ego dead, and the man has become "a Christ", or an adept: that is to say, one in whom the [6th] Christ principle has taken form.

It will readily be seen that this process is more difficult to accomplish than merely to go to church, to pay the dues to the priest, attend to prayer-meetings, and perform the prescribed ceremonies. To accomplish this process requires a constant meditation of the highest kind, and a continual employment of will-power to keep away the disturbing elements of evil, which, in a person who strives for light, are still more boisterous than in one who is indifferent; for, as soon as the spiritual light kindled in the centre begins to radiate its life-giving rays throughout our interior world, the "dwellers of the threshold," the evil Egos, created by evil thoughts and selfish desires floating at the periphery of the soul-sphere like clouds sailing through the atmosphere of our earth, begin to feel the destroying influence of the central sun, and battle for their existence. Still this atmosphere of evil must be penetrated before we can reach the luminous centre and the tranquil heaven within, and this is done by clinging to the principle of good and virtue, whose rays radiate from the centre. This principle will at first be felt only intuitionally, but as we feed it with good thoughts it grows, and the interior spiritual senses become opened, so that we may see and hear its voice distinctly, and without any fear of misunderstanding its meaning.

The "below" is always in exact correspondence to and related to the "above". We are immersed in an all-surrounding but invisible ocean, of life, whose waves pervade our psychic organisation, in the same sense as the volumes of air enter our lungs, and as the latter stimulates the life of the body, likewise the former stimulates the growth of the elements of the spirit, which draw their substance from the lower animal principles. In the same way the caloric rays of the sun enter the body of plants and stimulate the assimilation of the elements which are drawn from earth, water, and air.

Those who have gone through that occult process will require no proof of the truth of these assertions, because they know it is true by experiment, but the "exoteric Christian" and sceptic, having no such experience to assist his faith, may arrive at a certain degree of conviction by using his reasoning powers and logic in conjunction with the teachings of the Bible. Christ is reported to have said, "Except ye eat the flesh of the Son of Man and drink

His blood, ye have no life in you" (John vi. 53), and again, "I am the living bread, which came down from heaven; if any man eat of this bread he shall live for ever" (John vi. 51). Now, this seems plain enough to every student of occultism, and if translated into scientific language of modern occultists, it would mean, "Unless you absorb and assimilate within your psychic organisation the sixth principle (the Christ), which is the only permanent and immortal principle in the constitution of man, you will have no sixth principle developed in you, and consequently possess no immortal life, at least as far as your personality is concerned (for the divine and now unconscious germ within you cannot die, but will re-incarnate again). But if you absorb the principle or spiritual life and develop the spirit within you, so that it grows through your flesh and blood, then you will have drunk from the Elixir of Life and received the Baptism of Blood and become a Christian, an Adept; for 'Christ' will have taken form in your body, and being Himself immortal, you will be immortal through Him".

These views are corroborated by the great Christian mystic, Jacob Boehme, by Jane Leade, Paracelsus, the Rosicrucians, and I can find nothing in these which would in any way conflict with the esoteric doctrine as taught by the Eastern Adepts. If any difference in opinion could arise it could only be in regard to the person of Jesus of Nazareth or Jehoshua, and whether he lived exactly at the time claimed by the modern Christians. This question I must leave to someone wiser than myself; but it seems of no great importance to me; for the existence of the Christ principle is disputed by none, and the man Jesus having died, can only be a Saviour to us at present, if we study His character and imitate His example.

Twelve Stages of Rosicrucian Initiation

From *Under the Adepts* elaborating on Mailänder's Soul Teaching statement 293.[217]

On the Twelve Stages of Rosicrucian Initiation
By Franz Hartmann M.D

The soul light is a spiritual force and is called "faith" by the Rosicrucians.

It is then asked why faith is called a "Light" and the answer is that it is a state of consciousness; but consciousness is life and light, beginning with the dawn of knowledge and ending with the full day of supreme self-consciousness, in which the sun of wisdom shines. Everything in creation is a form of consciousness, a thought of God, a light, which sends its rays from its center; everything is a Word in the language of Nature, which through its existence and essence proclaims its essence and being; and the more glorious a thing is, the higher is its power, the greater is its light, and the more sublime is the Word, which proclaims its existence and the essence of its origin. An old and true proverb says, "All true wisdom comes from God, is in God and leads back to God. To believe in God is to feel the existence of the Most High in the heart; faith is the consciousness of his omnipresence, which proves itself through its existence. The spark of God in the heart is the consciousness of the highest existence, a force which, as it grows, penetrates the mind, soul and body and, through its perfection, overpowers and expels all that is inferior.

That which a man loves most, and to which his soul is most attached, is his faith, even if he cannot at all comprehend it with his intellect; that which he does not love he cannot in truth believe,

---

[217] Franz Hartmann, ed., *Lotusblüten* 15 (1899): 238.

even if he intellectually comprehends it; for faith is the power of union, and where there is no love, no attraction, there is no union and consequently no self-knowledge possible; for no one can recognize a power as his own unless it has become his own by its union with him. He who loves something transitory only believes in transitoriness, unites himself with it, and is transformed again; for the state of consciousness into which he thereby falls is not of eternal existence; but he who loves the highest ideal above all else has the highest faith, the highest power; he is on the way to union with the highest ideal, and the highest ideal is realized in himself. Therefore, as the Bhagavad Gita teaches, the Godhead speaks to man: "He who loves me above all things enters into me, and my greatness, my being, my power and glory become his own." But in order not to misunderstand this, we must remember that the Godhead who speaks this to man is not a foreign God, but the Creator of all things, i.e. the source of all things and consequently also the source and reason of our own being and existence.

Imagination is a fleeting thing; it jumps in an instant to the most distant regions of space, but always falls back to earth. The love for a thing created in our imagination is not a love for the true, but for a fantasy, and changes with the creations of our imagination. The divine self-consciousness (faith), which springs from the steadfast love of truth, is not changeable; whoever has once attained it can never again lose it completely; for it is the Eternal in man himself which feels and recognizes the Eternal. The awakening of this power does not depend, as the leaps of the imagination do, on the arbitrariness of man, but as the plant grows without stretching of its own through the intake of food, so a slow and often imperceptible growth takes place in man through the inner intake of the spirit of self-knowledge, whereby the soul is carried up from never having to reach higher, from height to height, when it overcomes the resistance of the sensual, just as the plant does not grow by negligence, but makes its growth possible by eagerly searching with its roots between the stones for the food that is suitable for it.

Indian philosophy speaks of different states of consciousness or planes of existence which the human mind must penetrate and through which the human soul must grow to attain self-knowledge of the highest existence (Brahma- vidya), and these are described by Shankaracharya in his "Tattva Bodha" or "Awareness of Existence." Accordingly, the Rosicrucians have learned from their own inner experience twelve stages of faith or "soul consciousness."

These are indicated as follows:

First. The seed, i.e. the spark of spiritual life and knowledge of God contained in every human being. Since God is the sole true essence of all things, and everything that presents itself to us objectively is in itself nothing but an incorporeal appearance, God is also in all things; but only in those creatures which have reached the stage of mankind does the ability of divine self-knowledge become a force capable of development; in the lower creatures it is still asleep, i.e. it is only latently or "potentially" present in them and awaits development in the course of the future periods of evolution.

Second. Nourishment. We know that if there were no sun and sunshine, there would be no fire and light on earth; for when wood or coal is burned, it means nothing else but that the heat and light stored and bound in it are released again by the combustion. Likewise, if there were no Spirit of God in the universe, the same could not be revealed in man. But the Spirit of God is everywhere. The order in the universe and the effects of his law in nature bear witness to his presence, and everywhere like is nourished by like. A well-known proverb says, "As it is below, so it is above, and there is nothing so slight in the world that when the lower is stirring, the superior above it does not oppose it." If therefore the love of the highest stirs in man's heart, the love of the highest comes to meet him and God sacrifices himself.

Third. Knowledge. From the spiritual growth comes knowledge. The more man unites himself in his consciousness with the inherent divine nature through the power of love, the more he recognizes it as his own divine being. There is no talk of any objective recognition, neither externally nor internally. In order to recognize something objectively, it must be an object, i.e. something separated from us. The more we want to look at God objectively and to investigate him scientifically, the more we separate from Him, and fall prey to self-conceit and pride, which hides our true nature from us. The wisdom of God is not human wisdom. It is not the earthly man who recognizes God, but the God-man recognizes himself in Him.

Fourth. Purification. There is no more purifying agent than fire and light, both outside and inside. When the love of truth is kindled within, the light of knowledge springs forth from it, before whose rays the shadows of lies and error disappear. The fire is the will. If the will is good and strong, a purification takes place from the inside outwards. The false, false desires and imaginations of the illusory states of our being disappear and the true self comes to light. In order to make this clearer, we imagine that God is the true I of the universe, and every person is a personified thought of God, which through this personification attains its own I-ness. Accordingly, the only God would then be personified in countless appearances. Each of these personalities again has its own will and conception, from which again many "spirits" arise, whose creator is man himself, though without his knowing it, and each of these consciousnesses growing in him represents, as it were, an "illusory ego" in his world, which stands in a similar relationship to his ego as he stands to God. These false lives, the representatives of his desires and passions are removed by the power of the awakening true self-consciousness. Without this self-consciousness, man is not just a single personality, but an ever-changing series of such, of which sometimes one, sometimes the other appears. Through purification, man emerges from the multiplicity and returns to his own unity, i.e. to himself. If we take a comparison from outer nature, the clear sky represents the pure mind of man; the ever-changing clouds are the personalities. Man walking in spiritual darkness considers the cloud to be his own ego; man, in whose mind the sun of wisdom has risen, whose light divides the clouds, recognizes in himself the clarity of heaven and his true ego as the sun, whose light fills his heaven with its glory.

Occult philosophy teaches that the substance of the mind is extremely plastic and can take on different forms. Every thought imbued with will create a form in it, the shape of which corresponds to the character of the thought from which it springs. The sphere of man's thoughts is populated by such crystallized ideas, they are the inhabitants of his thought world. Noble thoughts take on a noble form, base ugly forms. Through the purifying influence of the Spirit of Truth, all ideas arising from self-delusion are driven out and destroyed.[218]

Since the mind (soul) is intimately connected to the material body through the astral body, the force that purifies the mind is

---

[218] (Original Hartmann footnote). This type of vision, which is visible to the eye of the seer, can even be made outwardly visible. This explains the various benign and malignant phenomena in the lives of the saints, of which s. B. in Görres "Christian mysticism" a lot of examples can be found. See J. Joseph Görres, *On Christian Mysticism*, 4 vols., 1879.

also transferred to the physical body and can cause states in it whose observation would lead us away from the main point here.

Fifth. Transfiguration. When the impure is removed, heavenly peace and clarity enters the mind, which is also reflected in the outward appearance of man. It takes place when man overcomes his self-delusion and no longer works for his personal advantage, but only for the good of the whole. At this stage, the feeling of humanity in man becomes powerful and, he recognizes himself as a totality in the whole and thereby enters into intercourse with the gods, because this transfiguration also extends to his spiritual powers of perception.

Sixth. The Mystical Death. The consequence of this state is the complete death of all selfish inclinations, desires and passions. Man, who has come to the self-knowledge of his higher I, is no longer under the dominion of his lower nature. He recognizes his position in the universe and sees that his personal appearance on earth is only his own shadow. He has risen from the grave. His body walks on earth. He himself is an inhabitant of the world of heaven. For him there is no death.

Seventh. Justice. He who has grasped the spirit of the whole also grasps the law, and this law is the love of the good in everything, which makes no discrimination, and favours no creature to the detriment of change, but makes justice happen for all. In this state there is no longer any doubt about what is right or wrong. Here prevails complete impartiality of justice and judgment, which cannot be bent or falsified, but judges all things rightly, and weighs all things in the balance of equity; also opposing all oppression, cruelty, and deceit.

Eight. Consecration or Initiation, or in another word, sanctification. Man has not only overcome his sinful nature, but the same nature, filled with the power of goodness, resists sin.

This power overcomes all opposing forces and forms a protective wall around the soul, so to speak, through which nothing belonging to evil can penetrate.

Ninth. Rebirth, i.e. transition from the corruptible into the imperishable. The heavenly man is revealed in the earthly man. The spirit penetrates and enlivens the inner being and transforms the lower perishable soul forces into imperishable higher ones. Man reborn in the spirit behaves to his mortal personality in a manner similar to how the rose does to the bush on which it grew, or like the fruit to the tree. Both are a substance of one, and yet completely different from one another in their characteristics. Man reborn in the Spirit of God is the flower that the tree of his life has born, and also the ripe fruit that has carried the seed for future generations (incarnations).

This seed is the Word of God in man, or the spark of God's eternal love, without which man would be nothing more than an intellectual animal, and not capable of true spiritual progress. It is the Spirit of God in man, and apart from this there is no other spirit in man in truth; for that which intellectual man calls his own spirit is nothing other than a thinking activity stimulated by the Spirit of God and often applied wrongly, comparable to a drop of thaw that sparkles and flashes in the sunlight in many different colours

Tenth. Spiritual Vision. When the heaven of the mind has become clear in man, and man has come to divine self-knowledge through rebirth in the spirit of God, then everything in the kingdom of the spirit is also clear to him, because he sees everything in the light of the sun of wisdom, which has risen in his inner being. His spiritual (heavenly) senses are opened, not only the eye, but also the ear, feeling, smell and taste, and the spiritual world no longer has any unfathomable secrets for him.

Eleventh. Harmony or Union. In this state of perfection, which is not transient but permanent, man recognizes his own divine self as the Creator in all creatures, not only in all men, whether good or bad, but also in all animals, gods, angels, and demons, in everything, for everything comes forth from this self. This self-knowledge is for him no longer the result of logical speculation, but self-realization, and puts an end to all discord, disharmony and division, which are an obstacle to inner peace and quiet.

Twelve. God, that is, Perfection. The last shadow of singularity disappears. Man who has become one with God is omniscient, omnipresent, and omnipotent in the Spirit of God. It is the highest state of self-knowledge and bliss, called Sat-chit-ananda (existence-knowledge-bliss) in Indian.

It will now be clear that the Rosicrucians were not so much concerned with intellectual research and knowing what to do, but rather with divine self-knowledge, and the power of true faith that leads to this knowledge of God! For in comparison with the knowledge of the true self of all beings, which is the Lord of heaven and earth, all human knowledge has only a most insignificant and trivial value, and without this higher knowledge it is completely worthless, which is why one of the old Rosicrucian mottos was "I seek nothing, and want nothing, and desire to possess and know nothing, in heaven or on earth, but Christ crucified in me." But they were not at all modest with this, as one might believe, for he who in his inner being comes to know the Lord of his self, the God-man, which can only happen by becoming one with him, recognizes and possesses everything in him; he has found himself as his Lord, the Master who teaches him everything and the light which illuminates everything.

Part Six

Mailänder's Path According to Gustav Meyrink

Gustav Meyrink's Transfiguration of the Blood

From Meyrink's "Verwandlung des Blutes," found in his bequest:[219]

Annie Besant now rewarded me for my zeal by admitting me into a certain inner circle of the T. S., whose center is in Adyar in India. I gradually received instructional letters from her concerning yoga. From that moment until my resignation about three months later, you would say I led the life of a quite insane person. Following the regime, I lived only on vegetables, hardly slept, "enjoyed" a tablespoonful of acacia gum dissolved in soup twice a day (this was warmly recommended to me by a French occultist for the awakening of astral clairvoyance), I practiced asana (Asian sitting postures with legs folded) night after night for eight hours, holding my breath until I felt the shivers of death. Then, when the new moon came, I rode out in the deepest darkness to secret myself at a hill called the Cave of

---

[219] See Meyrink, "Die Verwandlung des Blutes," 12. My own translation.

St. Prokop, which is far from Prague, and there tied my horse to a tree, sat in asana and devotedly stared at a certain point in the sky until dawn broke. The regime to undertake all this I is what had fished out, insofar as I could not get them, from Annie Besant, and from books of Indian or medieval provenance. And whenever my confidence threatened to be dashed out so that despair might overcome me, then suddenly some antiquarian bookseller would send me a catalogue in which some hitherto unknown works on yoga, magic, and the like would get my hopes up again.

One night, I was sitting on a bench by the Vltava River and because it was winter riding out to my preferred hill seemed impossible because of the deep snow. Behind me was an old bridge tower with a large clock. I had already been sitting there for several hours, and despite being wrapped thickly in my fur coat I was still shivering from the cold, staring at the dark grey sky, struggling in every possible way to attain what Mrs. Besant had explained to me in a letter as the inner sight. All in vain. Up to that time, and indeed from my earliest childhood, I had an astonishing lack of the one ability which many people have, which is being able to imagine things, such as a picture or a familiar face with closed eyes. It was completely impossible for me to say whether one of my acquaintances had blue, brown or grey eyes, dark or light hair, a straight or a curved nose, if I had not first expressly looked at it. In other words, I was used to thinking in words and not in pictures. I sat down on that aforementioned bench with the firm decision not to get up until I had succeeded in opening up the inner sight, remembering the sublime example of Buddha Gautama, who had once sat down under the bodhi tree having made a similar decision. Of course, I only lasted about five hours and not days and nights like him.

Then the question suddenly came to me, "what time is it?" There, just in this moment of being torn out of my contemplation, I saw a mental image with a sharpness and clarity, as I never before in my life remember to have perceived any real object, a huge clock glaring brightly in the sky. The hands pointed: twelve minutes to two. The impression was so powerful that I felt how my very heartbeat became extraordinarily slow. As if a hand were holding it steady. I turned around, to look at the tower clock, which until then had been behind me. The fact that I could have turned around earlier and thereby could have gained a clue as to how late it was, was completely impossible, because I had sat motionless on the bench for the five hours, as strictly prescribed for such concentration exercises!

So it was that the tower clock also showed, just like the visionary one in the sky, twelve minutes to two! I was downright blissful. Just then a slight fear arose, "Will the inner eye remain open?" I resumed my exercise and for a while. The sky remained dark grey and closed, like before. Suddenly it occurred to me to attempt at making my heart beat so calmly again and so I worked at bringing it to the peaceful state it had done by itself during the vision or perhaps, most probably, even before the vision.

This was not so much an insight of an ordinary kind, but rather a half felt guidance I took from the meaning of a sentence of the Buddha, which impressed itself on me as if it came from the invisible mouth of the Hooded One. The sentence was, "From the heart things proceed, are heart-born and heart-bound." At that time, this sentence was deeply imprinted in my blood!

It is not merely a beautiful sentence that one reading it can simply feel as such or should allow its words to pass from one ear and out the other. No! It is the epitome of a whole philosophy, a realization that everything that we think to perceive here on earth and in the material cosmos as objectively existing outside of us is not substance, but a condition of ourselves.

Furthermore, the sentence formulates a subtle key to the true magic and includes not only theoretical realizations in itself. Many times in my life, when I thought I was lost, it helped me like a strong hand holding itself out to me for support. Many years later, when I once fell three hundred meters from the Dent de Jaman mountain, I remember just when I first began to fall on my left shoulder I was still able to give myself a different direction by twisting my body, which meant that I did not end up landing in a quarry, as would have otherwise been inevitable, but fell into in a gorge packed full of soft snow. Whether the sentence saved me, or whether it was He who gave me that idea in lightning speed, "Turn your body!?" Who could say that with certainty? But it seems to me that such was the case.

I sat on that stone bench and again stared at the sky. At last, I had succeeded in bringing rest to my chest and the calm in my heart that I had before attained. The result was immediate.

It was as if a circular piece of the night sky receded, and it had detached itself from the atmosphere and expandingly slipped into ever more immeasurably deep distances of space. I observed myself as sharply as I could. Soon it became clear to me, all this was happening only for the purpose, so that you set the gaze of the eye to the horizon. At the same time, I remembered reading in books that the gaze of somnambulists in their state of ecstasy was always like looking into the distance. It was not long before I succeeded in controlling not only the heartbeat, to a small but sufficient extent, but also the direction of my eyes, and what I had never known or witnessed before in my life now occurred almost instantaneously: geometric shapes were first formed in the circular section of the sky.

The first sign to appear was the so called "In hoc signo vinces," being a cross standing in a Latin capital H. I witnessed it with calm and with an uninvolved heart, no trace of self-conceit or the like seized me. Incidentally, I had little understanding for Christian ecstasies even at that time. It interested me only as a spectator then. With this time honoured sigil a series of visions began so that other colourless geometrical figures appeared, some resembling magical signs as one sees in medieval Faust grimoires.

Only much later did colourful and luminous images appear to me. Very often they were Greek statues, such as those of Pallas Athena. All these images had one thing in particular in common. They were of such a sharpness, colourfulness, and brightness that things of this earth comparatively appeared faded and blurred against them. As difficult as it is to comprehend, at times I could see them from all sides or angles at once, as if the inner eye were not a lens, but a circle, as it were, drawn around the visionary image. Eventually I got so much practice in the Inner Sight that I could conjure up the vision of an image at will, even when I was not at all externally relaxed, but, for instance when talking indifferently in some way with someone random. A favourite exercise for me was, while reading the newspaper in a coffee house, to look at a large, tangled ball of rope that often appeared to me, and then to unravel it loop by loop in my mind, as clearly as if it were actually present before me, until at last it lay before me curled up in a circle, like a wound anchor rope on a ship. A circumstance to which I attach great importance, since it proves to me that it is not of the outer man alone, that there is something deeper that causes the images: even today I cannot conjure up arbitrary visions before my eyes completely at will. It would be worthless if I could. It would have diverted from its actual purpose as a communication for me. Only the day consciousness would then speak to me of what I already know in other words!

The ability of the inner sight, which I acquired on that winter night, was the first step in my destiny, which made me, so to speak, suddenly jerk out of being a merchant and into a writer, for my imagination now became objective. Before I had thought in words. From then onwards I could also think in pictures. These images I saw as if they were bodily. No! A hundred times more bodily and more real than any physical thing. "Visions," it has become a catch phrase in the mouths of the multitude. Few have experienced them, but they all claim to know exactly what a vision is supposed to look like. Wispy, veiled, that's how they blather. I too used to talk like that when my eyes were still blind.

Consider how a person is celebrated as a poet if their keen observation of nature is puts to paper with ink. He is a miserable photographer, nothing more. Such means have nothing to do with the arts. With theatre, perhaps. Vision has the greatest influence in painting, provided that it takes hold not only of the eye and innermost feeling, but also of the hand, so that one is capable of reproducing the image. I know many painters and I have tried to clarify to almost every one of them that they would not need a model at all if only they knew how to open the inner eye. Still, they listen to me without understanding. Not a single one has tried what I have advised. They prefer to skim through nature, bewitched by the silly doctrine that nature (the outer one, that is) is the teacher of all art.

After that experience on the stone bench, I wrote a letter to Mrs. Beasant. Yet she was silent for a long time. Then I got the answer, "Try to tear the veil." I did not understand what she meant, so I asked again and again. From the embarrassing phrases she wrote me in reply I soon concluded that Mrs. Besant had no idea of what further to do with me. Then, a strange event, connected with further visions I experienced finally cut the bond that tied me to the Theosophical Society.

Still, I continued my own research in the field of yoga. This led me into the path of Bhakti Yoga, as it is called in India. This is the yoga of seeking after God by fervour and by religious ecstasies. The hooded one, or a kind fortune, saved me from being overcome by such ecstasies and from being crushed or torn apart like all the unfortunate ones (or fortunate ones, if they should reach the goal) who suffer from the ensuing splitting of the consciousness or seeing the "Light," like Ruysbroeck. Such as these become disenchanted in it, thinking they have found God as an object, forgetting that the God they always talk about can only always be subject. They seem to me like unfortunately mothers who carry and yet they die upon giving birth to their child. Who knows whether changelings are not sometimes born in the invisible world of causes, and then growing to Molochs, let trickle poison from that realm into the brains of mankind, which we call mental illness?

Before being accepted into the inner circle of the Theosophical Society, I too received the urgent warning: "Whoever does not hold fast to the end will be exposed to unheard of dangers in the spiritual realm." When I informed Mrs. Besant of my resignation, she answered me briefly:

"I know the snakes of Mara are many." Mara is the Indian term for the tempter.

I will briefly indicate the main experience which led me to leave the Theosophical Society. The real purpose of the three-month probationary period which precedes final acceptance into the "Inner Circle" is to find a guide. A guide, in fact, is indispensable on the path of yoga and magic.

Having assumed that through the visionary images, such as those which appeared to me, I would receive a hint or indication of the way in which I could find a guide, I ceaselessly endeavored to bring forth ever new visions from within myself by calming the heartbeat and straightening the eye axis.

Then one night, again at about two o'clock, I was sitting in my bachelor room in the well-known yoga position of Padmasana and practicing the Pranayam according to the Hamsa outline. This consists in rhythmically drawing in and expelling the breath alternately through the left and then right nostril. For me, a peculiar drowsiness in the head used to be the consequence of this exercise. I did not know then, that is to say, fortunately I did not know, that the secret purpose of Hamsa pranayam is to induce a kind of self-hypnosis. This I later found out only in 1914 when a young Brahmin whom I met told me. During these exercises I instinctively fought the anesthesia. If I had not done it, I would probably be an unhappy medium today, or otherwise suffer from having a split consciousness, perhaps even from religious insanity. But throughout this path I held onto one precious insight, an insight which forms a gem in Buddhist teachings, that one must always remain conscious!

Sitting motionless, I looked steadfastly at a large black circle on the wall, which I had left constantly hanging there for practice purposes. Suddenly this paper circle became bright. It was as if a luminous disk had slid in front of it. I was completely awake and sober. Then a life-size figure of a grown man appeared in it, dressed in white, but without a head! At that time, I had already read a vast number of books with occult content, and since I have possessed an excellent memory ever since I was a young man, I immediately remembered a passage from one such writing, in which it is expressly stated, that appearances of human-like beings "without heads" mean extreme danger for the one who sees them. Although an uneasy feeling came over me, I nevertheless continued to stare at the illuminated disk, and then asked myself the question, "Why is this happening to me? I do not partake of any drugs like the morphine addict who has such visions of people decapitated figures at the end of their life?"

In the meantime, a face formed under a turban, separated from the torso by a gap the width of a finger, and soon the features became visible. It was a face so aged that it would be difficult for me to find a comparison. For some while the vision remained, then with a sudden jolt it vanished. Yet for almost a whole day the impression remained, as if it had burned into my consciousness. I could not dismiss such a thing as I had previously done with earlier visions. It was a most sickening feeling, which gave way only when at night, in the open air on the deserted street while walking home from a meeting of the Theosophical Society Lodge, which I had founded, I indulged in a new exercise of contemplation concerning the search for a guru (guide). Again, I calmed my heart, and then, although the street was well lit by lanterns and I was walking quite fast, a greenish ray of light, as thick as a man, burst into appearance and shot down from the sky a few meters in front of me. Where it struck the earth, the green light split into three parts forming the shape of a three-pointed anchor.

I paused to look at the phenomenon coldly and calmly. Not for a moment I had the sensation that it could have been something other than a vision. Here my innermost aversion to allow myself to be disturbed by visions proved itself again. I held my heart with force because I felt that the presence of this ray of light sought to work a stronger effect upon me than had ever been the case with my visions before. Imagine what happens when a person who has never had any such experience in this field encounters something like this. They can fall into the delusion that they have received a so-called divine revelation. From then on they drift out into the boundless sea of theistic delusion without any support or docking rope. I would like to expressly here state that in my personal opinion absolutely anything and also everything connected with theism is false light! I want to unsettle its position out of its pious faith or make it sway! I already stated earlier I do not accept the belief that for those who are indifferent to everything occult, and remain materialistically minded to the bone, there is only complete ruin, and they shall only stagger through life. At the same time, far be it from me to assume that the enthusiastic "hot ones," or those who think theistically, will be spat out the mouth of life. If I am to make a confession of faith, it would perhaps be best stated like this: who is the Jacob of the Old Testament, who wrestled with the angel of the Lord all night long until he prevailed over him? Answer: One who does not take the torturous path of martyrdom in the theistic faith!

The English scholar Max Müller in London emphasized the high importance of Ramakrishna, the last Indian prophet. This Ramakrishna, a Bhakti yogi kat exochen, once said, "For a long time man serves his God, obeys what He tells him, and does all his deeds only for His sake and for His glory, and yet remains less to Him than a slave. But then one day God will hand over all His power to the faithful servant and sets him upon His own throne." Although there will not be too many of such, this here is noted for those who walk or long for the path of the Bhakta!

When that bright green light, as described, manifested before me, I asked myself, "What does this mean? What should be communicated to me with it?" I could not even remotely think of rejoicing at its sight, as a pious person might have done. Then immediately a "thought" came to me in reply. I call it a thought because I cannot find another expression. Actually, it was almost the hearing of a voice. It clarified to me, "The anchor means as much as holding on or hoping. The three prongs, wait three days."

After three days something so strange happened that I hardly dare to even write this down here, fearing that people might think I was speaking untruths and making fun of all who read what I write. Shall I affirm that it is not so? You may believe me or not. It is up to you.

On the third morning after that night, I went very early to my store, an exchange office in Prague. The assistant was sweeping the store, and apart from him no other staff was present. I was a little surprised to see a gentleman sitting in the waiting room despite the early hour, so I asked what he wanted. He was a well-dressed middle-aged man with glasses and squinting eyes.

He mumbled a few unintelligible words in answer to my question, then pulled himself together and said with a hint of volcanic determination, "I don't wish anything from you. I believe you wish something from me!" Immediately I recalled the phrase that had come at the sight of the anchor, "Wait three days!" The conversation with the strange gentleman, which was conducted quickly and without any gaps, revealed his name was "O.K." He had been a professor or teacher of chemistry in Japan for a long time, had been living in Dresden for a long time and he was a spiritualist. He was not a spiritualist in the common sense, but rather a "pious one," or a Bhakta yogi in the Christian way. The gift of automatic writing was a talent of his since childhood. Yet it was not spirits who made themselves known by writing through his hand. No! It was none other than Jesus Christ himself! I listened politely and soon found out that this time I was not dealing with a swindler, as often had occurred in previous cases, but at worst he might have been a religious enthusiast.

I will state that at that time, despite my youth, I possessed an uncommonly sharp awareness of human nature and was able to distinguish lies from truth with unerring accuracy. That is no wonder, considering the young age I had entered the banking profession as young as I did. It grants you the keen awareness to start reading people's hearts like an open book.

I asked Professor K. to come with me to my apartment, since a money changer's store did not seem to me the right place to discuss questions about occultism, yoga or prophecy. Upon arriving there, Mr. K. told me that at exactly three days ago he had been doing his usual automatic writing at night, when suddenly his hand resisted to finish a sentence he had begun. Instead, his hand wrote a new sentence of instruction "Go to Prague to a banker named M. (to me namely), so that you can be with him on the third day early in the morning!" K. assured me that he had never heard my name before. He did not know that this was the hour which coincided with that of my vision!

Therefore, he had come to Prague entirely randomly and had come to see me. When I asked him what he had to tell me, he said that he did not know exactly, but he had the feeling that I was in great danger and that he should save me. He suspected that I had fallen into the hands of "Asian devils." In fact, until then I had not remotely hinted to him with any word that I was engaged in yoga.

I remained together with K. the whole day and listened to the strange, I almost want to say rapturous speeches he gave me. He insisted the only way to become a spiritually more valuable person from a dull ordinary man was the way of revelation, which would be granted if one followed certain pious Christian apocryphal instruction, which were most aptly called Rosicrucian, since they were foreign to both the Protestant and the Catholic Church. He gave me such instructions. Since he had an astonishing knowledge and seemed to be a scholar in the best sense of the word, he gradually cast a spell over me, I being much younger than him anyway and therefore not as self-confident as I should have been.

I am not surprised about this today. After all, theism is in the blood of every person who has been brought up as a Christian from childhood. In those who do not deal with spiritual matters in the course of later life, something that like atheism takes the place of theism. I only suspect that such atheism is rarely genuine. Mostly it is buried theism. During K's speeches, the theism of my childhood years awoke in me again, became all the more awake in me, as the memory of the vision of the man with the cut-off head suddenly seemed take on a deep meaning for me. It reminded me as if that experience had been something similar, even if only in a small way, that Paul had before Damascus.

K. mentioned to me a number of books that would be particularly beneficial for me. They were the works of a certain Jakob Lorber. I immediately acquired and read them thoroughly. If ever a person felt sick, it was me when I read them. But I lied to myself about the situation with a perseverance that I no longer can understand today, by trying to believe that what was written there, with sweetened rose water, was somehow the epitome of salvation.

If the meeting with Professor K. had ended with nothing more than a reference to the godly Jakob Lorber, it would still have been at least bearable for me. Although I would probably never have grasped the meaning of the appearance of the headless one,

293

if I had it later would spared me from the long thorny path. A thorny path that took a full thirteen years of my life.

The matter of his visit that day ended like this: K. had boarded the train back to Dresden in the afternoon, when he suddenly turned around and said, "Right, one thing, and the most important, as I just remembered, and I forgot to tell you. There is a man named X.Y. living in Vienna. He and many other former Theosophists, Germans, and Englishmen, even an Indian Brahmin named Babajee have become the disciples of a real Rosicrucian, who is a simple craftsman like the once the famous Jakob Böhme. This Rosicrucian is said to live somewhere in Hessen and knows and teaches the true Yoga, as it is concealed and underlying in the New Testament."

It was like I had been struck by lightning. The mentioned X.Y. in Vienna was also a friend of mine of quite a long time. Moreover, K. had also named him together with X.Y Dr. Franz Hartmann, who I knew had gossiped to the Theosophists about belonging to the most "initiated of initiates" in yoga. If he and X.Y. and still others, whose names I will not mention here, were disciples of this indicated Rosicrucian, then at last, in accordance with the prophecy of the inner circle of Theosophical Society, I had finally found the expected "Guru."

I immediately went to Vienna and visited my friend X.Y. Staying as a guest was also an Englishman named G. R. S. Mead, who was Secretary of the Theosophical Society in Adyar in India. By a sign indicated with his hand he let me know that he was also a member of the "Eastern School" (Inner Circle). I revealed that I had undergone a certain experience recently and asked if I could speak openly in front of X. Y. Mead nodded. I began to describe the apparition of the man without a head. Suddenly Mead asked if the man had worn a white Brahmin cord from shoulder to hip.

I answered in the affirmative. Then Mead asked if I would have noticed the tightening of a knot in the cord. I closed my eyes to recall the image from that night. Immediately and accurately saw that knot and indicated the nature of how it was knotted. Mead arose to touch his forehead and said, "T" is the Master!" I glanced over at X.Y. and it seemed to me that he was suppressing a mocking smile.

When I then began to describe my experience with Professor K., X.Y. became more and more serious. At the mention of Professor K's last words concerning the Rosicrucian guru, X.Y. quickly put his finger to his lips, telling me to be silent immediately.[220] I broke off my sentence with a few phrases. Later X.Y. took me aside and told me things about the Theosophical Society that made my hair stand on end. I believed them! The evasive answers that Mrs. Besant had given me to my questions by letter concerning Yoga, the ghastly rubbish that had sometimes appeared in Theosophical Siftings. This and many other things strengthened me in the assumption that everything X.Y. told me was correct. In addition to this, a short time before I had

---

[220] Eckstein doesn't want Mead to know about Mailänder, to conceal him from the Adyar T.S. Interestingly, Mailänder's Soul Teaching statement 63, "What is the Will o' the Wisps? The wrong thoughts in the inner person," contains a unique symbolism that the wisps are misleading notions. But G.R.S Mead mentions wisps in the same way, in Lucifer, the theosophical journal, in 1893. Wahle published his version in 1896 in Vienna, writing, "They occur, of course, in such a way that the concept of a knowing could develop prematurely and without justification, and 'concepts' have sprouted up to bring light into these events, but they are will-o-the-wisps, souls of the desires for knowing, pitiful postulates of an empty form of knowledge, saying nothing in their evidence." Rudolf Steiner references the Wahle version many times as the first of stages of Rosicrucian initiation. See G.R.S. Mead, "Fierce Impetuosity," *Theosophical Journal Lucifer* 13, no. 74 (1893): 109; Richard Wahle, *Das Ganze der Philosophie und ihr Ende: Ihre Vermächtnisse an die Theologie, Physiologie, Ästhetik und Staatspädagogik* (W. Braumüller, 1894).

received a letter from William Judge of New York (Judge was considered a direct initiate of the so-called Mahatmas of Tibet) to the effect that the "Masters" did not recognize Mrs. Besant in any way as President of the Society and had expressly authorized him to communicate this to the members of the "Eastern School." Everything I had believed up to that point wavered beneath me. I spent the whole night in exercises of contemplation. No image appeared to provide any hint for me. The hooded man seemed to have withdrawn his hand from me. Professor K. had vaccinated me against it and consequently the rash was breaking out.

The next day I told my friend X.Y. that I was ready to acknowledge the leadership of the "Rosicrucian" (his name was given to me). When X. Y. had finished listening to my words with great attention, he showed me a telegram which he claimed to have received only shortly before. It roughly read that I had already been accepted by the "Guru" a few days prior. The date of this acceptance coincided with the day I saw my vision of the anchor. X.Y assured me that this certain Rosicrucian was a seer in the spiritual realm, that sometimes even physical phenomena occurred around him, and I could firmly rely on the fact that the "new student" meant me and nobody else.

Full of jubilation, I wrote to Annie Besant that in accordance with the prophecy she had given me right at the beginning, I had found the one who was secretly to be understood in the title of the "Guru." Mrs. Besant's answer, that "The snakes of Mara are many," which I mentioned earlier pursed the matter on its heels. The man without any head immediately came to mind. I asked myself, "Who was this suspicious man without a head?" A symbol, of course, what else! But what did the symbol want me to understand? It announced disaster. This I could feel. But what is the use of such an announcement if no way of escaping the danger is given? What did the hooded ruler of my destiny intend to warn me about by revealing that appearance of the Brahmin without a a head? I asked myself and asked myself and yet could not find the answer! Was the "Eastern School" the man without head? Or was it to be this newly found Rosicrucian leader?! I wavered back and forth. In the thirteen years in the thorny path that followed, I asked myself again and again. I asked without getting an answer, at least not an answer I wanted, which would be clear, distinct, and not to be misunderstood. "Answers" I got well enough. Yet even the oracle Pythian said one thing and another time the opposite. Only today, after all which transpired years ago, have I come to know the true meaning of that ominous image of the decapitated man. If you consider it, you can easily find out the answer for yourself. I myself am afraid to say it openly. You can guess if you have carefully read what I have written.

A few weeks later I drove to the location in Hessen, where the Rosicrucian lived. He had once been a weaver, could neither read nor write, and had undergone strange experiences in the field of spiritualism, but called this the "preschool of true knowledge," which only could come from the heart when it began to speak. This speaking of the heart he called the Inner Word. It awakened with time and was bestowed with "grace" in the Christian sense. He instructed his numerous disciples by giving them sentences to inwardly whisper, sentences he received, as he said, through his inner voice for each student. By such inward whispering the speech of one's own heart soon awoke, besides a certain transformation of the body went with it, until at the end of the path the immortality of Christ was instilled in the disciple, and with it eternal life. In his view, the physical body was the place to begin with. Piety in the ecclesiastical sense meant very little to him if not accompanied with the aforementioned transformation of the body.

If I had learned nothing else from this man, other than the knowledge that the body had to be involved in the transformation of man through yoga, I would already be obliged to thank him for my whole life with this knowledge alone!

To achieve such a transformation of the body merely from one's own intellectual knowledge and effort, he said, was completely impossible. He was right in that, too. "There must be something from above that brings about the change," he said.

He, of course, meant Jesus Christ with this "from above" statement, the resurrected Jesus Christ, who has overcome death and is around us every day, and not the form of the crucified Jesus. For those who only look at that crucified Christ, as practiced by Catholic monks, especially the Jesuits, and do not follow the living, risen one, would have their "bones broken" or would be left hanging with him on the cross.

As an example, he liked to name Katharina Emmerich, the well-known stigmatized.

His teaching concerning the transformation of the body was extremely profound and strange. It often reminded me of the Gnostics and their claims.

He said, "Baptism, foot-washing, the Lord's Supper, and the crucifixion in its exact course, as recorded in the Gospels, all of this has to be experienced literally on one's own body, otherwise it would remain only a theory, just something heard or read, and would only have the value of Christian edification."

I got to know many of his 54 students. There was not one among them I could refer to as a bigot, with the possible exception of one old lady. Most were elegant, distinguished people, apart from a few simple craftsmen. There was no trace of asceticism or the like, neither in the "Führer" (Guide) nor in any of the students! All the more strange, was that almost everybody, over time, experienced on themselves these event type "processes," the "J...," as we generally called the leader, considered so important. These processes came in visions or, mostly in dreams, but not only, for they also occurred on the body. Even though no one knew beforehand what would happen! It was strictly forbidden for anyone to tell the other person whatever he was experiencing, for the reason that autosuggestion would be ruled out.

I want to mention such a "process" here, which was that letters appeared on the skin. Each such letter had a definite meaning and indicated the stage of development of each person concerned. The layman might now easily lean towards a superficial opinion that it might have been a worthless rapture or the like. Such a view would be completely wrong! On the contrary, I must confirm that the teaching method of that "guide" aroused an inner life, the richness and value of which cannot be understood by those who have not experienced anything similar for themselves. The change in my blood, which compelled me to become a writer, also took place during that period of my esoteric apprenticeship. This was quite apart from other transformations I experienced, of which I cannot go into here."[221] It was the previously described experience of the"opening of my eyes" which occurred on the bench by the Vltava River in Prague that was the first real freeing of my inner self.

As to how much the practice of sentence whispering affects the human being and how thoroughly it can bring changes to the character, here is an example of it. One day Dr. Franz Hartmann, known from the history of the Theosophical Society, who was also one of my fellow students, came to the leader and

---

[221] Meyrink, "Die Verwandlung des Blutes," 13.

asked him to accept a young man as a student, who seemed to be quite suitable to become a partaker of the teaching as seldomly seen. He had been living like an ascetic of the strictest order and had withdrawn from the world for years like a saint. The guide thought for a while, apparently listening to his inner voice, and then said with great certainty: "You are mistaken, Franz (the guide was a Swabian), this man is not genuine. He only believes it!" Dr. Hartmann contented that he knew the young man very well and any opinion that he was a fake would surely be wrong. "Therefore, I will give him an exercise, so that you can see how it is with his innermost being," replied our guide. Half a year later, Hartmann met the young man in a big city transformed into an elegant dandy. Most astonished, Hartmann asked him what had happened. "Oh, I had hardly done the exercise you gave me on behalf of that Hessian fool for a few days when an epiphany came over me and I resolutely threw all that mystical garbage overboard," said the young man with a radiant smile. A few months later he died of syphilis. "You see. He has shown himself," said "J." thoughtfully, when Hartmann reported the incident to him, "Too bad, I couldn't help him!"

Of all the many disciples the leader had, only two experienced virtually next to nothing, in terms of such spiritual events.[222] One was my friend L. and the other was me. Brother L. has since died with the serenity of a saint in old age. Why he, who was a devout Christian, did not experience anything like that, despite the fact that the Leader always called him his favourite pupil, will remain a mystery to me. With me it is reasonably easy to explain, for despite such a frantic effort that I made to adopt and live by the notions of "J.", I never became a Paulus from a Saulus.

I have spent thirteen years in practice, day after day, without

---

[222] The original German word is "Vorgänge".

missing a single one. I often put aside the most important duties the outer life had put in front of me! I practiced the "mantras" eight hours a day. Not a single event occurred. Whenever I complained of my misery, the Leader always looked at me gravely and said: "You must be patient." The only thing I experienced was strange, piercing pains in the surfaces of my hands and feet, as faint signs of the stigmata. Others had them much clearer. In some the stigmata were in the form of red circular patches. "Crucifixion pains," called the Leader them, signs of the change in the blood. There were no ecstasies in my classmates. Had it been the case, the leader would have expressed his strongest disapproval. For the main thing in his teaching was that clear daytime awareness should be sharpened and not divided or weakened. And this attitude of staying in the body, in contrast to "stepping out of the body," as taught, for example in the Mysteries of the ancient Greeks, is another foundation, valuable in the path of true yoga like no other, which the Guide gave me like a jewel to hold for life.

There is, in fact, a method of "leaving the body during one's lifetime," as common among occultists who consider it, so to speak, an initiation. In reality, it is the worst schizophrenia imaginable. It leads sooner or later to a high degree of mediumship and an incurable splitting of consciousness. Thus, the ancient Greeks, strange as it may sound, were in their mysteries nothing else than victims of a disease, except those who could make the leap over the chasm: "My God, why hast thou forsaken me?"

The doctrine of that Hessian simple man culminated in this: The soul of man lives in the body, not to leave it, as one who spins around to see that he has fallen into a dead end, but rather it is to transform the matter in which we are born!

In many of his experiences he resembled the seer Jacob

Boehme, who today is known to every educated human as a wonderful person. This teacher surpassed him as a clairvoyant in many degrees, but he surpassed him sky-high by this single realization that a departure from the world is wrong, however sublime and endearing this flight from the world may seem. [223]

Some will object on the part of those who have interest in mysticism. All mystics of whom the history tells, even the Gautama Buddha, preached and taught, "Flee from the world!"

The Buddha, for example, called it a burning house and said that fleeing from it, as hastily as possible, would grant truth, understanding and reason. I knew the teaching. Yet everything cried out in me: wrong, wrong, wrong! Although, there is a certain truth in this teaching I am convinced it must be interpreted quite differently! At least for a person of our present times!

We are free to think differently from the exalted models of the past. The pastis always poisonous if anyone makes a dogma.

I have mentioned that of all the students of the man in Hessen, along with my friend L., I was the only one who did not experience the transformation of the body under the direction of the "leader." His assuring comforting, that I had to wait patiently for success, made me languish in the fire of hope for thirteen years.

Later, after his death, which incidentally was a heavy blow to his disciples and their prophecies, Brother "L" one day told me that the Leader had confided to him that the lack of my ability to raise the fires of the exercises was due to the fact that in my innermost being I strived after completely different goals than the Christian one taught and preached by him. He saw it as a task to get me on the "right" path. I was very surprised when my friend told me so. I had never revealed, even with half clues, how alien the Christianity of the Church was to me, as was the

[223] Meyrink, "Die Verwandlung des Blutes," fol. 14.

Rosicrucian-Gnosticism taught by the Guide when I explored myself in hours of extreme frankness.[224]

Of course, I do not wish to disparage Christianity in any way by relating this. On the contrary, I am convinced that the world would be a wonderful place if there were more (real) Christians. I only want to confess that despite my most ardent efforts, I never succeeded in making the Christian faith my own, although I was educated in it from childhood. For those who are tepid, of course, such things may be child's play. But my approach at that was only lukewarm and flat in its growth.

I have called the thirteen years, during which I was the disciple of that leader, a thorny path. It truly was, but not only in the spiritual, no, also in the physical. It may sound strange when I make the statement that exercises, such as these described, not only these, but all exercises in yoga, whether they are incorrect or correct, do not only change the blood, but they also inevitably change one's external destiny![225]

Kerning claimed to have figured out how to use certain letters in order to bring about this "transformation of the blood," as I call it. In the work, one must whisper them like a litany! And, so did the late leader "J." prescribe exercises in similar way! Strange! "J.." could neither read nor write, did not know anything about Kerning at the beginning of his development, and nevertheless came to almost the same system "by himself!" The common explanation for such occurrences, that knowledge can be transferred only from mouth to ear or by the reading of traditions is refuted here as clear as daylight.[226]

---

[224] Meyrink exaggerates. In a letter October 13, 1900, Mailänder writes to Meyrink: "...Why do you not believe in Christ? Just because you do not recognize him. If you took the trouble to look for him in the truth, you would soon come to believe that he is in you and you in him..." Dilloo-Heidger *44 Letters to Gustav Meyrink*.

[225] Meyrink, "Die Verwandlung des Blutes," fol. 15.

Meyrink's Prediction for the Restoration of the Tradition

From Meyrink's *The White Dominican,* 1921.

The most profound secret of all secrets, the most hidden mystery off all mysteries, is the alchemical transformation of the external form. – This I say to you who have put your hand at my disposal, as a token of my thanks for writing this down for me.

The hidden path leading to rebirth in the spirit, which is talked about in the Bible, is the transformation of the body and not of the spirit. The spirit expresses itself through the physical form; it is constantly moulding and carving it; the more rigid and incomplete the form; the more rigid and incomplete the manner of its revelation; the more responsive and subtle the form, the more manifold its manifestation.

It is God alone, the all-pervading spirit, who transforms it and spiritualizes our bodies so that our innermost, primal being does not send its prayer outside, but worships its own form, limb by limb, as if each part were a different image of the divinity residing and concealed within.

---

[226] Meyrink was mistaken in writing that Mailänder did not know Kerning's teachings and came to almost the same system "by himself." Meyrink's typoscript was written quite late in his life, approximately 1927-1928 while Hübbe-Schleiden's above quoted notebook dates from 1884-85. There Hübbe-Schleiden mentions two books from Kerning, plus a third by Kerning's disciple. Then, Hartmann's lecture "Practical Occultism in Germany" dates to 1885 and describing Mailänder's path therein he also refers to Kerning elements such as the vowel letters IAO and consonants being used in the body. Furthermore, because Hübbe-Schleiden stated that such books can be borrowed from Gabele it becomes apparent that Mailänder cannot have come into possession of Kerning's books from Hübbe-Schleiden himself. See Hübbe-Schleiden, "Wilhelm Hübbe-Schleiden's Notebooks," 1884 1885; Hartmann, "Practical Occultism in Germany."

The change in physical form that I am talking about only becomes visible to the eye when the alchemical process of transformation is approaching completion. Its origins lie hidden in the magnetic currents which determine the axis of our physique. It is our way of thinking, our inclinations and instincts which are transformed first of all, followed by a change in our behaviour and, with that, the metamorphosis of the physical form until it becomes the body of the resurrection from the Gospel.

It is as if a statue of ice were to begin to melt from within.

The time is coming when the doctrine of this alchemy will be erected once more for many.[227]

Meyrink's Final Realization of Mailander's Path

Typescript from August 7, 1930.

Today on August 7th 30 in the morning at 10 am, after a long agonizing night, suddenly it was as if scales had fallen from my eyes and I now know what the real purpose of all existence is in truth. We are not to change ourselves through yoga, but we are, so to speak, to build a God, or otherwise in Christian terms: we are not to follow Christ but must take Him down from the cross!!! I am to crown the old man, whom I always see in the far distance, and dress him with purple and make him the ruler of my life.

I see him now also crowned and clothed in purple. The more perfect he becomes, the sooner he will and can help me. So HE then is the adept and I will participate in it only insofar as he will merge with me one day, because essentially he is my own self.

"He will grow, but I will dwindle!!!" This is the meaning of the speech of the Baptist! Only now I realize that until now I had

[227] Meyrink. *The White Dominican*. (Dedalus, Translated Mike Mitchel. 1994). Page 112.

been severely wrong and the cause of all my suffering was that I did not know all this clearly but instead believed: "I" had to perfect myself, me and not Him!

The Tantric exercises, like everything of asceticism, are therefore wrong, lead into the abyss and are actually the blackest magic! Now I realize why the old man always remained so motionless like a picture! It was because I was working on myself and not on him!

The stupid Bo Yin Ra represented things in such a way that we ought to devour everything we come across as if it might nourish ourselves as we feed on it! It's just the other way around! So the old man is the Christos and we have to untie him and make him mighty, only then can he do miracles.

That working of miracles will pass into to us once the schizophrenia has been lifted away and we no longer concern ourselves with it. For example, the stigmatized Konnersreuth woman should try to spiritually untie the one she sees suffering, instead of always suffering with him! She but goes always around in circles.[228]

(Actually, I ought to now work on all these realizations in novel form!!! It would be the most interesting topic imaginable. Maybe our circumstances will change now, that I will finally be able to work as I always wanted to! I can by no means call everything I have tried and did in yoga throughout my life a mistake. I think such efforts were necessary to realize what became clear to me today on Aug. 7).

---

[228] Meyrink is referring to Therese Neumann (1898-1962). I added the word "stigmatized" to clarify her reason for fame.

Hübbe-Schleiden Formenlehre and Seelenlehre
mentioned directly from the diary autumn 1896

REFERENCES LIST

Adamson, Henry. *The Muses Threnodie, or, Mirthfull Mournings, on the Death of Master Gall.* Edinburgh: King Iames College, 1638.

Bock, Emil. *Rudolf Steiner: Studien zu seinem Lebensgang und Lebenswerk : Vortrage vor Mitgliedern der Anthroposophischen Gesellschaft.* Stuttgart: Verlag Freies Geistesleben, 1961.

―――. *The Life and Times of Rudolf Steiner.* Vol. 1. 2 vols. Edinburgh: Floris Books, 2008.

Butler, Hiram. "Key to the Spriritual World (English Translation)." Translated by C. Wieland. *The Esoteric* 1, no. 8 (February 1888): 276–79.

―――, ed. *The Esoteric* 2 (1888).

―――, ed. *The Esoteric* 8 (1894).

Dornseiff, Franz. *Das Alphabet in Mystik und Magie.* B.G. Teubner, 1922.

Dussler, Hildebrand. *Johann Michael Feneberg und die Allgäuer Erweckungsbewegung Ein kirchengeschichtl. Beitr. aus d. Quellen zur Heimatkunde d. Allgäus.* Kempten (Allgäu): Verl. f. Heimatpflege, 1959.

Findmitteldatenbank Der Staatlichen Archive Bayerns, Bezirksamt Kempten (No. 1-2788).

Görres, J. Joseph. *On Christian Mysticism.* 4 vols., 1879.

Hahn, Rahel Christine. "'Ach, er ist ein armer Sünder und hätte verzweifeln müssen': zu Theologie und Frömmigkeit des katholischen

Priesters Martin Boos (1762-1825)." Master Thesis, University of
Vienna; Evangelisch-Theologische Fakultät, 2015.

Hartmann, Franz. *Der weisse und schwarze Magie oder das Gesetz des
Geistes in der Natur.* Leipzig: Friedrich, 1894.

———. *In the Pronaos of the Temple of Wisdom: Containing the
History of the True and the False Rosicrucians : With an Introduction
Into the Mysteries of the Hermetic Philosophy.* Theosophical Pub.
Society, 1890.

———. *Magic, White and Black: Or, The Science of Finite and Infinite
Life.* 3rd ed. London, 1888.

———. "Practical Occultism in Germany." *The Theosophist* 8, no. 86
(November 1886).

———. "The Correlation of Spiritual Forces." *The Esoteric* 10 (1896).

———. *Unter den Adepten und Rosenkreuzer.* München: Verlag
Heliakon, 2013.

———. "Unter den Adepten: vertrauliche Mittheilungen aus
den Kreisen der indischen Adepten und christlichen Mystiker."
Lotusblüten 16 (1900): 648–81.

———. "What Is True Christianity." *Theosophical Siftings* 1, no. 4
(1888).

———. *With the Adepts: An Adventure Among the Rosicrucians.*
London.: W. rider, 1910.

———. *The Theosophist* 6, no. 12 (September 1885).

———, ed. *Lotusblüten* 15 (1899).

———, ed. *Lotusblüten* 16 (1900).

Heil, Roger. "Okkultistische Sekte im Dreieichenhain der Jahrhundertwende." *Landschaft Dreieich*, 1990, 120–25.

Hübbe-Schleiden, Wilhelm. *Indisches Tagebuch 1894/1896: Mit Anmerkungen und einer Einleitung herausgegeben von Norbert Klatt.* Göttingen: Norbert Klatt Verlag, 2009.

———. "Tagebuch von Wilhelm Hübbe Schleiden (Diaries)." SUB Göttingen Cod. MS W Hübbe Schleiden 1013: 15 1896.

———. "Tagebuch von Wilhelm Hübbe Schleiden (Diaries)." SUB Göttingen Cod. MS W Hübbe Schleiden 1013: 16 1896.

———. "Tagebuch von Wilhelm Hübbe Schleiden (Diaries)." SUB Göttingen Cod. MS W Hübbe Schleiden 1013: 18 1896.

———. "Wilhelm Hübbe-Schleiden's Notebooks." SUB Göttingen, 1884/85 numbered Cod. MS Hübbe Schleiden 1012: 4.

———. "Wilhelm Hübbe-Schleiden's Notebooks." SUB Göttingen, 1886/87 numbered Cod. MS Hübbe Schleiden 1012: 6.

———. "Wilhelm Hübbe-Schleiden's Estate." SUB Göttingen, 1886/87 numbered Cod. MS Hübbe Schleiden 2081 Seelenlehr

———. "Wilhelm Hübbe-Schleiden's Estate." SUB Göttingen, 1886/87 numbered Cod. MS Hübbe Schleiden 2081 Formen Lehr

Kerning, J.B. *Briefe über die Königliche Kunst.* Edited by Gottfried Buchner. Renatus Verlag Lorch, 1912.

Kerning, J.B., and Richard Cloud. *Kerning's Testament*, 2017.

Kiesewetter, Karl. *John Dee and the Angel from the Western Window.* Leipzig: Spohr, 1895.

Kneipp, Sebastian. *Meine Wasser-Kur.* Kempten, 1889.

Kolb, Karl. *Die Wiedergeburt, das innere wahrhaftige Leben, oder Wie wird der Mensch selig?* Lorch: Karl Rohm, 1919.

Lead, Jane. *A Fountain of Gardens.* London: Printed, and sold by the Booksellers of London and Westminster, 1697.

———. *The Enochian Walks with God.* Printed and sold by D. Edwards, 1694.

———. *The Heavenly Cloud Now Breaking: The Compiled Works of Jane Lead.* Broken Bread Publishing, n.d.

———. *The Messenger of an Universal Peace: Or a Third Message to the Philadelphian Society.* London: Printed for the Booksellers of London and Westminster, 1698.

———. *The Resurrection of Life or the Royal Characteristics and Identifying Marks.* Reverse-Translation (Old German to English)., 1705.

———. *The Revelation of Revelations: The Compiled Works of Jane Lead.* Broken Bread Publishing, n.d.

Liljestrom, Birgit. "On the Quest for Olympus: The Family Gebhard-L'Estrange - Pilgrims, Patrons and Founders, Part 1." *Farther Magazine* 2nd edition (2021).

Lorber, Jakob. *Bischof Martin: die Entwicklung einer Seele im Jenseits.* 4th ed. Bietigheim-Bissingen: Lorber-Verlag, 2003.

———. *Die drei Tage im Tempel Durch das innere Wort empfangen und niedergeschrieben.* Bietigheim/Württbg: Lorber, 1952.

———. *Die geistige Sonne Bd. 2.* Bietigheim Württ.: Neu-Salems-Verl., 1929.

———. *The Household of God.* Vol. 1. 3 vols. Bietigheim: Lorber Verlag, 1995.

———. *The Household of God.* Vol. 2. 3 vols. Bietigheim: Lorber Verlag, 1995.

Lorber, Jakob, and Karl Gottfried von Leitner. *Briefe Jakob Lorbers: Urkunden und Bilder aus seinem Leben.* Bietigheim/Württemberg: Lorber-Verlag, 1931.

Mailänder, Alois. *Nachlass: Briefe und Karten von Alois Mailänder an Gustav Meyrink - BSB Meyrinkiana I.2. Gabriele an Ruben.* Bayerische Staatsbibliothek, 1893.

———. *Nachlass: Briefe und Karten von Alois Mailänder an Gustav Meyrink - BSB Meyrinkiana I.2. Johannes an Ruben.* Bayerische Staatsbibliothek, 1893.

———. *Seelenlehre - Formenlehre.* Edited by Christine Eike and Erik Dilloo-Heidger. 1st edition. BoD – Books on Demand, 2021.

Mailänder, Alois, Erik Dilloo-Heidger, and Chris Allen. *44 Letters to Gustav Meyrink (English Translation).* Norderstedt: Books on Demand, 2020.

"Mailander SMF002318110516330 Kempten File." Stadtarchiv Kempten, n.d.

Mead, G.R.S. "Fierce Impetuosity." *Theosophical Journal Lucifer* 13, no. 74 (1893): 106–11.

Meyrink, Gustav. "Die Verwandlung des Blutes. Meyrinkiana." In *Nachlass von Gustav Meyrink (1868-1932) – BSB Meyrinkiana,* Bayerische Staatsbibliothek. Vol. VI:14. Repertorium des Nachlasses von Gustav Meyrink (1868-1932), Sonst Nummer: BSB-Hss Meyrinkiana. BSB-ID: 12773438. München, 1970.

———. "Hochstapler der Mystik." *Allgemeine Zeitung*. 1927.

———. *The White Dominican*. England; USA: Dedalus; Ariadne, 1994.

Meyrink, Gustav, and Eduard Frank. *Fledermäuse: Erzählungen, Fragmente, Aufsätze*. Frankfurt: Ullstein, 1992.

Sam, Martina Maria. "Beiträge aus dem Rudolf Steiner Archiv: Alois Mailänder und die frühe theosophische Bewegung." *ARCHIVMAGAZIN*, no. 11 (2021).

Schmidt, Gernot. *Dreieichenhain Beiträge zur Geschichte von Burg und Stadt Hayn in der Dreieich*. Dreieich: Hayner Burg-Verlag, 1983.

Schmidt, Gernot, and Roger Heil. *Feste Mauern, enge Gassen: Dreieichenhain in der Erinnerung*. Stadt und Landschaft Dreieich. Hayner Burg-Vlg, 1983.

Schrödter, Willy. *A Rosicrucian Notebook: The Secret Sciences Used by Members of the Order*. York Beach, Me: Weiser, 1992.

Shirley, Ralph, ed. "Autobiography of Dr. Franz Hartmann." *The Occult Review* 7, no. 1 (January 1908): 7–35.

Silberer, Dr. Herbert. *Problems of Mysticism and Its Symbolism*. New York: Moffat, Yard and Company, 1917.

Speckner, Rolf. "Friedrich Eckstein Als Okkultist." *Der Europäer* 18, no. 09/10 (2014).

Steiner, Rudolf, and Marie Steiner-Von Sivers. *Correspondence and Documents 1901-1925*. London: Steiner Press, 1988.

Surya, G.W. *Der Triumph der Alchemie (Die Transmutation der Metalle)*. Leipzig: Altmann, 1908.

"Theosophische Rundschau - Deutsches Organ Der Theosoph." *Gesellschaft* XII. Jahrgang, no. 6 (1924).

Wahle, Richard. *Das Ganze der Philosophie und ihr Ende: Ihre Vermächtnisse an die Theologie, Physiologie, Ästhetik und Staatspädagogik.* W. Braumüller, 1894.

Weihrauch, Wolfgang. "Eine Reise Nach Wien: Bei Den Quellen Des O.T.O.: Interview Mit Josef Dvorak." *Flensburger Hefte*, no. 4 (1998).

Weinfurter, Karel. *Der brennende Busch: der entschleierte Weg der Mystik.* Bietigheim, Württemberg: K. Rohm Verlag, 1980.

———. *History of Occultism,* 1932.

———. *Man's Highest Purpose: The Lost Word Regained.* Kila, Mont.: Kessinger, 2010.

———. *Mystische Fibel: Ein Handbuch Für Den Schüler Der Praktischen Mystik.* Sersheim: Osiris-Verlag, 1954.

Weinfurter, Karel, and Erich Sopp. *Der Königsweg: der goldene Pfad der praktischen Mystik.* Freiburg: Bauer, 1976.

The Theosophist 6, no. 72 (1885).

The Theosophist 7, no. 80 (May 1886): 534–37.

Langener Zeitung, September 24, 1890.

Zentralblatt Für Okkultismus: Monatsschrift Zur Erforschung Der Gesamten Geheimwissenschaften 25 (1932 1931).

9780645394603